New
Mediterranean Diet
Cookbook for Beginners 2025

Ruth S. Reed

2000+ Days Quick and Mouthwatering Mediterranean Recipes for Effortless Living

and Lifelong Health (Includes BONUS 30-Day Meal Plan)

TABLE OF
CONTENTS

Introduction

Welcome to my culinary journey, a celebration of family tradition and timeless flavors. This collection of recipes is more than just a collection of dishes; it's a tribute to my deep connection with my heritage and the generations of women who have shaped my love for cooking.

From my earliest memories, the kitchen has been a vibrant collection of sights, sounds, and scents. I remember watching my grandmother and mother transform simple ingredients into extraordinary meals. Each dish they created was a testament to their skill and passion, and every recipe came with its own story, representing cherished memories and pieces of our family history.

As I grew older, I immersed myself in these culinary traditions, eager to learn the techniques and secrets that had been lovingly handed down through the generations. Every dish I now prepare is infused with the wisdom and flavors of my ancestors. I've mastered the art of blending traditional methods with my own modern twists, creating a unique culinary style that honors the past while embracing the present.

In this book, I'm excited to share a selection of recipes that reflect my journey—a journey of learning, loving, and creating. Each recipe is a doorway to the past, inviting you to experience the rich heritage of my family's cooking. From cherished classics to innovative adaptations, these dishes offer a taste of history and a celebration of tradition.

Join me as I share these beloved recipes, each one a delicious link in a chain of family legacy. I hope you experience the warmth and joy that has been passed down through the generations, and that these dishes bring as much happiness to your table as they have to mine.

Why Choose The Mediterranean Diet?

The Mediterranean diet has long been celebrated for its numerous health benefits, vibrant flavors, and enjoyable eating habits. But beyond the scientific studies and nutritional guidelines, why should you consider embracing this diet in your daily life? Let's delve into the reasons why the Mediterranean diet stands out as a choice for both health and pleasure.

First and foremost, the Mediterranean diet is rooted in tradition and history. Originating from the countries bordering the Mediterranean Sea—such as Italy, Greece, Spain, and Morocco—it reflects centuries of culinary practices that emphasize fresh, seasonal ingredients and simple cooking techniques. This diet isn't just about what you eat; it's about how you eat and live. Meals are often enjoyed leisurely with family and friends, fostering social connections and a sense of well-being. By adopting the Mediterranean diet, you're not only embracing a way of eating but also a way of living that values connection and mindfulness.

Health-wise, the Mediterranean diet is renowned for its potential to improve overall well-being. It is characterized by a high intake of fruits, vegetables, whole grains, nuts, and seeds, which are rich in essential vitamins, minerals, and antioxidants. These components play a crucial role in reducing inflammation, combating oxidative stress, and supporting cardiovascular health. The diet also emphasizes the consumption of healthy fats, particularly from olive oil and nuts, which are known to improve cholesterol levels and heart function.

Moreover, the Mediterranean diet includes moderate amounts of fish and poultry, providing high-quality protein and omega-3 fatty acids that are beneficial for brain health and reducing the risk of chronic diseases. Red meat is consumed sparingly, which helps to lower the intake of saturated fats and reduce the risk of conditions such as hypertension and diabetes. By focusing on nutrient-dense, unprocessed foods and healthy fats, the Mediterranean diet promotes balanced nutrition and weight management.

Another significant advantage of the Mediterranean diet is its sustainability. Unlike many fad diets that may promise quick results but are difficult to maintain long-term, the Mediterranean diet offers a flexible and enjoyable approach to eating. It encourages variety and creativity in the kitchen, allowing you to explore an array of flavors and ingredients. This makes it easier to stick to in the long run, as you're more likely to enjoy and look forward to your meals.

Furthermore, the Mediterranean diet has been linked to a reduced risk of several chronic conditions, including heart disease, stroke, and certain cancers. Its emphasis

on whole foods, healthy fats, and a balanced approach to eating aligns with the principles of modern nutritional science and offers a holistic approach to health. By adopting this diet, you're making a proactive choice to invest in your long-term health and well-being.

In addition to its health benefits, the Mediterranean diet is a celebration of culinary richness and diversity. It encourages the use of fresh herbs, spices, and aromatic ingredients that not only enhance the flavor of your dishes but also offer their own health benefits. Ingredients like garlic, basil, and rosemary are known for their anti-inflammatory and antimicrobial properties, adding both taste and therapeutic value to your meals.

Finally, choosing the Mediterranean diet is about more than just food; it's about embracing a lifestyle that values balance, moderation, and enjoyment. It encourages a mindful approach to eating, where meals are savored and appreciated rather than rushed. It also promotes physical activity as an integral part of daily life, further enhancing your overall health and quality of life.

In conclusion, the Mediterranean diet offers a wealth of benefits that go beyond just nutrition. Its roots in tradition, emphasis on whole, fresh ingredients, and holistic approach to health make it an appealing choice for those looking to improve their well-being while enjoying delicious and varied meals. By choosing the Mediterranean diet, you're not only adopting a healthy eating pattern but also embracing a way of life that values connection, balance, and joy.

Health Benefits Of The Mediterranean Diet

The Mediterranean diet is more than just a culinary trend; it's a time-tested approach to eating that boasts a wealth of health benefits. Rooted in the traditional dietary patterns of countries bordering the Mediterranean Sea, this diet is celebrated not only for its vibrant flavors but also for its profound positive impact on overall health. Here's a closer look at the remarkable health benefits associated with the Mediterranean diet.

1. Cardiovascular Health:

One of the most well-documented benefits of the Mediterranean diet is its positive effect on heart health. This diet emphasizes the consumption of healthy fats, particularly from sources like olive oil, nuts, and fatty fish, which are rich in monounsaturated fats and omega-3 fatty acids. These fats are known to help reduce levels of LDL (bad) cholesterol while increasing HDL (good) cholesterol. Studies have shown that adhering to the Mediterranean diet can significantly lower the risk of heart disease, stroke, and high blood pressure. The diet's focus on fresh fruits, vegetables, and whole grains also provides essential antioxidants and fiber that support cardiovascular health.

2. Weight Management:

The Mediterranean diet promotes a balanced and sustainable approach to weight management. By prioritizing whole, nutrient-dense foods and healthy fats, the diet helps to regulate appetite and reduce cravings. Unlike restrictive diets that may lead to nutrient deficiencies and unsustainable weight loss, the Mediterranean diet offers a satisfying and enjoyable way to maintain a healthy weight. Its emphasis on portion control and mindful eating also contributes to long-term success in weight management.

3. Diabetes Prevention and Management:

Adopting the Mediterranean diet can be beneficial for those at risk of or managing diabetes. The diet's emphasis on whole grains, legumes, fruits, and vegetables helps to stabilize blood sugar levels and improve insulin sensitivity. The high fiber content from these foods aids in glucose regulation and reduces the risk of type 2 diabetes. Additionally, the diet's moderate consumption of healthy fats supports overall metabolic health and can help prevent the development of diabetes-related complications.

4. Enhanced Cognitive Function:

Emerging research suggests that the Mediterranean diet may play a role in supporting brain health and cognitive function. The diet's rich supply of antioxidants, omega-3 fatty acids, and healthy fats is believed to protect against oxidative stress and inflammation, both of which are linked to cognitive decline and neurodegenerative diseases. Some studies have found that individuals who follow the Mediterranean diet have a lower risk of developing conditions such as Alzheimer's disease and age-related cognitive decline.

5. Reduced Inflammation:

Chronic inflammation is a contributing factor to many health conditions, including heart disease, arthritis, and certain cancers. The Mediterranean diet's focus on anti-inflammatory foods—such as olive oil, nuts, fatty fish, and a variety of fruits and vegetables—helps to combat inflammation and support overall health. The diet's abundant supply of polyphenols, which are naturally occurring compounds found in plant-based foods, contributes to its anti-inflammatory effects.

6. Longevity and Quality of Life:

Research has consistently shown that the Mediterranean diet is associated with increased longevity and improved quality of life. The diet's nutrient-dense foods and healthy fats support overall well-being and help to prevent chronic diseases. Additionally, the Mediterranean lifestyle promotes social interactions, physical activity, and a balanced approach to living, all of which contribute to a healthier and more fulfilling life.

7. Digestive Health:

The Mediterranean diet's high fiber content, derived from whole grains, legumes, fruits, and vegetables, supports digestive health by promoting regular bowel movements and maintaining a healthy gut microbiome. Fiber-rich foods help to prevent constipation and reduce the risk of gastrointestinal disorders.

In summary, the Mediterranean diet offers a multitude of health benefits that extend beyond just physical well-being. Its focus on nutrient-rich foods, healthy fats, and a balanced approach to eating contributes to improved cardiovascular health, weight management, diabetes prevention, cognitive function, and overall quality of life. By adopting this diet, you're not only nourishing your body but also embracing a lifestyle that supports long-term health and vitality.

The Mediterranean Diet Food Pyramid

The Mediterranean Diet Food Pyramid serves as a visual guide to understanding the balance and variety of foods central to this celebrated eating pattern. Unlike typical food pyramids, the Mediterranean model emphasizes a lifestyle as much as it does dietary choices, offering a holistic approach to health and well-being.

At the base of the pyramid, you'll find a strong foundation of fruits and vegetables. These are the cornerstones of the Mediterranean diet, consumed in abundant amounts. Fresh, seasonal produce provides essential vitamins, minerals, and antioxidants that support overall health and reduce the risk of chronic diseases. A wide array of colorful fruits and vegetables ensures a rich supply of nutrients and health-promoting compounds.

Moving up, whole grains occupy the next level. Foods such as whole wheat, brown rice, barley, and oats are staples in the Mediterranean diet. These grains are valued for their high fiber content, which aids digestion, supports heart health, and helps maintain stable blood sugar levels. Whole grains serve as a vital energy source and contribute to a balanced diet.

The middle section of the pyramid highlights healthy fats and nuts. Central to the Mediterranean diet is the use of olive oil, a primary source of monounsaturated fats known for their heart-protective properties. Nuts, including almonds, walnuts, and pistachios, provide additional healthy fats, protein, and essential nutrients. These fats are beneficial for reducing inflammation and supporting overall cardiovascular health.

Legumes also play a significant role, positioned in the same tier as nuts. Beans, lentils, and chickpeas offer plant-based protein and are rich in fiber. They are a valuable component of the diet, helping to keep meals satisfying and nutritionally complete while contributing to heart health and blood sugar control.

Fish and seafood are featured prominently in the upper sections of the pyramid. These foods are recommended several times a week and are prized for their omega-3 fatty acids, which support brain function and cardiovascular health. Fish such as salmon, sardines, and mackerel are particularly beneficial.

Poultry, eggs, and dairy products like yogurt and cheese are included in moderate amounts. These provide additional protein and essential nutrients but are consumed less frequently than the base foods. Opting for low-fat or reduced-fat options can enhance the diet's heart-healthy benefits.

At the peak of the pyramid, you'll find red meat and sweets, which are enjoyed sparingly. These are considered occasional indulgences rather than staples, reflecting the diet's emphasis on moderation and balance.

Lastly, the Mediterranean diet pyramid incorporates physical activity and social connections as integral elements of a healthy lifestyle. Regular exercise and shared meals with family and friends are encouraged, promoting both physical and emotional well-being.

In essence, the Mediterranean Diet Food Pyramid encapsulates a holistic approach to eating that prioritizes plant-based foods, healthy fats, and balanced portions of animal products, all while supporting an active and social lifestyle.

Classical Ingredients in the Mediterranean Diet

The Mediterranean Diet is renowned for its delicious, vibrant, and healthful ingredients. Central to its appeal is the use of fresh, high-quality ingredients that not only contribute to the diet's rich flavors but also offer a range of nutritional benefits. Here's a look at some of the classical ingredients that define this culinary tradition:

Olive Oil

Olive oil is perhaps the most iconic ingredient in the Mediterranean diet. Its rich, fruity flavor and high monounsaturated fat content make it a cornerstone of Mediterranean cooking. Used for everything from sautéing vegetables to drizzling over salads, olive oil is celebrated for its heart-healthy benefits and antioxidant properties. Extra-virgin olive oil, in particular, is prized for its purity and higher levels of beneficial compounds.

Fruits and Vegetables

Fresh fruits and vegetables are abundant in the Mediterranean diet, showcasing a diverse array of colors and flavors. Tomatoes, bell peppers, cucumbers, and leafy greens like spinach and kale are commonly used. Seasonal and local produce is emphasized, ensuring meals are not only flavorful but also packed with vitamins, minerals, and antioxidants. Fruits such as figs, grapes, and citrus are enjoyed for their natural sweetness and health benefits.

Legumes

Legumes like chickpeas, lentils, and beans are fundamental to Mediterranean cuisine. They serve as excellent sources of plant-based protein, fiber, and essential nutrients. These ingredients are used in a variety of dishes, from hearty stews and soups to fresh salads and dips like hummus.

Whole Grains

Whole grains are a staple in the Mediterranean diet, providing a rich source of fiber, vitamins, and minerals. Common grains include barley, farro, bulgur, and brown rice. Whole grain breads and pasta are also integral parts of this diet, offering complex carbohydrates that help sustain energy and support digestive health.

Nuts and Seeds

Nuts and seeds, such as almonds, walnuts, and sunflower seeds, add both texture and nutritional value to Mediterranean dishes. They are high in healthy fats, protein, and essential minerals. These ingredients can be used in salads, as snacks, or incorporated into sauces and dressings.

Herbs and Spices

Herbs and spices are essential for imparting the distinctive flavors of Mediterranean cuisine. Fresh herbs like basil, oregano, thyme, rosemary, and parsley are frequently used to enhance dishes. Spices such as cumin, coriander, and paprika add depth and complexity to the flavor profile of Mediterranean meals.

Fish and Seafood

Fish and seafood are frequently featured in Mediterranean meals, offering high-quality protein and beneficial omega-3 fatty acids. Varieties like salmon, sardines, and shrimp are commonly prepared in a range of dishes, from grilled fillets to seafood stews.

Cheese

Cheeses such as feta, ricotta, and goat cheese are enjoyed in moderation within the Mediterranean diet. These cheeses add creamy texture and tangy flavor to salads, pastries, and various other dishes. They provide protein and calcium while keeping meals flavorful and satisfying.

Wine

Moderate wine consumption, particularly red wine, is a traditional aspect of Mediterranean dining. Rich in antioxidants and enjoyed in social settings, wine complements the diet's emphasis on enjoying meals with family and friends. The key is moderation, aligning with the diet's overall focus on balance and enjoyment.

These classical ingredients not only define the essence of Mediterranean cooking but also contribute to the diet's renowned health benefits. By incorporating these fresh and flavorful components, the Mediterranean diet promotes a nourishing and enjoyable approach to eating that has stood the test of time.

Foods To Eat And Avoid

The Mediterranean diet emphasizes a balance of wholesome, nutrient-dense foods, while also suggesting certain foods be limited or avoided for optimal health. Understanding which foods to embrace and which to limit can help you make the most of this beneficial eating plan.

Foods to Embrace

Fruits and Vegetables

Fruits and vegetables form the backbone of the Mediterranean diet. Aim to include a variety of colorful produce, such as leafy greens, tomatoes, bell peppers, and berries. These foods are rich in vitamins, minerals, and antioxidants, which support overall health and well-being.

Whole Grains

Opt for whole grains like quinoa, brown rice, farro, and barley. These grains provide essential fiber, vitamins, and minerals, contributing to digestive health and sustained energy levels. They should be a regular feature in your meals, replacing refined grains.

Legumes

Incorporate legumes such as chickpeas, lentils, and beans into your diet. These plant-based proteins are packed with fiber and essential nutrients, making them excellent choices for both their health benefits and versatility in various dishes.

Nuts and Seeds

Nuts and seeds, including almonds, walnuts, and chia seeds, are valuable sources of healthy fats, protein, and vital minerals. They add texture and flavor to meals, whether as a topping for salads or a satisfying snack.

Olive Oil

Use extra-virgin olive oil as your primary fat source. It is rich in monounsaturated fats and antioxidants, offering numerous health benefits, including supporting heart health and reducing inflammation. Use it for cooking, dressings, and drizzling over dishes.

Fish and Seafood

Enjoy a variety of fish and seafood, such as salmon, sardines, and shrimp. These foods are high in omega-3 fatty acids, which are beneficial for heart health. Aim to include fish in your diet at least a few times a week.

Herbs and Spices

Flavor your meals with a wide range of herbs and spices like basil, oregano, rosemary, and garlic. These ingredients not only enhance the taste of your food but also provide additional health benefits through their anti-inflammatory and antioxidant properties.

Foods to Limit or Avoid

Refined Grains

Minimize your intake of refined grains such as white bread, white rice, and pastries. These processed foods lack the fiber and nutrients found in whole grains and can contribute to blood sugar spikes and overall poor health.

Added Sugars

Avoid foods and beverages high in added sugars, such as sugary drinks, candies, and desserts. Excessive sugar intake can lead to weight gain, increased risk of diabetes, and other health issues.

Red and Processed Meats

Limit consumption of red meats, such as beef and pork, as well as processed meats like sausages and deli meats. These can be high in saturated fats and sodium, which are linked to various health problems, including heart disease.

High-Sodium Foods

Be cautious with foods high in sodium, including certain canned goods, processed snacks, and salty condiments. Excessive sodium intake can contribute to high blood pressure and other cardiovascular issues.

Fried Foods

Avoid or significantly reduce the consumption of fried foods. These items are often high in unhealthy fats and calories, which can undermine the health benefits of the Mediterranean diet.

Sugary Drinks

Stay away from sugary beverages like sodas and sweetened coffee drinks. These can add unnecessary calories and sugar to your diet without providing nutritional value.

By focusing on foods that are fresh, whole, and nutrient-rich while limiting those that are processed and high in unhealthy components, you can fully embrace the Mediterranean diet and enjoy its numerous health benefits.

Some Tips On The Mediterranean Diet

Embracing the Mediterranean diet can be a delightful and enriching experience. To make the most of this heart-healthy and flavorful eating plan, here are some practical tips to help you integrate Mediterranean principles into your daily life:

1. Prioritize Fresh and Seasonal Produce

Focus on incorporating a variety of fresh, seasonal fruits and vegetables into your meals. Seasonal produce often has superior flavor and nutritional value. Visit local farmers' markets or join a community-supported agriculture (CSA) program to get the freshest ingredients.

2. Choose Whole Grains

Opt for whole grains over refined grains to maximize fiber intake and maintain stable blood sugar levels. Brown rice, quinoa, bulgur, and whole wheat pasta are excellent choices. Experiment with different grains to keep your meals interesting and diverse.

3. Embrace Healthy Fats

Incorporate healthy fats from sources like extra-virgin olive oil, avocados, nuts, and seeds. Use olive oil as your primary cooking fat and for salad dressings. These fats support heart health and provide essential nutrients.

4. Enjoy Fish and Seafood Regularly

Aim to include fish and seafood in your diet at least twice a week. Choose fatty fish such as salmon, sardines, and mackerel for their high omega-3 content. Cooking methods like grilling, baking, or steaming can enhance their natural flavors without adding excessive fat.

5. Use Herbs and Spices for Flavor

Instead of relying on salt, use a variety of herbs and spices to flavor your dishes. Fresh herbs like basil, parsley, and cilantro, along with spices such as cumin, paprika, and cinnamon, can add depth and complexity to your meals.

6. Practice Portion Control

Even with healthy foods, portion control is essential. Be mindful of serving sizes, especially with calorie-dense items like nuts and oils. Balancing portions ensures that you enjoy the benefits of the Mediterranean diet without overeating.

7. Incorporate Legumes and Nuts

Add legumes like beans, lentils, and chickpeas to your meals as a source of plant-based protein. Nuts and seeds make great snacks or can be used as toppings for salads and yogurt. They offer a satisfying crunch and nutritional benefits.

8. Savor Your Meals

Adopt a mindful approach to eating by savoring each bite. Take time to enjoy your food, eat slowly, and appreciate the flavors and textures. This practice not only enhances the dining experience but can also aid in digestion and satiety.

9. Stay Hydrated

Drink plenty of water throughout the day to stay hydrated. While moderate consumption of red wine is traditional in the Mediterranean diet, it's important to prioritize water as your primary beverage. Herbal teas can also be a refreshing choice.

10. Make Meals a Social Event

One of the hallmarks of the Mediterranean lifestyle is the emphasis on social dining. Share meals with family and friends to enhance your eating experience and foster a sense of community and connection.

11. Balance is Key

The Mediterranean diet is about balance and variety, not strict rules. Enjoy a wide range of foods and flavors while maintaining a focus on healthful choices. Flexibility allows for a more sustainable and enjoyable approach to eating.

By incorporating these tips into your routine, you can more easily embrace the Mediterranean diet and reap its numerous health benefits. Remember, the goal is to create a nourishing and pleasurable eating experience that supports long-term well-being.

Chapter 1: Morning Meals

Greek Egg and Tomato Scramble

Serves: 4 / Prep time: 10 minutes / Cook time: 25 minutes

- ¼ cup extra-virgin olive oil, divided
- 1½ cups chopped fresh tomatoes
- ¼ cup finely minced red onion
- 2 garlic cloves, minced
- ½ teaspoon dried oregano or 1 to 2 teaspoons chopped fresh oregano
- ½ teaspoon dried thyme or 1 to 2 teaspoons chopped fresh thyme
- 8 large eggs
- ½ teaspoon salt
- ¼ teaspoon freshly ground black pepper
- ¾ cup crumbled feta cheese
- ¼ cup chopped fresh mint leaves

1. In a large skillet, heat the olive oil over medium heat. Add the chopped tomatoes and red onion, and sauté until the tomatoes are soft, about 10-12 minutes.
2. Add the garlic, oregano, and thyme, sautéing for another 2-4 minutes until fragrant and the liquid reduces.
3. In a medium bowl, whisk together the eggs, salt, and pepper.
4. Pour the eggs into the skillet, lower the heat, and scramble until set and creamy, stirring constantly for 3-4 minutes.
5. Remove from heat, fold in the feta and mint, and serve warm.

Per Serving: Calories: 355 / Fat: 29g / Protein: 17g / Carbs: 6g / Fiber: 1g / Sodium: 695mg

Peach Sunrise Smoothie

Serves: 14 / Prep time: 10 minutes / Cook time: 0 minutes

- 1 large unpeeled peach, pitted and sliced (about ½ cup)
- 6 ounces (170 g) vanilla or peach low-fat Greek yogurt
- 2 tablespoons low-fat milk
- 6 to 8 ice cubes

1. Place all the ingredients in a blender and blend until smooth and creamy.
2. Serve immediately.

Per Serving: Calories: 228 / Fat: 3g / Protein: 11g / Carbs: 42g / Fiber: 3g / Sodium: 127mg

Mini Shrimp Frittata

Serves: 4 / Prep time: 15 minutes / Cook time: 20 minutes

- 1 teaspoon olive oil, plus more for spraying
- ½ small red bell pepper, finely diced
- 1 teaspoon minced garlic
- 1 (4-ounce / 113-g) can of tiny shrimp, drained
- Salt and freshly ground black pepper, to taste
- 4 eggs, beaten
- 4 teaspoons ricotta cheese

1. Spray four ramekins with olive oil.
2. Heat 1 teaspoon of olive oil in a medium skillet over medium-low heat. Add the bell pepper and garlic, sautéing until the pepper softens, about 5 minutes.
3. Add the shrimp, seasoning with salt and pepper, and cook until warmed through, about 1-2 minutes. Remove from heat.
4. Stir the shrimp mixture into the beaten eggs.
5. Divide the egg mixture evenly among the ramekins.
6. Bake two ramekins in an air fryer at 350°F (177°C) for 6 minutes.
7. Stir each frittata, top with 1 teaspoon of ricotta cheese, and continue baking for another 4-5 minutes until the eggs are set and lightly browned.
8. Repeat with the remaining two ramekins.

Per Serving: Calories: 114 / Fat: 6g / Protein: 12g / Carbs: 1g / Fiber: 0g / Sodium: 314mg

Egg Salad with Red Pepper and Dill

Serves: 6 / Prep time: 5 minutes / Cook time: 10 minutes

- 6 large eggs
- 1 cup water
- 1 tablespoon olive oil
- 1 medium red bell pepper, seeded and chopped
- ¼ teaspoon salt
- ¼ teaspoon ground black pepper
- ½ cup low-fat plain Greek yogurt
- 2 tablespoons chopped fresh dill

1. Prepare a large bowl of ice water. Place the rack or egg holder into the bottom of the Instant Pot®.
2. Arrange the eggs on the rack, add water, close the lid, and set the steam release to Sealing. Press the Manual button and set the timer for 5 minutes.
3. After the timer beeps, let the pressure release naturally for 5 minutes, then quick-release the remaining pressure.
4. Transfer the eggs to the ice water and let them cool for 10 minutes. Peel and chop the eggs, then place them in a medium bowl.
5. Clean out the Instant Pot®, then heat the olive oil using the Sauté function. Add the bell pepper, salt, and black pepper, cooking until the bell pepper is tender, about 5 minutes. Add to the bowl with the eggs.
6. Stir in the yogurt and dill, folding to combine. Cover

and chill for 1 hour before serving.

Per Serving: Calories: 111 / Fat: 8g / Protein: 8g / Carbs: 3g / Fiber: 0g / Sodium: 178mg

Savory Breakfast Oats

Serves: 2 / Prep time: 10 minutes / Cook time: 15 minutes

- ½ cup steel-cut oats
- 1 cup water
- 1 large tomato, chopped
- 1 medium cucumber, chopped
- 1 tablespoon olive oil
- Freshly grated, low-fat Parmesan cheese
- Flat-leaf parsley or mint, chopped, for garnish
- Sea salt and freshly ground pepper, to taste

1. Bring the oats and water to a boil in a medium saucepan over high heat.
2. Continue stirring for about 15 minutes until the water is absorbed.
3. Divide the oatmeal between two bowls.
4. Top with the chopped tomato and cucumber.
5. Drizzle with olive oil, sprinkle with Parmesan, and garnish with parsley or mint.
6. Season to taste and serve immediately.

Per Serving: Calories: 240 / Fat: 10g / Protein: 8g / Carbs: 32g / Fiber: 6g / Sodium: 10mg

Egg Baked in Avocado

Serves: 2 / Prep time: 5 minutes / Cook time: 15 minutes

- 1 ripe large avocado
- 2 large eggs
- Salt
- Freshly ground black pepper
- 4 tablespoons jarred pesto, for serving
- 2 tablespoons chopped tomato, for serving
- 2 tablespoons crumbled feta, for serving (optional)

1. Preheat your oven to 425°F (220°C).
2. Halve the avocado, removing the pit, and scoop out about 1-2 tablespoons from each half to create a hole for the egg.
3. Place the avocado halves on a baking sheet, cut-side up. Crack one egg into each half and season with salt and pepper.
4. Bake for 10-15 minutes until the eggs are set to your desired doneness.
5. Remove from the oven and top each avocado half with 2 tablespoons of pesto, 1 tablespoon of chopped tomato, and 1 tablespoon of crumbled feta, if desired.

Per Serving: Calories: 248 / Fat: 23g / Protein: 10g / Carbs: 2g / Fiber: 1g / Sodium: 377mg

Ricotta and Fruit Bruschetta

Serves: 2 / Prep time: 5 minutes / Cook time: 0 minutes

- ¼ cup full-fat ricotta cheese
- 1½ teaspoons honey, divided
- 3 drops almond extract
- 2 slices whole-grain bread, toasted
- ½ medium banana, peeled and sliced
- ½ medium pear, thinly sliced
- 2 teaspoons chopped walnuts
- 2 pinches ground cinnamon

1. Mix the ricotta cheese with ¼ teaspoon honey and almond extract in a small bowl until well combined.
2. Spread 1½ tablespoons of the ricotta mixture onto each slice of toasted bread.
3. Layer the banana and pear slices on top of the ricotta.
4. Drizzle the remaining honey equally over each slice and sprinkle with chopped walnuts and a pinch of cinnamon.

Per Serving: Calories: 207 / Fat: 7g / Protein: 8g / Carbs: 30g / Fiber: 4g / Sodium: 162mg

Greek Yogurt Parfait

Serves: 1 / Prep time: 5 minutes / Cook time: 0 minutes

- 2 tablespoons heavy whipping cream
- ½ cup plain whole-milk Greek yogurt
- ¼ cup frozen berries, thawed with juices
- ½ teaspoon vanilla or almond extract (optional)
- ¼ teaspoon ground cinnamon (optional)
- 1 tablespoon ground flaxseed
- 2 tablespoons chopped nuts (walnuts or pecans)

1. In a small bowl or glass, mix the Greek yogurt, heavy whipping cream, thawed berries with their juices, flaxseed, and vanilla or almond extract (if using). Stir until smooth.
2. Sprinkle with chopped nuts and enjoy.

Per Serving: Calories: 333 / Fat: 27g / Protein: 10g / Carbs: 15g / Fiber: 4g / Sodium: 71mg

Sunny-Side Up Baked Eggs with Swiss Chard, Feta, and Basil

Serves: 4 / Prep time: 15 minutes / Cook time: 10 to 15 minutes

- 1 tablespoon extra-virgin olive oil
- 1 large shallot, finely chopped
- 1 small garlic clove, minced
- 1 bunch Swiss chard, ribs removed, coarsely chopped
- 1 tablespoon unsalted butter
- 4 large eggs
- 2 ounces (57 g) feta cheese, crumbled

- Chopped fresh basil leaves, for garnish
- Sea salt and freshly ground black pepper, to taste

1. Preheat the oven to 425°F (220°C).
2. In a large, ovenproof skillet, heat the olive oil over medium heat.
3. Add the shallot and sauté until softened, about 5 minutes.
4. Add the garlic, cooking until fragrant, about 1 minute.
5. Stir in the Swiss chard, cooking until wilted, about 5 minutes.
6. Stir in the butter, mixing until melted.
7. Use a spoon to create 4 wells in the Swiss chard mixture. Crack an egg into each well.
8. Sprinkle with feta, salt, and pepper.
9. Bake until the egg whites are set but the yolks are still runny, about 8 to 10 minutes.
10. Garnish with fresh basil and serve immediately.

Per Serving: Calories: 208 / Fat: 17g / Protein: 11g / Carbs: 4g / Fiber: 2g / Sodium: 372mg

Yogurt with Granola and Citrus Compote

Serves: 4 / Prep time: 5 minutes / Cook time: 10 minutes

- 1 medium orange, peeled and sectioned
- 1 small grapefruit, peeled and sectioned
- ½ cup sugar
- 2 cups plain Greek yogurt
- ½ cup granola

1. In a medium saucepan, combine the orange and grapefruit sections with sugar over medium heat.
2. Bring the mixture to a boil, stirring until the sugar is dissolved.
3. Reduce heat to medium-low, simmering for 3 minutes until the citrus thickens slightly.
4. Remove from heat and allow the compote to cool for 5 minutes.
5. Divide the yogurt among four bowls, topping with granola and citrus compote.

Per Serving: Calories: 238 / Fat: 3g / Protein: 14g / Carbs: 45g / Fiber: 2g / Sodium: 57mg

Amaranth Chocolate Almond Bowl

Serves:6 / Prep time: 10 minutes / Cook time: 6 minutes

- 2 cups amaranth, rinsed and drained
- 2 cups almond milk
- 2 cups water
- ¼ cup maple syrup
- 3 tablespoons cocoa powder
- 1 teaspoon vanilla extract
- ¼ teaspoon salt
- ½ cup toasted sliced almonds

- ⅓ cup miniature semisweet chocolate chips

1. Add the amaranth, almond milk, water, maple syrup, cocoa powder, vanilla, and salt to the Instant Pot®. Mix everything together.
2. Secure the lid, set the steam release to Sealing, press the Rice button, and set the timer for 6 minutes. Once the timer goes off, quick-release the pressure until the float valve drops. Press the Cancel button, open the lid, and stir the mixture.
3. Serve the amaranth bowl hot, topped with the toasted almonds and chocolate chips.

Per Serving: Calories: 263 / Fat: 12g / Protein: 5g / Carbs: 35g / Fiber: 5g / Sodium: 212mg

Nutty Pear Oatmeal

Serves: 2 / Prep time: 10 minutes / Cook time: 7 minutes

- 1 cup rolled oats
- 1¼ cups water
- ¼ cup orange juice
- 1 medium pear, peeled, cored, and cubed
- ¼ cup dried cherries
- ¼ cup chopped walnuts
- 1 tablespoon honey
- ¼ teaspoon ground ginger
- ¼ teaspoon ground cinnamon
- ⅛ teaspoon salt

1. Combine oats, water, orange juice, pear, cherries, walnuts, honey, ginger, cinnamon, and salt in the Instant Pot®. Mix well.
2. Close the lid, set the steam release to Sealing, press the Manual button, and cook for 7 minutes. After the cooking time, let the pressure release naturally for about 20 minutes. Press the Cancel button, open the lid, and give the oatmeal a good stir.
3. Serve the oatmeal warm.

Per Serving: Calories: 362 / Fat: 8g / Protein: 7g / Carbs: 69g / Fiber: 8g / Sodium: 164mg

Blue Cheese and Apricot Toast

Serves: 2 / Prep time: 5 minutes / Cook time: 5 minutes

- 2 thick slices of whole-wheat bread
- 1 tablespoon olive oil
- 2 apricots, sliced into ¼-inch pieces
- 2 ounces (57 g) blue cheese
- 2 tablespoons honey
- 2 tablespoons toasted slivered almonds

1. Preheat the broiler to high. Brush the bread slices with olive oil on both sides.
2. Arrange the slices on a baking sheet and broil them for about 2 minutes on each side until lightly browned.
3. Place the apricot slices on the toasted bread,

distributing them evenly. Sprinkle blue cheese on top, dividing equally.

4. Return the baking sheet to the broiler and broil for 1 to 2 minutes until the cheese melts and just starts to brown. Remove from the oven and drizzle with honey, then garnish with toasted almonds.

Per Serving: Calories: 379 / Fat: 20g / Protein: 13g / Carbs: 40g / Fiber: 4g / Sodium: 595mg

Hearty Veggie Breakfast

Serves: 4 / Prep time: 20 minutes / Cook time: 10 minutes

- 1 tablespoon olive oil
- 1 small sweet onion, diced
- 2 large carrots, diced
- 2 medium potatoes, diced
- 1 stalk celery, diced
- 1 large red bell pepper, diced
- 1 tablespoon low-sodium soy sauce
- ¼ cup water
- 1 cup diced zucchini or summer squash
- 2 medium tomatoes, diced
- 2 cups cooked brown rice
- ½ teaspoon ground black pepper

1. Press the Sauté button on the Instant Pot® and add the olive oil. Once heated, cook the onion until just tender, about 2 minutes.
2. Add the carrots, potatoes, celery, and bell pepper and cook for another 2 minutes. Stir in soy sauce and water, then press the Cancel button.
3. Close the lid, set the steam release to Sealing, press the Manual button, and cook for 2 minutes. Quick-release the pressure until the float valve drops, and then press Cancel.
4. Open the lid and add the zucchini or squash and tomatoes. Stir to combine. Close the lid again, set the steam release to Sealing, press the Manual button, and cook for 1 minute. Quick-release the pressure until the float valve drops, press Cancel, and open the lid.
5. Serve the vegetable mixture over cooked brown rice and season with black pepper.

Per Serving: Calories: 224 / Fat: 5g / Protein: 6g / Carbs: 41g / Fiber: 5g / Sodium: 159mg

Powerhouse Peach Smoothie Bowl

Serves: 2 / Prep time: 15 minutes / Cook time: 0 minutes

- 2 cups frozen peaches, partially thawed
- ½ cup plain or vanilla Greek yogurt
- ½ ripe avocado
- 2 tablespoons flax meal
- 1 teaspoon vanilla extract
- 1 teaspoon orange extract
- 1 tablespoon honey (optional)

1. Blend the peaches, yogurt, avocado, flax meal, vanilla extract, orange extract, and honey until smooth.
2. Pour the smoothie mixture into two bowls and add any desired toppings.

Per Serving: Calories: 213 / Fat: 13g / Protein: 6g / Carbs: 23g / Fiber: 7g / Sodium: 41mg

Tuna and Pepper Spanish Tortilla

Serves: 4 / Prep time: 15 minutes / Cook time: 15 minutes

- 6 large eggs
- ¼ cup olive oil
- 2 small russet potatoes, diced
- 1 small onion, chopped
- 1 roasted red bell pepper, sliced
- 1 (7-ounce / 198-g) can tuna in water, drained and flaked
- 2 plum tomatoes, diced
- 1 teaspoon dried tarragon

1. Preheat the broiler on high. Whisk the eggs in a large bowl until just combined.
2. Heat the olive oil in a large oven-safe, nonstick or cast-iron skillet over medium-low heat.
3. Add the diced potatoes and cook until they begin to soften, about 7 minutes. Add the onion and roasted pepper, and continue to cook until soft, 3–5 minutes more.
4. Stir in the tuna, tomatoes, and tarragon, then pour the eggs into the skillet. Cook for 7–10 minutes until the eggs are set at the bottom and just starting to bubble.
5. Transfer the skillet to the oven and broil on one of the top racks until the eggs are fully set and the top is slightly browned.
6. Slice into wedges and serve warm or at room temperature.

Per Serving: Calories: 247 / Fat: 14g / Protein: 12g / Carbs: 19g / Fiber: 2g / Sodium: 130mg

Egg and Veggie Pita

Serves: 4 / Prep time: 10 minutes / Cook time: 10 minutes

- 2 pita breads
- 2 tablespoons olive oil
- 1 red or yellow bell pepper, diced
- 2 zucchini, quartered lengthwise and sliced
- 4 large eggs, beaten
- Sea salt
- Freshly ground black pepper
- Pinch dried oregano
- 2 avocados, sliced
- ½ to ¾ cup crumbled feta cheese
- 2 tablespoons chopped scallion, green part only
- Hot sauce, for serving

1. Warm the pita breads in a large skillet over medium heat until lightly toasted, about 2 minutes. Remove

and set aside.

2. In the same skillet, heat olive oil over medium heat. Sauté the bell pepper and zucchini for 4 to 5 minutes. Add the beaten eggs, season with salt, pepper, and oregano, and cook, stirring, for 2 to 3 minutes until the eggs are fully cooked.
3. Slice the pitas in half and fill each half with the egg and veggie mixture. Add avocado slices and feta to each pita half. Garnish with scallion and serve with hot sauce.

Per Serving: Calories: 476 / Fat: 31g / Protein: 17g / Carbs: 36g / Fiber: 11g / Sodium: 455mg

Red Pepper Feta Egg Cups

Serves: 6 / Prep time: 5 minutes / Cook time: 8 minutes

- 1 tablespoon olive oil
- ½ cup crumbled feta cheese
- ¼ cup chopped roasted red peppers
- 6 large eggs, beaten
- ¼ teaspoon ground black pepper
- 1 cup water

1. Brush silicone muffin or poaching cups with olive oil. Evenly distribute the feta and roasted red peppers among the cups.
2. In a bowl with a pour spout, beat the eggs with black pepper.
3. Pour the egg mixture into the cups. Place a rack in the Instant Pot® and add water. Set the cups on the rack. Close the lid, set the steam release to Sealing, press the Manual button, and cook for 8 minutes.
4. When the timer beeps, quick-release the pressure until the float valve drops. Open the lid, carefully remove the silicone cups, and slide the egg bites onto plates. Serve warm.

Per Serving: Calories: 145 / Fat: 11g / Protein: 10g / Carbs: 3g / Fiber: 1g / Sodium: 294mg

Tahini and Apple Toast

Serves: 1 / Prep time: 10 minutes / Cook time: 0 minutes

- 2 tablespoons tahini
- 2 slices whole-wheat bread, toasted
- 1 small apple, cored and thinly sliced
- 1 teaspoon honey

1. Spread tahini over the toasted bread slices.
2. Lay apple slices on top of the tahini and drizzle with honey. Serve immediately.

Per Serving: Calories: 439 / Fat: 19g / Protein: 13g / Carbs: 60g / Fiber: 10g / Sodium: 327mg

Quinoa Breakfast Bowl with Figs and Walnuts

Serves: 4 / Prep time: 10 minutes / Cook time: 12 minutes

- 1½ cups quinoa, rinsed and drained
- 2½ cups water
- 1 cup almond milk
- 2 tablespoons honey
- 1 teaspoon vanilla extract
- ½ teaspoon ground cinnamon
- ¼ teaspoon salt
- ½ cup low-fat plain Greek yogurt
- 8 fresh figs, quartered
- 1 cup chopped toasted walnuts

1. Combine quinoa, water, almond milk, honey, vanilla extract, cinnamon, and salt in the Instant Pot®. Stir well, close the lid, set the steam release to Sealing, press the Rice button, and cook for 12 minutes. Once the timer beeps, allow the pressure to release naturally for about 20 minutes.
2. Press the Cancel button, open the lid, and fluff the quinoa with a fork. Serve warm, topped with yogurt, figs, and walnuts.

Per Serving: Calories: 413 / Fat: 25g / Protein: 10g / Carbs: 52g / Fiber: 7g / Sodium: 275mg

Sweet Potato Toast with Spinach and Pesto

Serves: 4 / Prep time: 5 minutes / Cook time: 15 minutes

- 2 large sweet potatoes, sliced lengthwise
- 2 plum tomatoes, halved
- 1 cup fresh spinach
- 8 medium asparagus, trimmed
- 4 large cooked eggs (poached, scrambled, or fried)
- 1 cup arugula
- 4 tablespoons pesto
- 4 tablespoons shredded Asiago cheese
- 6 tablespoons extra-virgin olive oil, divided
- Salt
- Freshly ground black pepper

1. Preheat the oven to 450°F (235°C). Place the plum tomato halves on a baking sheet, brush with 2 tablespoons of olive oil, and season with salt and pepper. Roast for 15 minutes, then remove from the oven and set aside.
2. Arrange the sweet potato slices on another baking sheet, brushing each side with 2 tablespoons of olive oil, and season with salt and pepper. Bake for about 15 minutes, flipping once after 5 to 7 minutes, until tender. Set aside.
3. In a skillet, heat the remaining 2 tablespoons of olive oil over medium heat and sauté the spinach until wilted. Transfer to a paper towel-lined dish. Use the same pan to sauté the asparagus, turning occasionally, and then transfer to a paper towel-lined dish.
4. Place the sweet potato slices on serving plates, and evenly distribute the spinach and asparagus over

them. Top each slice with a cooked egg and ¼ cup of arugula.
5. Finish by drizzling 1 tablespoon of pesto and sprinkling 1 tablespoon of Asiago cheese over each slice. Serve with a roasted plum tomato.

Per Serving: Calories: 441 / Fat: 35g / Protein: 13g / Carbs: 23g / Fiber: 4g / Sodium: 481mg

Mediterranean Pita Breakfast Sandwiches

Serves: 2 / Prep time: 5 minutes / Cook time: 7 minutes

- 2 eggs
- 1 small avocado, peeled, halved, and pitted
- ¼ teaspoon fresh lemon juice
- Pinch of salt
- ¼ teaspoon freshly ground black pepper
- 1 (8-inch) whole-wheat pocket pita bread, halved
- 12 (¼-inch thick) cucumber slices
- 6 oil-packed sun-dried tomatoes, rinsed, patted dry, and halved
- 2 tablespoons crumbled feta
- ½ teaspoon extra virgin olive oil

1. Boil water in a small saucepan over medium heat. Carefully lower the eggs into the water and boil for 7 minutes. Remove the eggs and place them in cold water.
2. In a small bowl, mash the avocado with lemon juice and salt.
3. Peel and slice the eggs, then sprinkle with black pepper.
4. Spread half of the avocado mixture on one pita half. Top with 6 cucumber slices, 6 sun-dried tomato pieces, and 1 sliced egg.
5. Sprinkle 1 tablespoon of crumbled feta over the top and drizzle ¼ teaspoon of olive oil. Repeat with the other pita half and serve immediately.

Per Serving: Calories: 427 / Fat: 28g / Protein: 14g / Carbs: 36g / Fiber: 12g / Sodium: 398mg

Smoked Trout and Avocado Toast

Serves: 2 / Prep time: 10 minutes / Cook time: 0 minutes

- 1 avocado, peeled and pitted
- 2 teaspoons lemon juice, plus extra for serving
- ¾ teaspoon ground cumin
- ¼ teaspoon kosher salt
- ¼ teaspoon red pepper flakes, plus more for sprinkling
- ¼ teaspoon lemon zest
- 2 slices whole-wheat bread, toasted
- 1 (3.75-ounce/106-g) can smoked trout

1. Mash the avocado in a medium bowl with lemon juice, cumin, salt, red pepper flakes, and lemon zest.
2. Spread half of the avocado mixture on each slice of toast.

3. Top each slice with half of the smoked trout.
4. Garnish with additional red pepper flakes and/or lemon juice, if desired.

Per Serving: Calories: 300 / Fat: 20g / Protein: 11g / Carbs: 21g / Fiber: 6g / Sodium: 390mg

Italian-Style Egg Cups

Serves: 4 / Prep time: 5 minutes / Cook time: 10 minutes

- Olive oil
- 1 cup marinara sauce
- 4 eggs
- 4 tablespoons shredded Mozzarella cheese
- 4 teaspoons grated Parmesan cheese
- Salt and freshly ground black pepper, to taste
- Chopped fresh basil, for garnish

1. Lightly coat 4 ramekins with olive oil spray. Pour ¼ cup of marinara sauce into each ramekin.
2. Crack one egg into each ramekin, on top of the marinara.
3. Sprinkle 1 tablespoon of Mozzarella and 1 tablespoon of Parmesan over each egg. Season with salt and pepper.
4. Cover each ramekin with aluminum foil and place two in the air fryer basket.
5. Air fry at 350°F (177°C) for 5 minutes. Remove the foil and continue air frying for 2 to 4 more minutes, until the egg white is cooked. For a firmer yolk, cook an additional 3 to 5 minutes.
6. Repeat with the remaining ramekins. Garnish with basil before serving.

Per Serving: Calories: 123 / Fat: 7g / Protein: 9g / Carbs: 6g / Fiber: 1g / Sodium: 84mg

Tropical Peach Smoothie Bowl

Serves: 2 / Prep time: 15 minutes / Cook time: 0 minutes

- 2 cups frozen peaches, slightly thawed
- ½ cup Greek yogurt (plain or vanilla)
- ½ avocado
- 2 tablespoons flax seeds
- 1 teaspoon vanilla extract
- 1 teaspoon orange extract
- 1 tablespoon honey (optional)

1. Blend all ingredients together until smooth.
2. Divide the mixture between two bowls and, if desired, add your favorite toppings.

Per Serving: Calories: 213 / Fat: 13g / Protein: 6g / Carbs: 23g / Fiber: 7g / Sodium: 41mg

Avocado Toast with Flax Seed Bread

Prep time: 10 minutes / Cook time: 10 minutes / Makes: 4 toasts

- Bread Base:
- ¼ cup flax seed meal
- 2 tablespoons coconut flour
- 2 teaspoons psyllium husk powder
- ⅛ teaspoon baking soda
- Optional: ½ teaspoon dried herbs, ¼ teaspoon paprika or turmeric
- Salt and black pepper, to taste
- ¼ teaspoon apple cider vinegar
- 1 teaspoon extra-virgin olive oil or ghee, plus extra for greasing
- 1 large egg
- 2 tablespoons water
- Avocado Topping:
- 1 large ripe avocado
- ¼ small red onion or 1 spring onion, finely chopped
- 1 tablespoon extra-virgin olive oil
- 1 tablespoon fresh lemon juice
- Salt, black pepper, and/or chili flakes, to taste
- 2 teaspoons chopped fresh herbs (e.g., parsley or chives)
- Optional: 2 ounces smoked salmon and/or poached egg

1. Prepare the bread base: Combine dry ingredients in a bowl. Mix in wet ingredients and let sit for 5 minutes. Divide the mixture between two greased ramekins and microwave on high for about 2 minutes, checking every 30 to 60 seconds. If too dry, add 1 tablespoon of water and microwave for another 30 seconds. Cool slightly, slice widthwise, and toast in a nonstick pan for 1 to 2 minutes per side. Set aside.
2. For the topping: Mash avocado with onion, oil, lemon juice, salt, pepper, and chili flakes. Spread over toasted bread and top with fresh herbs. Optionally, add smoked salmon.

Per Serving: Calories: 112 / Fat: 10g / Protein: 3g / Carbs: 4g / Fiber: 3g / Sodium: 71mg

Smoked Trout Crostini

Serves: 4 / Prep time: 10 minutes / Cook time: 5 minutes

- ½ French baguette, sliced into 1-inch pieces
- 1 tablespoon olive oil
- ¼ teaspoon onion powder
- 1 (4-ounce / 113-g) can smoked trout
- ¼ cup crème fraîche
- ¼ teaspoon chopped fresh dill, for garnish

1. Brush both sides of the baguette slices with olive oil and sprinkle with onion powder.
2. Toast the bread slices in a skillet over medium heat until golden brown on both sides, about 3 to 4 minutes.
3. Arrange toasted bread on a serving plate, place 1 or 2 pieces of smoked trout on each slice, and top with crème fraîche. Garnish with dill and serve immediately.

Per Serving: Calories: 206 / Fat: 10g / Protein: 13g /

Carbs: 15g / Fiber: 1g / Sodium: 350mg

Almond Banana Cocoa Smoothie

Serves: 1 / Prep time: 5 minutes / Cook time: 0 minutes

- ¾ cup almond milk
- ½ medium banana (preferably frozen)
- ¼ cup frozen blueberries
- 1 tablespoon almond butter
- 1 tablespoon unsweetened cocoa powder
- 1 tablespoon chia seeds

1. Combine all ingredients in a blender and process until smooth.

Per Serving: Calories: 300 / Fat: 16g / Protein: 8g / Carbs: 37g / Fiber: 10g / Sodium: 125mg

Spiced Berry Smoothie

Serves: 1 / Prep time: 5 minutes / Cook time: 0 minutes

- ⅔ cup plain kefir or yogurt
- ½ cup frozen mixed berries
- ½ cup chopped cucumber
- ½ cup baby spinach
- 2 tablespoons unsweetened shredded coconut
- ¼ teaspoon grated ginger
- ¼ teaspoon ground cinnamon
- ¼ teaspoon ground nutmeg
- ⅛ teaspoon ground cardamom
- ¼ teaspoon vanilla extract (optional)

1. Blend all ingredients until well mixed.

Per Serving: Calories: 165 / Fat: 7g / Protein: 7g / Carbs: 20g / Fiber: 4g / Sodium: 100mg

Greek Tomato and Egg Cups

Serves: 4 / Prep time: 5 minutes / Cook time: 10 minutes

- Olive oil
- 1 cup marinara sauce
- 4 eggs
- 4 tablespoons shredded Mozzarella cheese
- 4 teaspoons grated Parmesan cheese
- Salt and freshly ground black pepper, to taste
- Chopped fresh basil, for garnish

1. Lightly coat 4 ramekins with olive oil. Pour ¼ cup marinara sauce into each ramekin.
2. Crack an egg into each ramekin over the sauce. Top with 1 tablespoon of Mozzarella and 1 tablespoon of Parmesan cheese. Season with salt and pepper.
3. Cover ramekins with aluminum foil and air fry at 350°F (177°C) for 5 minutes. Remove foil and continue cooking for an additional 2 to 4 minutes, or longer if firmer yolks are preferred.
4. Garnish with basil before serving.

Per Serving: Calories: 123 / Fat: 7g / Protein: 9g / Carbs: 6g / Fiber: 1g / Sodium: 84mg

Tomato and Feta Egg Skillet

Serves: 2 / Prep time: 5 minutes / Cook time: 10 minutes

- 2 tablespoons finely chopped onion (any type)
- 2 teaspoons extra virgin olive oil
- 1 medium tomato, chopped
- 2 eggs
- ¼ teaspoon fine sea salt, divided
- 1 ounce (28 g) crumbled feta cheese
- ½ teaspoon dried oregano
- 1 teaspoon chopped fresh mint
- Pinch of freshly ground black pepper

1. In a small skillet over medium heat, warm the olive oil until it shimmers. Add the onions and ⅛ teaspoon of sea salt, and cook for about 3 minutes until the onions are tender.
2. Add the chopped tomatoes, stir, then reduce heat to low and simmer for about 8 minutes until the mixture thickens.
3. While the tomato mixture simmers, beat the eggs in a separate bowl.
4. Once the tomatoes are thickened, pour the eggs into the pan and increase the heat to medium. Cook, stirring continuously with a spatula, for 2–3 minutes until the eggs are fully set. Remove from heat.
5. Stir in the crumbled feta, oregano, and mint.
6. Transfer to plates, sprinkle with the remaining ⅛ teaspoon of sea salt and a pinch of black pepper. Serve immediately.

Per Serving: Calories: 156 / Fat: 12g / Protein: 8g / Carbs: 4g / Fiber: 1g / Sodium: 487mg

Sweet Potato Toast with Spinach and Eggs

Serves: 4 / Prep time: 5 minutes / Cook time: 15 minutes

- 2 large sweet potatoes, sliced lengthwise
- 6 tablespoons extra-virgin olive oil, divided
- Salt and freshly ground black pepper
- 2 plum tomatoes, halved
- 1 cup fresh spinach
- 8 medium asparagus spears, trimmed
- 4 large cooked eggs or egg substitute (poached, scrambled, or fried)
- 1 cup arugula

- 4 tablespoons pesto
- 4 tablespoons shredded Asiago cheese

1. Preheat the oven to 450°F (235°C). Brush the tomato halves with 2 tablespoons of olive oil and season with salt and pepper. Roast the tomatoes on a baking sheet for about 15 minutes, then remove and let cool.
2. Brush the sweet potato slices with 2 tablespoons of olive oil on both sides, and season with salt and pepper. Bake on a separate baking sheet for approximately 15 minutes, flipping once halfway through, until tender. Remove from oven and set aside.
3. Heat the remaining 2 tablespoons of olive oil in a sauté pan over medium heat. Sauté the spinach until wilted, then transfer to a paper-towel-lined plate. In the same pan, sauté the asparagus until tender and then place on a paper-towel-lined plate.
4. Arrange the sweet potato slices on serving plates. Top each slice with a portion of spinach and asparagus, and place a cooked egg on top. Add ¼ cup of arugula over each egg.
5. Drizzle with 1 tablespoon of pesto and sprinkle with 1 tablespoon of Asiago cheese. Serve with roasted tomato halves.

Per Serving: Calories: 441 / Fat: 35g / Protein: 13g / Carbs: 23g / Fiber: 4g / Sodium: 481mg

Farro Breakfast with Fruit and Nuts

Serves: 8 / Prep time: 10 minutes / Cook time: 20 minutes

- 16 ounces (454 g) farro, rinsed
- 4½ cups water
- ¼ cup maple syrup
- ¼ teaspoon salt
- 1 cup dried mixed fruit
- ½ cup chopped toasted mixed nuts
- 2 cups almond milk

1. In an Instant Pot®, combine farro, water, maple syrup, and salt. Stir well, close the lid, set the steam release to Sealing, select the Multigrain setting, and cook for 20 minutes. Allow the pressure to release naturally for about 30 minutes.
2. Open the lid, add dried fruit, and let it sit on the Keep Warm setting for an additional 20 minutes.
3. Serve the farro warm, topped with nuts and almond milk.

Per Serving: Calories: 347 / Fat: 7g / Protein: 9g / Carbs: 65g / Fiber: 9g / Sodium: 145mg

Chapter 2: Delicious Grains and Beans

Arborio Rice and Leeks

Serves: 6 / Prep time: 10 minutes / Cook time: 12 minutes

- 6 large leeks
- 4 scallions, chopped
- ¼ cup chopped fresh mint
- ½ tablespoon dried thyme
- ½ teaspoon salt
- ¼ teaspoon ground black pepper
- 1 cup Arborio rice
- ⅓ cup extra-virgin olive oil
- 3 tablespoons lemon juice
- 5 cups water
- ⅓ cup chopped fresh dill

1. Slice the white parts of the leeks into thick rounds, discarding the green tops.
2. In the Instant Pot®, combine the leeks, water, scallions, dill, mint, thyme, salt, and pepper. Stir well, then add the rice and mix to combine.
3. Secure the lid, set the steam release valve to Sealing, press the Rice button, and adjust the timer to 12 minutes. When cooking is complete, let the pressure release naturally for 10 minutes before performing a quick release to remove any remaining pressure.
4. Open the lid, stir the mixture, then incorporate the olive oil and lemon juice. Serve warm.

Per Serving: Calories: 224 / Fat: 12g / Protein: 4g / Carbs: 28g / Fiber: 4g / Sodium: 408mg

Cilantro and Lime Brown Rice

Serves: 8 / Prep time: 10 minutes / Cook time: 32 minutes

- 2 tablespoons extra-virgin olive oil
- ½ medium yellow onion, chopped
- 2 cloves garlic, minced
- ½ cup chopped fresh cilantro, divided
- 2 cups brown rice
- 2 tablespoons lime juice
- ¼ teaspoon salt
- ½ teaspoon ground black pepper
- 2¼ cups water
- 1 tablespoon lime zest

1. Set the Instant Pot® to Sauté mode and heat the olive oil. Sauté the onion until softened, about 6 minutes. Add the garlic and ¼ cup of cilantro and cook for another 30 seconds until fragrant. Stir in the rice and cook, stirring frequently, for about 3 minutes until lightly toasted. Press Cancel to stop Sauté mode.
2. Add water to the pot and stir well. Seal the lid, set the steam release valve to Sealing, select Manual, and set the cooking time to 22 minutes. Once the timer goes off, let the pressure release naturally for 10 minutes before performing a quick release.

3. Fluff the rice with a fork and mix in the remaining ¼ cup of cilantro, lime juice, lime zest, salt, and pepper. Serve warm.

Per Serving: Calories: 95 / Fat: 4g / Protein: 1g / Carbs: 14g / Fiber: 1g / Sodium: 94mg

South Indian Pigeon Peas and Vegetable Stew

Serves: 6 / Prep time: 20 minutes / Cook time: 4½ to 6½ hours

- For the Sambar Masala:
- 1 teaspoon rapeseed oil
- 3 tablespoons coriander seeds
- 2 tablespoons split gram
- 1 teaspoon black peppercorns
- ½ teaspoon fenugreek seeds
- ½ teaspoon mustard seeds
- ¼ teaspoon cumin seeds
- For the Sambar:
- 1½ cups split yellow pigeon peas, rinsed
- 2 fresh green chilies, sliced
- 2 garlic cloves, chopped
- 4 to 5 tablespoons sambar masala
- 2 teaspoons salt
- 1 to 2 carrots, peeled and chopped
- 1 red potato, peeled and diced
- 1 white radish, peeled and cut into 2¾-inch sticks
- 1 tomato, chopped
- 2 to 3 moringa seed pods or ⅓ pound green beans or asparagus, cut into 2¾-inch pieces
- 2 tablespoons tamarind paste
- ½ teaspoon asafetida
- 1 teaspoon mustard seeds
- 2 dried red chilies
- Fresh coriander leaves, chopped (optional)
- To Prepare the Sambar Masala:
- 12 dried red chilies
- 6 pearl onions
- 4 cups water
- 2 teaspoons coconut oil
- 20 curry leaves

1. Heat the rapeseed oil in a medium nonstick skillet. Add coriander seeds, split gram, black peppercorns, fenugreek seeds, mustard seeds, cumin seeds, and dried red chilies. Roast the spices for a few minutes until they become fragrant and slightly browned, taking care not to burn them.
2. Remove from heat, let cool, then grind into a powder using a spice grinder or mortar and pestle. Set aside.

To Prepare the Sambar:

3. In a slow cooker, combine pigeon peas, green chilies, garlic, pearl onions, sambar masala, salt, carrots, potatoes, radish, tomato, and water.
4. Cover and cook on high for 4 hours or low for 6 hours.

5. Add the moringa pods or green beans/asparagus, tamarind paste, and asafetida. Cook for an additional 30 minutes.
6. Heat coconut oil in a frying pan, add mustard seeds, curry leaves, and dried red chilies. Once the seeds pop, pour the tempering over the sambar. Garnish with fresh coriander leaves if desired and serve.

Per Serving: Calories: 312 / Fat: 7g / Protein: 12g / Carbs: 59g / Net Carbs: 43g / Sugars: 12g / Fiber: 16g / Sodium: 852mg / Cholesterol: 0mg

Bulgur Wheat with Lentils and Caramelized Onions

Serves: 6 / Prep time: 10 minutes / Cook time: 50 minutes

- ½ cup extra-virgin olive oil
- 4 large onions, chopped
- 2 teaspoons salt, divided
- 6 cups water
- 2 cups brown lentils, rinsed
- 1 teaspoon freshly ground black pepper
- 1 cup bulgur wheat

1. Heat olive oil in a medium pot over medium heat. Cook the onions, stirring frequently, for 7 to 10 minutes until they are browned at the edges.
2. Increase heat to high, add water and 1 teaspoon of salt, and bring to a boil. Boil for about 3 minutes.
3. Stir in the lentils, reduce heat to medium-low, cover, and cook for 20 minutes, stirring occasionally.
4. Add bulgur wheat, cover, and cook for an additional 20 minutes.
5. Fluff with a fork, and let stand covered for another 5 minutes. Serve topped with the reserved caramelized onions.

Per Serving: Calories: 479 / Fat: 20g / Protein: 20g / Carbs: 60g / Fiber: 24g / Sodium: 789mg

Vegetable Barley Casserole

Serves: 6 / Prep time: 10 minutes / Cook time: 6 to 8 hours

- 1 cup raw barley (not quick-cooking)
- 3 cups low-sodium vegetable broth
- 3 garlic cloves, minced
- 2 bell peppers, any color, seeded and chopped
- 1 small onion, chopped
- 2 ounces (57 g) mushrooms, sliced
- 1 teaspoon extra-virgin olive oil
- 2 tablespoons Italian seasoning
- 1 teaspoon sea salt
- ¼ teaspoon freshly ground black pepper

1. In a slow cooker, combine barley, vegetable broth, garlic, bell peppers, onion, mushrooms, olive oil, Italian seasoning, salt, and black pepper. Stir to mix.
2. Cover and cook on Low for 6 to 8 hours.

Per Serving: Calories: 147 / Fat: 2g / Protein: 5g / Carbs: 30g / Fiber: 8g / Sodium: 464mg

Polenta with Blue Cheese, Figs, and Arugula

Serves: 4 / Prep time: 15 minutes / Cook time: 40 minutes

- 1 cup coarse-ground cornmeal
- ½ cup oil-packed sun-dried tomatoes, chopped
- 1 teaspoon fresh thyme (or ¼ teaspoon dried thyme)
- ½ teaspoon table salt
- ¼ teaspoon black pepper
- 3 tablespoons extra-virgin olive oil, divided
- 2 ounces baby arugula
- 4 figs, cut into ½-inch wedges
- 1 tablespoon balsamic vinegar
- 2 ounces blue cheese, crumbled (½ cup)
- 2 tablespoons toasted pine nuts

1. Place the trivet from the Instant Pot® in the base of the insert and add 1 cup of water. Create a sling by folding a piece of aluminum foil to a 16 by 6-inch size, then position a 1½-quart round soufflé dish in the center of the sling. In a bowl, whisk together 4 cups of water, cornmeal, tomatoes, thyme, salt, and pepper, then pour the mixture into the soufflé dish. Use the sling to lower the soufflé dish onto the trivet inside the pot, allowing the sling edges to rest on the sides.
2. Lock the lid in place, set the steam release valve to Sealing, select the high-pressure cook setting, and set the timer for 40 minutes. Once done, turn off the Instant Pot and perform a quick release of the pressure. Carefully open the lid, directing steam away from you.
3. Use the sling to transfer the soufflé dish to a wire rack. Whisk 1 tablespoon of olive oil into the polenta to smooth out any lumps, and let it sit for about 10 minutes to thicken slightly. Season with additional salt and pepper if desired.
4. Toss the arugula and figs with balsamic vinegar and the remaining 2 tablespoons of olive oil, seasoning with salt and pepper to taste. Spoon the polenta onto serving plates and top with the arugula mixture, crumbled blue cheese, and pine nuts. Serve warm.

Per Serving: Calories: 360 / Fat: 21g / Protein: 7g / Carbs: 38g / Fiber: 8g / Sodium: 510mg

Spanish-Style Rice

Serves: 4 / Prep time: 10 minutes / Cook time: 20 minutes

- 2 tablespoons extra-virgin olive oil
- 1 medium onion, finely chopped
- 1 large tomato, finely diced
- 2 tablespoons tomato paste
- 1 teaspoon smoked paprika
- 1 teaspoon salt
- 1½ cups basmati rice
- 3 cups water

1. Heat olive oil in a medium pot over medium heat. Add the onion and tomato, cooking for 3 minutes.
2. Mix in the tomato paste, paprika, salt, and rice. Cook for 1 minute.
3. Pour in the water, cover the pot, and reduce the heat to low. Cook for 12 minutes.
4. Gently fluff the rice, cover, and let it sit for an additional 3 minutes.

Per Serving: Calories: 328 / Fat: 7g / Protein: 6g / Carbs: 60g / Fiber: 2g / Sodium: 651mg

Chicken, Spinach, and Chickpea Quinoa Salad

Serves: 6 / Prep time: 15 minutes / Cook time: 18 minutes

- 4 tablespoons olive oil, divided
- 1 medium yellow onion, chopped
- 2 cloves garlic, minced
- 4 cups fresh baby spinach
- ½ teaspoon salt
- ¼ teaspoon black pepper
- 1½ cups quinoa, rinsed
- 2 cups vegetable broth
- 1⅓ cups water
- 1 tablespoon apple cider vinegar
- 1 (15-ounce / 425-g) can chickpeas, drained and rinsed
- 1 (6-ounce / 170-g) boneless, skinless chicken breast, cooked and shredded

1. Set the Instant Pot® to Sauté mode and heat 2 tablespoons of olive oil. Add the onion and cook until tender, about 3 minutes. Stir in the garlic, spinach, salt, and pepper, and cook until the spinach has wilted, about 3 minutes. Transfer the spinach mixture to a large bowl. Press Cancel to stop Sauté mode.
2. Add quinoa, vegetable broth, and water to the Instant Pot®. Close the lid, set the steam release valve to Sealing, press the Rice button, and set the timer for 12 minutes.
3. While the quinoa is cooking, mix the remaining 2 tablespoons of olive oil, apple cider vinegar, chickpeas, and shredded chicken into the spinach mixture.
4. When the cooking cycle ends, let the pressure release naturally for about 20 minutes. Open the lid and fluff the quinoa with a fork. Let it cool for 10 minutes, then add it to the bowl with the chicken mixture. Mix well and serve warm, at room temperature, or chilled.

Per Serving: Calories: 232 / Fat: 12g / Protein: 14g / Carbs: 20g / Fiber: 6g / Sodium: 463mg

Lemon Herb Orzo

Serves: 4 / Prep time: 10 minutes / Cook time: 10 minutes

- 2 cups orzo
- ½ cup fresh parsley, chopped
- ½ cup fresh basil, chopped
- 2 tablespoons lemon zest
- ½ cup extra-virgin olive oil
- ⅓ cup lemon juice
- 1 teaspoon salt
- ½ teaspoon black pepper

1. Boil a large pot of water, add the orzo, and cook for 7 minutes. Drain and rinse with cold water. Allow the orzo to cool and drain completely in a strainer.
2. Transfer the cooled orzo to a large bowl and mix in the parsley, basil, and lemon zest.
3. In a small bowl, whisk together the olive oil, lemon juice, salt, and pepper. Pour the dressing over the orzo and toss to combine. Serve at room temperature or chilled.

Per Serving: Calories: 568 / Fat: 29g / Protein: 11g / Carbs: 65g / Fiber: 4g / Sodium: 586mg

Greek Chickpeas and Rice with Lemon and Tahini

Serves: 2 / Prep time: 10 minutes / Cook time: 1 hour 45 minutes

- ¾ cup dried chickpeas
- 1 tablespoon tahini
- 3 tablespoons fresh lemon juice plus juice of 1 lemon for serving
- 4 tablespoons water
- 2 tablespoons extra-virgin olive oil
- 1 medium onion, chopped
- 1 garlic clove, minced
- ¾ cup medium-grain rice
- ¾ teaspoon fine sea salt
- ½ teaspoon black pepper
- 1 bay leaf
- 2½ cups reserved chickpea cooking water
- 4 teaspoons chopped fresh parsley

1. Soak the chickpeas in a large bowl of cold water for 12 hours or overnight to expand.
2. In a small bowl, mix tahini with lemon juice and 4 tablespoons of water. Set aside.
3. Drain and rinse the chickpeas. In a large pot, cover the chickpeas with cold water and bring to a boil. Reduce heat to medium-low and simmer until tender, 60–90 minutes, checking after 30 minutes. Reserve 2½ cups of the cooking water and drain the chickpeas.
4. Heat olive oil in a medium pot over medium heat. Sauté the onions until soft, about 4–5 minutes. Add garlic and cook for another minute. Stir in rice until coated with oil.
5. Add the tahini-lemon mixture, salt, black pepper, bay leaf, and 1½ cups of the reserved cooking water (or tap water if using canned chickpeas). Reduce heat to medium-low and simmer for about 10 minutes. Add chickpeas and cook until rice is tender and water is absorbed, about 10 minutes, adding more water if

necessary.

6. Discard the bay leaf and divide the mixture into bowls. Squeeze lemon juice over each serving and sprinkle with parsley. Store leftovers in the refrigerator for up to 3 days.

Per Serving: Calories: 842 / Fat: 25g / Protein: 25g / Carbs: 134g / Fiber: 27g / Sodium: 863mg

Kale and White Bean Stew

Serves: 2 / Prep time: 15 minutes / Cook time: 7½ hours

- 1 onion, chopped
- 1 leek (white part only), sliced
- 2 celery stalks, sliced
- 2 garlic cloves, minced
- 1 cup dried white lima beans or cannellini beans, rinsed and sorted
- 2 cups vegetable broth
- ½ teaspoon salt
- ½ teaspoon dried thyme leaves
- ⅛ teaspoon freshly ground black pepper
- 3 cups torn kale

1. Combine all ingredients except the kale in the slow cooker.
2. Cover and cook on low for 7 hours, or until beans are tender.
3. Stir in the kale and cover. Cook on high for 30 minutes, or until the kale is tender yet firm.
4. Serve.

Per Serving: Calories: 176 / Fat: 1g / Protein: 9g / Carbs: 36g / Fiber: 9g / Sodium: 616mg

Hearty Lentil Soup

Serves: 6 / Prep time: 10 minutes / Cook time: 6 to 8 hours

- 1 cup dried lentils (any color), rinsed and sorted
- 3 cups low-sodium vegetable broth
- 1 (15-ounce/425-g) can no-salt-added diced tomatoes
- 1 small onion, chopped
- 3 celery stalks, chopped
- 3 carrots, chopped
- 3 garlic cloves, minced
- 2 tablespoons Italian seasoning
- 1 teaspoon sea salt
- ½ teaspoon freshly ground black pepper
- 2 bay leaves
- 1 tablespoon freshly squeezed lemon juice

1. Combine lentils, vegetable broth, tomatoes, onion, celery, carrots, garlic, Italian seasoning, salt, pepper, and bay leaves in a slow cooker. Mix well.
2. Cover and cook on low for 6 to 8 hours.
3. Stir in lemon juice before serving.

Per Serving: Calories: 152 / Fat: 1g / Protein: 10g / Carbs: 29g / Fiber: 13g / Sodium: 529mg

Tomato Sauce Lentils

Serves: 6 / Prep time: 10 minutes / Cook time: 11 minutes

- 2 cups dried lentils (red, green, or brown), rinsed and drained

- ½ teaspoon salt
- 4 cups water
- 1 (24-ounce / 680-g) jar marinara sauce
- 1 tablespoon extra-virgin olive oil
- 1 tablespoon fresh oregano, chopped
- 1 teaspoon ground fennel
- ¼ teaspoon black pepper
- ½ cup grated Parmesan cheese
- ½ cup fresh flat-leaf parsley, minced

1. Place lentils, salt, and water in the Instant Pot®. Close the lid, set the steam release to Sealing, press Manual, and set the timer for 6 minutes. Once cooking is complete, quick-release the pressure. Open the lid and drain any excess liquid.
2. Stir in marinara sauce, olive oil, oregano, fennel, and black pepper. Close the lid, set the steam release to Sealing, press Manual, and set the timer for 5 minutes. After cooking, allow the pressure to release naturally for 10 minutes, then quick-release any remaining pressure. Open the lid and top with Parmesan cheese and parsley.

Per Serving: Calories: 342 / Fat: 8g / Protein: 21g / Carbs: 48g / Fiber: 9g / Sodium: 640mg

Chickpeas with Sage and Coriander

Serves: 6 to 8 / Prep time: 20 minutes / Cook time: 22 minutes

- 1½ tablespoons table salt (for brining)
- 1 pound (454 g) dried chickpeas, rinsed and sorted
- 2 tablespoons extra-virgin olive oil, plus extra for drizzling
- 2 onions, halved and thinly sliced
- ¼ teaspoon table salt
- 1 tablespoon coriander seeds, cracked
- ¼–½ teaspoon red pepper flakes
- 2½ cups chicken broth
- ¼ cup fresh sage leaves
- 2 bay leaves
- 1½ teaspoons grated lemon zest
- 2 teaspoons lemon juice
- 2 tablespoons fresh parsley, minced

1. Dissolve 1½ tablespoons salt in 2 quarts of cold water and soak chickpeas for 8 to 24 hours. Drain and rinse.
2. Heat oil in the Instant Pot® on the highest sauté setting until shimmering. Add onions and ¼ teaspoon salt; cook until softened and browned, about 10-12 minutes. Add coriander and pepper flakes, cooking until fragrant, about 30 seconds. Add broth, scraping up any browned bits, then stir in chickpeas, sage, and bay leaves.
3. Lock the lid and close the pressure release valve. Select low pressure and cook for 10 minutes. Let the pressure release naturally for 15 minutes, then quick-release any remaining pressure. Open the lid and

remove the bay leaves. Stir in lemon zest, juice, and season with salt and pepper to taste. Garnish with parsley and serve with a drizzle of extra olive oil.

Per Serving: Calories: 190 / Fat: 6g / Protein: 11g / Carbs: 40g / Fiber: 1g / Sodium: 360mg

Spiced Quinoa Salad

Serves: 6 / Prep time: 15 minutes / Cook time: 17 minutes

- 2 tablespoons vegetable oil
- 1 medium white onion, chopped
- 2 garlic cloves, minced
- ½ teaspoon ground cumin
- ½ teaspoon ground coriander
- ½ teaspoon smoked paprika
- ½ teaspoon salt
- ¼ teaspoon black pepper
- 1½ cups quinoa, rinsed and drained
- 2 cups vegetable broth
- 1⅓ cups water
- 2 cups fresh baby spinach
- 2 plum tomatoes, seeded and chopped

1. Set the Instant Pot® to Sauté and heat the oil. Cook onion until tender, about 3 minutes. Add garlic, cumin, coriander, paprika, salt, and pepper; cook until fragrant, about 30 seconds.
2. Add quinoa, stirring to coat in the spice mixture. Cook for 2 minutes to lightly toast the quinoa. Add broth and water, scraping the bottom and sides of the pot to loosen any browned bits. Press Cancel.
3. Close the lid and set the steam release to Sealing. Press the Rice button and set the timer for 12 minutes. After cooking, let the pressure release naturally for about 20 minutes. Open the lid, add spinach and tomatoes, and fluff the quinoa with a fork. Serve warm, at room temperature, or chilled.

Per Serving: Calories: 215 / Fat: 7g / Protein: 7g / Carbs: 32g / Fiber: 4g / Sodium: 486mg

Pearled Barley Risotto

Serves: 6 / Prep time: 10 minutes / Cook time: 30 minutes

- 1 large onion, diced
- 1 stalk celery, finely chopped
- 1½ cups pearl barley, rinsed
- 4 cups low-sodium chicken broth
- 1 cup grated Parmesan cheese
- 2 tablespoons fresh parsley, chopped
- ¼ teaspoon salt
- 1 clove garlic, minced
- 2 tablespoons olive oil
- ⅓ cup dried mushrooms
- 2¼ cups water

1. Set the Instant Pot® to Sauté and heat the olive oil. Add the onion and cook for 5 minutes. Incorporate the garlic and cook for an additional 30 seconds.
2. Stir in the celery, barley, mushrooms, broth, and water. Press Cancel.

3. Secure the lid, set the steam release to Sealing, select Manual, and cook for 18 minutes. Once the cooking is complete, quick-release the pressure and open the lid.
4. Drain any excess liquid, keeping enough to ensure a slightly soupy consistency. Press Cancel, then select Sauté and cook until the risotto thickens, about 5 minutes. Mix in the cheese, parsley, and salt. Serve immediately.

Per Serving: Calories: 175 / Fat: 9g / Protein: 10g / Carbs: 13g / Fiber: 2g / Sodium: 447mg

Lentil Spread

Serves: 12 / Prep time: 10 minutes / Cook time: 34 minutes

- 2 tablespoons olive oil, divided
- 1 cup yellow onion, diced
- 3 cloves garlic, minced
- 1 teaspoon red wine vinegar
- 2 cups green lentils, rinsed
- 4 cups water
- 1 teaspoon salt
- ¼ teaspoon black pepper

1. Heat 1 tablespoon of olive oil in the Instant Pot® using the Sauté function. Cook the onion until translucent, about 3 minutes. Add garlic and vinegar, cooking for an additional 30 seconds.
2. Add the lentils, water, remaining olive oil, and salt to the pot, stirring well. Press Cancel.
3. Close the lid, set the steam release to Sealing, select the Bean function, and cook for 30 minutes. After cooking, let the pressure release naturally for 10 minutes. Quick-release any remaining pressure, then open the lid.
4. Transfer the lentil mixture to a food processor or blender and blend until smooth. Season with black pepper and serve warm.

Per Serving: Calories: 138 / Fat: 3g / Protein: 8g / Carbs: 20g / Fiber: 10g / Sodium: 196mg

Pilaf with Pistachios and Dates

Serves: 4 to 6 / Prep time: 15 minutes / Cook time: 6 minutes

- 2 tablespoons extra-virgin olive oil, plus extra for drizzling
- 1 shallot, minced
- 1½ teaspoons fresh ginger, grated
- ½ teaspoon salt
- ¼ teaspoon ground coriander
- ¼ teaspoon ground cumin
- ¼ teaspoon black pepper
- 1¾ cups water
- 1½ cups cracked freekeh, rinsed
- 3 ounces (85 g) pitted dates, chopped
- ¼ cup shelled pistachios, toasted and chopped

- 1½ tablespoons lemon juice
- ¼ cup fresh mint, chopped

1. Heat olive oil in the Instant Pot® on the highest sauté setting until it shimmers. Add shallot, ginger, salt, coriander, cumin, and pepper; cook until the shallot softens, about 2 minutes. Stir in the water and freekeh.
2. Lock the lid and close the pressure release valve. Set to high pressure and cook for 4 minutes. Turn off the Instant Pot and quick-release the pressure. Carefully remove the lid, allowing steam to escape away from you.
3. Mix in the dates, pistachios, and lemon juice. Fluff the freekeh with a fork and adjust seasoning if needed. Transfer to a serving dish, garnish with mint, and drizzle with extra olive oil. Serve.

Per Serving: Calories: 280 / Fat: 8g / Protein: 8g / Carbs: 46g / Fiber: 9g / Sodium: 200mg

Tri-Color Lentil Salad

Serves: 6 / Prep time: 15 minutes / Cook time: 12 minutes

- 2 cups tri-color dried lentils, rinsed
- ½ teaspoon salt
- 4 cups water
- 1 medium red onion, diced
- 1 stalk celery, diced
- 1 cup cherry tomatoes, sliced
- ½ yellow bell pepper, seeded and diced
- ¼ cup fresh cilantro, chopped
- ¼ cup extra-virgin olive oil
- ¼ cup red wine vinegar
- 1 tablespoon fresh oregano, chopped
- 1 teaspoon fresh thyme leaves
- ¼ teaspoon black pepper
- ½ cup feta cheese, crumbled
- ½ cup Kalamata olives, halved

1. Combine lentils, salt, and water in the Instant Pot®. Close the lid, set steam release to Sealing, press Manual, and cook for 12 minutes. Quick-release the pressure and drain any excess liquid. Let the lentils cool to room temperature, about 30 minutes.
2. Mix in the onion, celery, tomatoes, bell pepper, cilantro, olive oil, vinegar, oregano, thyme, and black pepper. Transfer to a serving bowl and garnish with feta and olives. Serve at room temperature or refrigerate for at least 2 hours.

Per Serving: Calories: 469 / Fat: 19g / Protein: 14g / Carbs: 62g / Fiber: 4g / Sodium: 730mg

Red Lentils with Feta and Kale

Serves: 6 / Prep time: 10 minutes / Cook time: 10 minutes

- 1 tablespoon olive oil
- 1 medium yellow onion, chopped
- 1 clove garlic, minced

- 3 cups chopped kale
- 1 cup dried red lentils, rinsed
- 2 cups water
- 3 tablespoons fresh mint, chopped
- 2 tablespoons fresh parsley, chopped
- 1 tablespoon lemon juice
- ¼ teaspoon ground allspice
- ¼ teaspoon salt
- ¼ teaspoon black pepper
- ½ cup feta cheese, crumbled

1. Heat olive oil in the Instant Pot® using the Sauté function. Add the onion and cook until tender, about 3 minutes. Stir in the garlic and cook until fragrant, about 30 seconds. Add the kale and cook until it begins to wilt, about 1 minute. Press Cancel.
2. Add the lentils and water. Close the lid, set the steam release to Sealing, select Manual, and cook for 5 minutes. After cooking, let the pressure release naturally for 5 minutes, then quick-release any remaining pressure. Open the lid and drain excess liquid.
3. Mix in mint, parsley, lemon juice, allspice, salt, and black pepper. Transfer to a serving bowl and top with feta. Serve warm or at room temperature.

Per Serving: Calories: 244 / Fat: 6g / Protein: 17g / Carbs: 33g / Fiber: 12g / Sodium: 338mg

Tomato Quinoa Salad

Serves: 4 / Prep time: 10 minutes / Cook time: 22 minutes

- 1 cup quinoa, rinsed
- 2 cups water
- 2 cloves garlic, minced
- 2 tablespoons olive oil
- 1 cup fresh tomatoes, diced
- ¼ cup Italian flat-leaf parsley, chopped
- 1 tablespoon lemon juice
- 1 teaspoon salt

1. Set the Instant Pot® to Sauté and heat the olive oil. Sauté the garlic for 30 seconds, then add the tomatoes, parsley, and lemon juice. Cook for an additional minute. Transfer the mixture to a small bowl and set aside. Press Cancel.
2. Add quinoa and water to the Instant Pot®. Close the lid, set the steam release to Sealing, press the Multigrain button, and set the cooking time to 20 minutes.
3. Once the timer goes off, let the pressure release naturally for about 20 minutes, then open the lid. Fluff the quinoa with a fork and mix in the tomato mixture and salt. Serve immediately.

Per Serving: Calories: 223 / Fat: 10g / Protein: 6g / Carbs: 29g / Fiber: 3g / Sodium: 586mg

Chickpea and Kale Stew

Serves: 6 / Prep time: 10 minutes / Cook time: 4 to 6 hours

- 1 to 2 tablespoons rapeseed oil
- 1 teaspoon mustard seeds
- 1 teaspoon cumin seeds
- 1 large onion, diced
- 4 garlic cloves, crushed
- 4 plum tomatoes, finely chopped
- 1 heaped teaspoon ground coriander seeds
- 1 fresh green chile, chopped
- 1 teaspoon chili powder
- 1 teaspoon turmeric
- 1 teaspoon salt
- 2 (16-ounce / 454-g) cans cooked chickpeas, drained and rinsed
- ¾ cup water
- 7 to 8 ounces (198 to 227 g) kale, chopped
- 1 fresh green chile, sliced, for garnish

1. Heat the rapeseed oil in a frying pan (or in the slow cooker if it has a sear setting). Add mustard seeds and cumin seeds, cooking until they pop and become fragrant.
2. Stir in the onion and cook, stirring occasionally, for 10 minutes. Add the garlic and cook for a few more minutes. Add the tomatoes, ground coriander, green chile, chili powder, turmeric, and salt.
3. Incorporate the chickpeas and water. Cover and cook on low for 6 hours or on high for 4 hours.
4. Add the chopped kale gradually, stirring between additions. Cook for an additional 10 to 15 minutes, until the kale is tender. Garnish with sliced green chile.

Per Serving: Calories: 202 / Fat: 6g / Protein: 10g / Carbs: 30g / Fiber: 10g / Sodium: 619mg

Greek Green Beans (Fasolakia)

Serves: 2 / Prep time: 5 minutes / Cook time: 45 minutes

- ⅓ cup olive oil
- 1 medium onion, chopped
- 1 medium russet or white potato, sliced into ¼-inch (.5 cm) thick slices
- 1 pound (454 g) green beans (fresh or frozen)
- 3 medium tomatoes, grated or 1 (15-ounce / 425-g) can crushed tomatoes
- ¼ cup fresh parsley, chopped
- 1 teaspoon granulated sugar
- ½ teaspoon salt
- ¼ teaspoon black pepper

1. Heat olive oil in a medium pot over medium-low heat. Once shimmering, add onions and sauté until soft, about 5 minutes.
2. Add the potato slices and continue to sauté for an additional 2–3 minutes.
3. Add the green beans, stirring to coat with the olive oil. Mix in the tomatoes, parsley, sugar, salt, and pepper. Stir well.
4. Pour in just enough hot water to cover half the beans. Cover and simmer for 40 minutes or until the beans are soft and there is no liquid left in the pot. Avoid

boiling.
5. Allow the beans to cool to warm or room temperature before serving. Refrigerate for up to 3 days.

Per Serving: Calories: 536 / Fat: 37g / Protein: 9g / Carbs: 50g / Fiber: 11g / Sodium: 617mg

Zucchini Boats with Lentils

Serves: 4 / Prep time: 15 minutes / Cook time: 50 minutes

- 1 cup dried green lentils, rinsed
- 2 cups water
- ¼ teaspoon salt
- 1 tablespoon olive oil
- ½ medium red onion, diced
- 1 clove garlic, minced
- 1 cup marinara sauce
- ¼ teaspoon crushed red pepper flakes
- 4 medium zucchini, halved lengthwise
- ½ cup shredded part-skim mozzarella cheese
- ¼ cup fresh parsley, chopped

1. Combine lentils, salt, and water in the Instant Pot®. Close the lid, set steam release to Sealing, press Manual, and set the timer for 12 minutes. Once cooking is complete, quick-release the pressure and open the lid. Drain any excess liquid and transfer lentils to a medium bowl. Set aside.
2. Set the Instant Pot® to Sauté and heat olive oil. Cook the onion until tender, about 3 minutes. Add garlic and cook until fragrant, about 30 seconds. Stir in the marinara sauce and crushed red pepper flakes. Press Cancel and mix in the lentils.
3. Preheat the oven to 350°F (180°C) and prepare a 9" × 13" baking dish with nonstick spray.
4. Hollow out each zucchini half with a teaspoon. Place the zucchini in the prepared baking dish and fill with the lentil mixture. Top with mozzarella cheese. Bake for 30–35 minutes, or until zucchini is tender and cheese is melted and golden. Garnish with parsley and serve hot.

Per Serving: Calories: 326 / Fat: 10g / Protein: 22g / Carbs: 39g / Fiber: 16g / Sodium: 568mg

Thyme-Infused Creamy Polenta

Serves: 6 / Prep time: 5 minutes / Cook time: 10 minutes

- 3½ cups water
- ½ cup coarse polenta
- ½ cup fine cornmeal
- 1 cup corn kernels
- 1 teaspoon dried thyme
- 1 teaspoon salt

1. Combine all ingredients in the Instant Pot® and stir well.
2. Close the lid, set steam release to Sealing, press Manual, and set the cooking time to 10 minutes. Once the timer goes off, quick-release the pressure and open the lid. Serve immediately.

Per Serving: Calories: 74 / Fat: 1g / Protein: 2g / Carbs: 14g / Fiber: 2g / Sodium: 401mg

Chapter 3: Poultry Recipes

Paella with Shrimp and Chicken

Serves: 6 / Prep time: 20 minutes / Cook time: 40 minutes

- 1 pound (454 g) chicken breasts, cubed
- 1 cup Arborio rice
- 1 teaspoon ground cumin
- 1 teaspoon smoked paprika
- ½ teaspoon ground turmeric
- 1½ cups low-sodium chicken broth
- 1 (14½-ounce / 411-g) can diced tomatoes, with juice
- 1 cup frozen peas, thawed
- 1 medium zucchini, diced
- 8 ounces (227 g) shrimp, peeled, deveined, and thawed
- 3 tablespoons olive oil
- 1 onion, chopped (about 2 cups)
- 5 garlic cloves, minced
- Zest and juice of 1 lemon
- ½ teaspoon salt
- 2 tablespoons fresh parsley, chopped

1. Heat 2 tablespoons of olive oil in a large saucepan over medium heat. Add the onion and cook, stirring occasionally, until softened, about 5 minutes. Mix in the garlic, chicken, rice, and remaining 1 tablespoon of olive oil, ensuring the rice is well coated.
2. Stir in the cumin, paprika, turmeric, chicken broth, tomatoes with juice, lemon zest, lemon juice, and salt. Spread the mixture evenly in the pan, bring to a boil, then reduce heat to medium-low. Cover and cook for 25 minutes without stirring.
3. Remove the cover and mix in the peas and zucchini. Place the shrimp on top of the rice, pressing them slightly into the mixture. Cover and cook for another 8 to 10 minutes. Let stand off heat for 10 minutes.
4. Garnish with parsley before serving.

Per Serving: Calories: 310 / Fat: 18g / Protein: 26g / Carbs: 18g / Fiber: 7g / Sodium: 314mg

Dill-Coated Chicken Strips

Serves: 4 / Prep time: 30 minutes / Cook time: 10 minutes

- 2 boneless, skinless chicken breasts (approximately 1 pound / 454 g each), sliced lengthwise
- 1 cup Italian dressing
- 3 cups crushed potato chips
- 1 tablespoon dried dill weed
- 1 tablespoon garlic powder
- 1 large egg, beaten
- 1 to 2 tablespoons oil

1. Marinate the chicken in Italian dressing by placing it in a large resealable bag and refrigerating for at least 1 hour.
2. Combine potato chips, dill, and garlic powder in a shallow dish. Place beaten egg in a second shallow dish.
3. Remove chicken from the marinade and coat thoroughly in the egg, then in the potato chip mixture.
4. Preheat the air fryer to 325°F (163°C) and line the basket with parchment paper. Arrange the coated chicken on the parchment and lightly spritz with oil.
5. Air fry for 5 minutes, flip the chicken, spritz with oil again, and cook for an additional 5 minutes until crispy and cooked through.

Per Serving: Calories: 349 / Fat: 16g / Protein: 30g / Carbs: 20g / Fiber: 2g / Sodium: 92mg

Roasted Greek Chicken and Potatoes

Serves: 4 / Prep time: 10 minutes / Cook time: 1 hour 20 minutes

- 2 pounds (907 g) potatoes (russet or white), peeled and cut into wedges
- 1½ pounds (680 g) chicken pieces (breasts, thighs, legs)
- ½ cup extra virgin olive oil
- 2 tablespoons fresh lemon juice
- 1 cup wine (any variety), for rinsing
- 1½ teaspoons freshly ground black pepper, divided
- 2 tablespoons dried oregano, divided
- 1 teaspoon salt, divided
- 2 to 3 allspice berries
- 2 to 3 cloves
- 2 garlic cloves, quartered

1. Preheat the oven to 375°F (190°C). Soak the peeled potatoes in cold water, then drain.
2. Rinse chicken pieces with wine, pat dry, and season with a rub made from 1 teaspoon pepper, 1 tablespoon oregano, and ½ teaspoon salt.
3. Dry the potatoes, toss with olive oil, lemon juice, remaining oregano, ½ teaspoon pepper, and ½ teaspoon salt. Place in a large baking dish.
4. Arrange the chicken on top of the potatoes. Scatter allspice berries, cloves, and garlic around the chicken.
5. Add hot water to the dish, tilting to distribute evenly without washing away the oil and spices. Roast for 20 minutes, then reduce temperature to 350°F (180°C) and continue roasting for 1 hour, or until the potatoes are golden and tender. Add more water if necessary.

Per Serving: Calories: 629 / Fat: 34g / Protein: 38g / Carbs: 43g / Fiber: 3g / Sodium: 761mg

Butternut Squash and Lentil Chicken

Serves: 4 / Prep time: 15 minutes / Cook time: 28 minutes

- 2 large shallots, thinly sliced
- 5 teaspoons extra-virgin olive oil, divided
- ½ teaspoon grated lemon zest
- 2 teaspoons lemon juice
- 1 teaspoon table salt, divided
- 4 bone-in chicken thighs (5 to 7 ounces / 142 to 198 g each)
- ¼ teaspoon black pepper
- 2 garlic cloves, minced
- 1½ teaspoons caraway seeds
- 1 teaspoon ground coriander
- 1 teaspoon ground cumin
- ½ teaspoon paprika
- ⅛ teaspoon cayenne pepper
- 2 cups chicken broth
- 1 cup French green lentils, rinsed
- 2 pounds (907 g) butternut squash, peeled, seeded, and cubed
- 1 cup fresh parsley or cilantro leaves

1. Mix half of the shallots with 1 tablespoon of olive oil, lemon zest, lemon juice, and ¼ teaspoon salt. Set aside. Season chicken with ½ teaspoon salt and pepper.
2. Heat 2 teaspoons of olive oil in the Instant Pot® on high sauté for 5 minutes, or until smoking. Brown chicken skin-side down for about 5 minutes, then transfer to a plate.
3. Add the remaining shallots and ¼ teaspoon salt to the pot, cooking until softened, about 2 minutes. Stir in garlic, caraway seeds, coriander, cumin, paprika, and cayenne, cooking until fragrant, about 30 seconds. Add broth and lentils, scraping up any browned bits.
4. Place chicken skin-side up into the pot, add accumulated juices, and arrange squash on top. Lock the lid and set to high pressure for 15 minutes.
5. Quick-release the pressure and carefully remove the lid. Discard chicken skin if desired. Season lentils with salt and pepper. Toss shallot mixture with parsley and serve with the chicken.

Per Serving: Calories: 513 / Fat: 14g / Protein: 42g / Carbs: 60g / Fiber: 17g / Sodium: 773mg

Turkey Breasts with Lemon and Basil

Serves: 4 / Prep time: 30 minutes / Cook time: 58 minutes

- 2 pounds (907 g) bone-in, skin-on turkey breasts
- 2 tablespoons olive oil
- Coarse sea salt and ground black pepper, to taste
- 1 teaspoon chopped fresh basil
- 2 tablespoons grated lemon zest

1. Rub olive oil over the turkey breasts and season with salt, pepper, basil, and lemon zest.
2. Place the turkey breasts skin-side up in the air fryer

basket lined with parchment paper.
3. Air fry at 330°F (166°C) for 30 minutes. Flip the turkey and cook for an additional 28 minutes.
4. Serve with lemon wedges if desired. Enjoy your meal!

Per Serving: Calories: 417 / Fat: 23g / Protein: 50g / Carbs: 0g / Fiber: 0g / Sodium: 134mg

Spiced Citrus Chicken

Serves: 8 / Prep time: 15 minutes / Cook time: 17 minutes

- 2 tablespoons olive oil
- 3 pounds (1.4 kg) boneless, skinless chicken thighs
- 1 teaspoon smoked paprika
- ½ teaspoon salt   • ⅛ teaspoon ground cinnamon
- ⅛ teaspoon ground ginger
- ⅛ teaspoon ground nutmeg
- ½ cup golden raisins   • ½ cup slivered almonds
- 1 cup orange juice   • ⅛ cup lemon juice
- ⅛ cup lime juice
- 1 pound (454 g) carrots, peeled and chopped
- 2 tablespoons water
- 1 tablespoon arrowroot powder

1. Turn on the Instant Pot® by pressing the Sauté button and heat the oil. Brown the chicken thighs for 2 minutes on each side.
2. Add the paprika, salt, cinnamon, ginger, nutmeg, raisins, almonds, orange juice, lemon juice, lime juice, and carrots. Press the Cancel button to stop the sauté function.
3. Close the lid, ensure the steam release is set to Sealing, press the Manual button, and set the cooking time to 10 minutes. Once cooking is complete, let the pressure release naturally for 5 minutes, then quick-release any remaining pressure. Open the lid once the float valve drops. Ensure the chicken's internal temperature is at least 165°F (74°C).
4. Using a slotted spoon, transfer the chicken, carrots, and raisins to a serving dish. Press Cancel to stop cooking.
5. In a small bowl, whisk the water and arrowroot powder to make a slurry. Add this mixture to the liquid in the Instant Pot®, stir well, and press the Sauté button. Adjust the temperature to Less and simmer uncovered for 3 minutes until the sauce thickens. Pour the sauce over the chicken and serve.

Per Serving: Calories: 332 / Fat: 14g / Protein: 36g / Carbs: 14g / Fiber: 3g / Sodium: 337mg

Roasted Cornish Hen with Fresh Figs

Serves: 2 / Prep time: 10 minutes / Cook time: 45 minutes

- 2 Cornish game hens   • 2 tablespoons olive oil
- 1 tablespoon Herbes de Provence
- Sea salt and freshly ground pepper, to taste
- 1 pound (454 g) fresh figs   • 1 cup dry white wine

1. Preheat the oven to 350°F (180°C).

2. Place the Cornish hens in a shallow roasting pan, then brush them with olive oil.
3. Generously season the hens with Herbes de Provence, sea salt, and freshly ground pepper. Roast the hens for 15 minutes or until they start to turn golden brown.
4. Add the figs and white wine to the roasting pan, then cover the hens with aluminum foil. Continue roasting for an additional 20–30 minutes until the hens are fully cooked. Let them rest for 10 minutes before serving.

Per Serving: Calories: 660 / Fat: 22g / Protein: 50g / Carbs: 48g / Fiber: 7g / Sodium: 166mg

Honey-Glazed Chicken Thighs

Serves: 4 / Prep time: 5 minutes / Cook time: 14 minutes

- Oil, for spraying
- 4 boneless, skinless chicken thighs, fat trimmed
- 3 tablespoons soy sauce
- 1 tablespoon balsamic vinegar
- 2 teaspoons honey
- 2 teaspoons minced garlic
- 1 teaspoon ground ginger

1. Preheat the air fryer to 400°F (204°C) and line the basket with parchment paper, lightly spraying it with oil.
2. Place the chicken thighs in the prepared basket.
3. Cook for 7 minutes, flip the thighs, and continue cooking for another 7 minutes or until the internal temperature reaches 165°F (74°C) and the juices run clear.
4. In a small saucepan, combine the soy sauce, balsamic vinegar, honey, garlic, and ginger, and warm over low heat for 1 to 2 minutes.
5. Transfer the chicken to a serving plate and drizzle with the sauce just before serving.

Per Serving: Calories: 286 / Fat: 10g / Protein: 39g / Carbs: 7g / Fiber: 0g / Sodium: 365mg

Chicken and Freekeh with Cilantro and Preserved Lemon

Serves: 4 / Prep time: 20 minutes / Cook time: 11 minutes

- 2 tablespoons extra-virgin olive oil, plus extra for drizzling
- 1 onion, finely chopped
- 4 garlic cloves, minced
- 1½ teaspoons smoked paprika
- ¼ teaspoon ground cardamom
- ¼ teaspoon red pepper flakes
- 2¼ cups chicken broth
- 1½ cups cracked freekeh, rinsed
- 2 (12-ounce / 340-g) bone-in split chicken breasts, halved crosswise and trimmed
- ½ teaspoon table salt
- ¼ teaspoon pepper
- ¼ cup chopped fresh cilantro

- 2 tablespoons toasted sesame seeds
- ½ preserved lemon, pulp and white pith removed, rind rinsed and minced (2 tablespoons)

1. Set the Instant Pot® to the highest sauté function and heat the oil until shimmering. Add the onion and cook for about 5 minutes until softened. Stir in the garlic, paprika, cardamom, and pepper flakes, and cook for about 30 seconds until fragrant. Add the broth and freekeh.
2. Season the chicken with salt and pepper and place it skin side up into the freekeh mixture. Lock the lid in place and close the pressure release valve. Select the high pressure cook function and set the cooking time to 5 minutes.
3. After cooking, turn off the Instant Pot® and quick-release the pressure. Carefully remove the lid. Transfer the chicken to a serving dish and discard the skin if desired. Tent with aluminum foil and let it rest while finishing the freekeh.
4. Fluff the freekeh with a fork. Place a clean dish towel over the pot, replace the lid, and let it sit for 5 minutes. Season with salt and pepper to taste. Serve the chicken and freekeh on a serving dish, sprinkling with cilantro, sesame seeds, and preserved lemon. Drizzle with extra oil before serving.

Per Serving: Calories: 346 / Fat: 15g / Protein: 43g / Carbs: 10g / Fiber: 2g / Sodium: 418mg

Greek-Inspired Turkey Burgers

Serves: 4 / Prep time: 10 minutes / Cook time: 10 minutes

- 1 pound (454 g) ground turkey
- 1 medium zucchini, grated
- ¼ cup whole-wheat bread crumbs
- ¼ cup red onion, minced
- ¼ cup crumbled feta cheese
- 1 large egg, beaten
- 1 garlic clove, minced
- 1 tablespoon fresh oregano, chopped
- 1 teaspoon kosher salt
- ¼ teaspoon freshly ground black pepper
- 1 tablespoon extra-virgin olive oil

1. In a large mixing bowl, combine the ground turkey, grated zucchini, bread crumbs, minced onion, feta cheese, beaten egg, minced garlic, chopped oregano, salt, and black pepper. Mix thoroughly and shape into 4 patties.
2. Heat the olive oil in a large nonstick grill pan or skillet over medium-high heat. Place the burgers in the pan and reduce the heat to medium. Cook for 5 minutes on one side, then flip and cook for another 5 minutes on the other side.

Per Serving: Calories: 285 / Fat: 16g / Protein: 26g / Carbs: 9g / Fiber: 2g / Sodium: 465mg

Spanish Garlic and Lemon Sautéed Chicken

Serves: 3 / Prep time: 10 minutes / Cook time: 15 minutes

- 2 large boneless, skinless chicken breasts
- ¼ cup extra virgin olive oil
- 3 garlic cloves, finely chopped
- 5 tablespoons fresh lemon juice
- Zest of 1 lemon
- ½ cup chopped fresh parsley
- ¼ teaspoon fine sea salt
- Pinch of freshly ground black pepper

1. Slice the chicken breasts crosswise into thin pieces, each about ¼-inch thick.
2. Heat the olive oil in a large pan over medium heat. When the oil shimmers, add the chopped garlic and sauté for about 30 seconds before adding the chicken slices.
3. Lower the heat to medium-low and sauté the chicken for about 12 minutes, stirring occasionally until the edges start to brown.
4. Add the lemon zest and juice, increase the heat to medium, and bring to a boil, using a wooden spatula to scrape any browned bits from the bottom of the pan. Cook for about 2 more minutes.
5. Stir in the chopped parsley, remove the pan from the heat, and transfer the chicken and juices to a platter.
6. Season with sea salt and black pepper, and serve immediately. Store leftovers in an airtight container in the refrigerator for up to 2 days.

Per Serving: Calories: 358 / Fat: 22g / Protein: 35g / Carbs: 4g / Fiber: 1g / Sodium: 269mg

Turkey Tenderloin with Paprika and Garlic

Serves: 4 / Prep time: 20 minutes / Cook time: 30 minutes

- Olive oil
- ½ teaspoon paprika
- ½ teaspoon garlic powder
- ½ teaspoon salt
- ½ teaspoon freshly ground black pepper
- Pinch cayenne pepper
- 1½ pounds (680 g) turkey breast tenderloin

1. Lightly spray the air fryer basket with olive oil.
2. In a small bowl, mix together the paprika, garlic powder, salt, black pepper, and cayenne pepper. Rub the spice mixture evenly over the turkey tenderloin.
3. Place the turkey in the air fryer basket and lightly spray with olive oil.
4. Air fry at 370°F (188°C) for 15 minutes. Flip the turkey, spray lightly with olive oil again, and continue air frying for an additional 10 to 15 minutes, or until

the internal temperature reaches at least 170°F (77°C).
5. Let the turkey rest for 10 minutes before slicing and serving.

Per Serving: Calories: 196 / Fat: 3g / Protein: 40g / Carbs: 1g / Fiber: 0g / Sodium: 483mg

Grilled Chicken Gyros with Vegetables and Tzatziki Sauce

Serves: 2 / Prep time: 15 minutes / Cook time: 15 minutes

- For the Chicken:
- 2 tablespoons freshly squeezed lemon juice
- 2 tablespoons olive oil, divided (plus extra for grilling)
- 1 teaspoon minced fresh oregano (or ½ teaspoon dried oregano)
- ½ teaspoon garlic powder   • ½ teaspoon salt, divided
- 8 ounces (227 g) chicken tenders
- For the Vegetables:
- 1 small zucchini, cut into ½-inch strips lengthwise
- 1 small eggplant, cut into 1-inch strips lengthwise
- ½ red pepper, seeded and halved lengthwise
- For the Tzatziki:
- ¾ cup plain Greek yogurt
- ½ English cucumber, peeled and minced
- 1 tablespoon minced fresh dill • 2 (8-inch) pita breads

1. In a medium bowl, mix the lemon juice, 1 tablespoon of olive oil, oregano, garlic powder, and ¼ teaspoon salt. Add the chicken and marinate for 30 minutes.
2. Place the zucchini, eggplant, and red pepper in a large bowl, season with salt, and toss with the remaining 1 tablespoon of olive oil. Let the vegetables sit while the chicken marinates.
3. In another bowl, mix the yogurt, cucumber, the remaining salt, and dill. Refrigerate until ready to use.
4. Preheat the grill to medium-high heat and lightly oil the grates.
5. Drain the vegetables and place them on the grill, followed by the marinated chicken tenders.
6. Grill the chicken and vegetables for 3 minutes per side, or until the chicken is cooked through and the vegetables are nicely charred.
7. Remove everything from the grill and warm the pitas on the grill for about 30 seconds, flipping them often.
8. Divide the chicken and vegetables between the pitas, top each with ¼ cup of tzatziki sauce, and roll up the pitas to serve.

Per Serving: Calories: 584 / Fat: 21g / Protein: 38g / Carbs: 64g / Fiber: 12g / Sodium: 762mg

Chicken Cacciatore with Fennel and Wild Mushrooms

Serves: 6 to 8 / Prep time: 10 minutes / Cook time: 1 hour and 10 minutes

- ½ ounce (14 g) dried porcini mushrooms
- 1 cup boiling water
- 2 tablespoons olive oil
- 12 boneless, skinless chicken thighs (about 3 pounds / 1.4 kg), trimmed
- 1 large green bell pepper, seeded and cut into rings
- 1 large onion, halved and thinly sliced
- 1 large fennel bulb, trimmed, halved, cored, and thinly sliced
- 3 garlic cloves, minced
- 1 tablespoon minced fresh rosemary
- 2 teaspoons freshly grated orange zest
- 1 teaspoon fresh thyme leaves
- 3 tablespoons red wine vinegar
- ¾ cup dry white wine
- 2 tablespoons tomato paste
- 1 teaspoon salt

1. Preheat the oven to 350°F (180°C). Soak the porcini mushrooms in boiling water for about 20 minutes.
2. Meanwhile, heat olive oil in a large skillet over medium-high heat. Brown the chicken thighs on all sides, working in batches if necessary. Transfer the browned chicken to a 9-by-13-inch baking dish.
3. Lower the heat to medium, add the bell pepper, onion, and fennel to the skillet, and cook until softened, about 5 minutes. Stir in the garlic, rosemary, orange zest, and thyme, and cook for another 30 seconds.
4. Stir in the vinegar, cooking for another minute. Remove from heat.
5. Remove the porcini mushrooms from the soaking liquid (reserving the liquid), chop them coarsely, and add them to the skillet along with the soaking liquid, wine, tomato paste, and salt. Bring to a simmer over medium heat.
6. Pour the hot mixture over the chicken in the baking dish, cover with aluminum foil, and bake for 45 minutes.
7. Let the dish rest for 5 to 10 minutes before serving.

Per Serving: Calories: 468 / Fat: 19g / Protein: 58g / Carbs: 9g / Fiber: 3g / Sodium: 527mg

Pesto Chicken with Slow-Cooked Potatoes

Serves: 6 / Prep time: 15 minutes / Cook time: 6 to 8 hours

- For the Pesto:
- 1 cup fresh basil leaves
- 1 garlic clove, crushed
- ¼ cup pine nuts
- ¼ cup grated Parmesan cheese
- 2 tablespoons extra-virgin olive oil (plus more as needed)
- 1 teaspoon sea salt
- ½ teaspoon freshly ground black pepper
- For the Chicken:
- Nonstick cooking spray

- 2 pounds (907 g) red potatoes, quartered
- 3 pounds (1.4 kg) boneless, skinless chicken thighs
- ½ cup low-sodium chicken broth

1. Make the Pesto: In a food processor, combine the basil, garlic, pine nuts, Parmesan cheese, olive oil, salt, and pepper. Pulse until smooth, adding more olive oil ½ teaspoon at a time if needed until any clumps are gone. Set aside.
2. Make the Chicken: Coat a slow cooker insert with cooking spray and add the quartered red potatoes.
3. Place the chicken thighs on top of the potatoes.
4. In a medium bowl, whisk together the prepared pesto and chicken broth until well combined, then pour the mixture over the chicken.
5. Cover the slow cooker and cook on Low for 6 to 8 hours.

Per Serving: Calories: 467 / Fat: 24g / Protein: 38g / Carbs: 25g / Fiber: 3g / Sodium: 819mg

Chicken and Vegetable Fajitas

Serves: 6 / Prep time: 15 minutes / Cook time: 23 minutes

- Chicken:
- 1 pound (454 g) boneless, skinless chicken thighs, cut crosswise into thirds
- 1 tablespoon vegetable oil
- 4½ teaspoons taco seasoning
- Vegetables:
- 1 cup sliced onion
- 1 cup sliced bell pepper
- 1 or 2 jalapeños, quartered lengthwise
- 1 tablespoon vegetable oil
- ½ teaspoon kosher salt
- ½ teaspoon ground cumin
- For Serving:
- Tortillas
- Sour cream
- Shredded cheese
- Guacamole
- Salsa

1. For the Chicken: In a medium bowl, combine the chicken, vegetable oil, and taco seasoning until evenly coated.
2. For the Vegetables: In a separate bowl, toss the sliced onion, bell pepper, and jalapeños with vegetable oil, salt, and cumin until well mixed.
3. Place the seasoned chicken in the air fryer basket. Set the air fryer to 375°F (191°C) and cook for 10 minutes. Add the vegetables to the basket, mix everything to blend the seasonings, and continue cooking for 13 more minutes. Use a meat thermometer to check that the chicken reaches an internal temperature of 165°F (74°C).
4. Transfer the cooked chicken and vegetables to a serving platter. Serve with tortillas and your preferred fajita toppings.

Per Serving: Calories: 151 / Fat: 8g / Protein: 15g / Carbs: 4g / Fiber: 1g / Sodium: 421mg

Cashew Chicken and Snap Peas

Serves: 2 / Prep time: 15 minutes / Cook time: 6 hours

- 16 ounces (454 g) boneless, skinless chicken breasts, cut into 2-inch pieces
- 2 cups sugar snap peas, strings removed
- 1 teaspoon grated fresh ginger
- 1 teaspoon minced garlic
- 2 tablespoons low-sodium soy sauce
- 1 tablespoon ketchup • 1 tablespoon rice vinegar
- 1 teaspoon honey • Pinch red pepper flakes
- ¼ cup toasted cashews
- 1 scallion, white and green parts, sliced thin

1. Place the chicken and sugar snap peas in the slow cooker.
2. In a small bowl or measuring cup, whisk together the ginger, garlic, soy sauce, ketchup, vinegar, honey, and red pepper flakes. Pour this mixture over the chicken and snap peas.
3. Cover the slow cooker and cook on low for 6 hours, until the chicken is cooked through and the snap peas are tender but still crisp.
4. Just before serving, stir in the toasted cashews and sliced scallion.

Per Serving: Calories: 463 / Fat: 14g / Protein: 59g / Carbs: 23g / Fiber: 5g / Sodium: 699mg

Chicken and Chickpea Skillet with Berbere Spice

Serves: 6 / Prep time: 15 minutes / Cook time: 45 minutes

- 2 tablespoons olive oil
- 1 (3-to 4-pound / 1.4-to 1.8-kg) whole chicken, cut into 8 pieces
- 3 teaspoons Berbere or baharat spice blend
- 1 large onion, thinly sliced into half-moons
- 2 garlic cloves, minced
- 2 cups 1-inch cubes peeled butternut squash, or 1 (12-ounce / 340-g) bag pre-cut squash
- 1 (15-ounce / 425-g) can no-salt-added chickpeas, undrained
- ½ cup golden raisins
- Hot cooked rice, for serving

1. In a 12-inch skillet, heat 1 tablespoon of olive oil over medium-high heat. Season the chicken with 2 teaspoons of the Berbere spice. Add half of the chicken pieces to the skillet and cook for 4 to 6 minutes per side until browned. Transfer the chicken to a plate and repeat with the remaining chicken.
2. In the same skillet, heat the remaining tablespoon of olive oil. Add the sliced onion and cook until softened, about 5 minutes. Stir in the remaining 1 teaspoon Berbere spice, garlic, butternut squash, chickpeas, and golden raisins. Mix well.

3. Return the chicken to the skillet, nestling the pieces among the vegetables. Bring the mixture to a boil, then reduce the heat to maintain a simmer. Cover the skillet tightly and cook for 20 to 25 minutes, or until the chicken is cooked through and the squash is tender. The chicken should reach an internal temperature of 165ºF (74ºC).
4. Serve over hot cooked rice.

Per Serving: Calories: 507 / Fat: 26g / Protein: 42g / Carbs: 33g / Fiber: 9g / Sodium: 218mg

Chicken and Olives with Couscous

Serves: 6 / Prep time: 15 minutes / Cook time: 1 hour

- 2 tablespoons olive oil, divided
- 8 bone-in, skin-on chicken thighs
- ½ teaspoon kosher salt
- ¼ teaspoon ground black pepper
- 2 cloves garlic, chopped
- 1 small red onion, chopped
- 1 red bell pepper, seeded and chopped
- 1 green bell pepper, seeded and chopped
- 1 tablespoon fresh thyme leaves
- 2 teaspoons fresh oregano leaves
- 1 (28-ounce / 794-g) can no-salt-added diced tomatoes
- 1 cup low-sodium chicken broth
- 1 cup pitted green olives, coarsely chopped
- 2 cups whole wheat couscous
- Chopped flat-leaf parsley, for garnish

1. Preheat the oven to 350°F (180°C).
2. In a large ovenproof or cast-iron skillet over medium heat, warm 1 tablespoon of olive oil. Pat the chicken thighs dry with a paper towel, then season with salt and black pepper. Cook the chicken, turning once, until golden and crispy, about 8 to 10 minutes per side. Remove the chicken from the skillet and set aside.
3. Add the remaining tablespoon of olive oil to the skillet. Sauté the chopped garlic, red onion, bell peppers, thyme, and oregano until softened, about 5 minutes. Stir in the diced tomatoes and chicken broth, bringing the mixture to a boil.
4. Return the chicken to the skillet, add the chopped olives, cover, and place the skillet in the oven. Roast for 40 to 50 minutes until the chicken is tender and a thermometer inserted into the thickest part registers 165°F (74ºC).
5. While the chicken is cooking, prepare the couscous according to package directions.
6. To serve, pile the couscous onto a serving platter, nestle the chicken pieces on top, and pour the cooked vegetables and pan juices over everything. Garnish with chopped parsley.

Per Serving: Calories: 481 / Fat: 15g / Protein: 29g / Carbs: 61g / Fiber: 11g / Sodium: 893mg

Herb-Marinated Grilled Lamb Loin Chops

Serves 4 to 6 / Prep time: 5 minutes / Cook time: 10 to 12 minutes

- 3 tablespoons olive oil   • Zest and juice of 1 lemon
- 2 tablespoons pomegranate molasses
- 1 cup finely chopped fresh mint
- ½ cup finely chopped fresh cilantro or parsley
- 2 scallions (green onions), finely chopped
- 6 lamb loin chops
- Freshly ground black pepper, to taste

1. In a small bowl, whisk together the olive oil, lemon zest, lemon juice, pomegranate molasses, mint, parsley, and scallions until well combined. Put the lamb in a large zip-top plastic bag. Add the marinade, seal the bag, and massage the marinade onto all sides of the chops. Refrigerate for at least 1 hour or up to overnight.
2. When ready to cook, heat a grill to medium.
3. Remove the chops from the marinade; discard the marinade. Season with pepper, if desired. Grill the chops for 10 to 12 minutes, turning once, for medium. Let rest for 10 minutes before serving.

Per Serving: Calories: 182 / Fat: 11g / Protein: 10g / Carbs: 10g / Fiber: 0g / Sodium: 46mg

Quinoa-Stuffed Pork Tenderloin

Serves: 6 / Prep time: 15 minutes / Cook time: 45 minutes

- 1 (1½-pound / 680-g) pork tenderloin
- ½ cup quinoa, rinsed and drained
- 2 tablespoons olive oil, divided
- 1 clove garlic, minced   • ½ medium tomato, diced
- ¼ cup chopped fresh flat-leaf parsley
- 1 tablespoon lemon juice   • 2 cups water, divided
- ¼ cup crumbled goat cheese
- ¼ teaspoon salt

1. Butterfly pork tenderloin. Open tenderloin and top with a sheet of plastic wrap. Pound pork out to ½" thick. Wrap and refrigerate until ready to use.
2. Press the Sauté button on the Instant Pot® and heat 1 tablespoon oil. Add garlic and cook 30 seconds, then add tomato, parsley, and lemon juice. Cook an additional minute. Transfer mixture to a small bowl. Press the Cancel button.
3. Add quinoa and 1 cup water to the pot. Close lid, set steam release to Sealing, press the Multigrain button, and set time to 20 minutes. When the timer beeps, let pressure release naturally, about 20 minutes, then open lid. Press the Cancel button. Fluff quinoa with a fork. Transfer

quinoa to bowl with tomato mixture and mix well.
4. Spread quinoa mixture over pork. Top with goat cheese. Season with salt. Roll pork over filling. Tie pork every 2" with butcher's twine to secure.
5. Press Sauté on the Instant Pot® and heat remaining 1 tablespoon oil. Brown pork on all sides, about 2 minutes per side. Press the Cancel button. Remove pork and clean out pot. Return to machine, add remaining 1 cup water, place rack in pot, and place pork on rack.
6. Close lid, set steam release to Sealing, Press the Manual button, and set time to 20 minutes. When the timer beeps, quick-release the pressure until the float valve drops. Open lid and transfer pork to cutting board. Let rest for 10 minutes, then remove twine and cut into 1" slices. Serve hot.

Per Serving: Calories: 207 / Fat: 9g / Protein: 25g / Carbs: 11g / Fiber: 1g / Sodium: 525mg

Lamb and Herb Stew

Serves: 8 / Prep time: 25 minutes / Cook time: 55 minutes

- 1 pound (454 g) boneless lamb shoulder, trimmed and cut into 1" pieces
- 2 tablespoons all-purpose flour • ¼ teaspoon salt
- ¼ teaspoon ground black pepper
- 2 tablespoons olive oil, divided
- 2 medium carrots, peeled and sliced
- 2 stalks celery, sliced
- 1 medium onion, peeled and chopped
- 3 cloves garlic, minced   • 4 thyme sprigs
- 1 sprig rosemary   • 1 bay leaf
- 2 tablespoons chopped fresh oregano
- 2 cups low-sodium chicken broth
- 1 cup tomato sauce
- 1 medium russet potato, cut into 1" pieces
- ¼ cup chopped fresh parsley

1. In a medium bowl, add lamb, flour, salt, and pepper. Toss until lamb is thoroughly coated. Set aside.
2. Press the Sauté button on the Instant Pot® and heat 1 tablespoon oil. Add half of the lamb pieces in a single layer, leaving space between each piece to prevent steaming, and brown well on all sides, about 3 minutes per side. Transfer lamb to a large bowl and repeat with remaining 1 tablespoon oil and lamb.
3. Add carrots, celery, and onion to the pot. Cook until tender, about 8 minutes. Add garlic and cook until fragrant, about 30 seconds. Add thyme, rosemary, oregano, and bay leaf. Stir well.
4. Slowly add chicken broth, scraping the bottom of the pot well to release any brown bits. Add tomato sauce,

potato, and browned lamb along with any juices. Press the Cancel button.

5. Close lid, set steam release to Sealing, press the Stew button, and set time to 40 minutes. When the timer beeps, quick-release the pressure until the float valve drops, open lid, and stir well. Remove and discard thyme, rosemary, and bay leaf. Sprinkle with parsley and serve hot.

Per Serving: Calories: 222 / Fat: 11g / Protein: 18g / Carbs: 11g / Fiber: 2g / Sodium: 285mg

Herb-Infused Lamb Meatballs

Serves: 4 / Prep time: 10 minutes / Cook time: 6 to 8 hours

- 1 (28-ounce / 794-g) can no-salt-added diced tomatoes
- 1 pound (454 g) raw ground lamb
- 2 garlic cloves, minced, divided
- 1 small onion, finely diced, or 1 tablespoon dried onion flakes
- 2 tablespoons bread crumbs
- 1 large egg
- 1 teaspoon dried basil
- 1 teaspoon dried oregano
- 1 teaspoon dried rosemary
- 1 teaspoon dried thyme
- 1 teaspoon sea salt
- ½ teaspoon freshly ground black pepper

1. In a slow cooker, combine the tomatoes and 1 clove of garlic. Stir to mix well.
2. In a large bowl, mix together the ground lamb, onion, egg, bread crumbs, basil, oregano, rosemary, thyme, salt, pepper, and the remaining 1 garlic clove until all of the ingredients are well-blended. Shape the meat mixture into 10 to 12 (2½-inch) meatballs. Put the meatballs in the slow cooker.
3. Cover the cooker and cook for 6 to 8 hours on Low heat.

Per Serving: Calories: 406 / Fat: 28g / Protein: 23g / Carbs: 16g / Fiber: 5g / Sodium: 815mg

Pork Milanese

Serves: 4 / Prep time: 10 minutes / Cook time: 12 minutes

- 4 (1-inch) boneless pork chops
- Fine sea salt and ground black pepper, to taste
- 2 large eggs
- ¾ cup powdered Parmesan cheese
- Chopped fresh parsley, for garnish
- Lemon slices, for serving

1. Spray the air fryer basket with avocado oil. Preheat the air fryer to 400°F (204°C).
2. Place the pork chops between 2 sheets of plastic wrap and pound them with the flat side of a meat tenderizer until they're ¼ inch thick. Lightly season both sides of the chops with salt and pepper.
3. Lightly beat the eggs in a shallow bowl. Divide the Parmesan cheese evenly between 2 bowls and set the bowls in this order: Parmesan, eggs, Parmesan. Dredge

a chop in the first bowl of Parmesan, then dip it in the eggs, and then dredge it again in the second bowl of Parmesan, making sure both sides and all edges are well coated. Repeat with the remaining chops.
4. Place the chops in the air fryer basket and air fry for 12 minutes, or until the internal temperature reaches 145°F (63°C), flipping halfway through.
5. Garnish with fresh parsley and serve immediately with lemon slices. Store leftovers in an airtight container in the refrigerator for up to 3 days. Reheat in a preheated 390°F (199°C) air fryer for 5 minutes, or until warmed through.

Per Serving: Calories: 349 / Fat: 14g / Protein: 50g / Carbs: 3g / Fiber: 0g / Sodium: 464mg

Greek-Style Pork Kebabs

Serves: 4 / Prep time: 1 hour 15 minutes / Cook time: 10 minutes

- 1½ pounds (680 g) pork loin
- ⅓ cup extra-virgin olive oil
- ⅓ cup lemon juice
- 2 tablespoons minced garlic
- 1 tablespoon dried oregano
- 1 teaspoon salt
- Pita bread and tzatziki, for serving (optional)

1. Slice the pork loin into 1-inch cubes and place them in a bowl or a resealable plastic bag.
2. In another bowl, combine the olive oil, lemon juice, garlic, oregano, and salt, mixing well.
3. Pour the marinade over the pork cubes and marinate for at least 1 hour.
4. Preheat your grill, grill pan, or a lightly oiled skillet to high heat. Thread the marinated pork onto wooden or metal skewers.
5. Grill the pork skewers for 3 minutes per side, cooking a total of 12 minutes.
6. Serve the grilled pork with pita bread and tzatziki sauce, if desired.

Per Serving: Calories: 393 / Fat: 25g / Protein: 38g / Carbs: 3g / Fiber: 0g / Sodium: 666mg

Tuscan Braised Pork

Serves: 4 / Prep time: 10 minutes / Cook time: 4⅓ hours

- 2½ pounds (1.1 kg) boneless pork shoulder
- Coarse sea salt and black pepper, to taste
- 2 tablespoons olive oil
- 1 large yellow onion, finely chopped
- 3 garlic cloves, minced
- 1 celery stalk, finely diced
- ¾ teaspoon fennel seeds
- ½ cup dry red wine
- 1 (28-ounce / 794-g) can crushed tomatoes
- 4 cups prepared hot couscous, for serving

1. Season the pork shoulder with salt and pepper.

2. Heat the olive oil in a large skillet over medium-high heat. Brown the pork on all sides, turning occasionally, for about 8 minutes. Transfer the pork to a slow cooker.
3. Reduce the skillet heat to medium and add the onion, garlic, celery, and fennel seeds. Cook, stirring frequently, until the onion softens, about 4 minutes.
4. Pour in the red wine, stirring and scraping up the browned bits from the bottom of the skillet. Cook until the wine reduces by half, about 2 minutes. Pour this mixture into the slow cooker and stir in the crushed tomatoes.
5. Cover the slow cooker and cook on high for 4 hours or on low for 8 hours until the pork is tender.
6. Move the pork to a cutting board and shred it into bite-sized pieces, discarding any fat.
7. Skim the fat from the sauce in the slow cooker, then return the shredded pork to the sauce and stir to combine. Cook for another 5 minutes to reheat.
8. Serve the braised pork hot over the couscous.

Per Serving: Calories: 669 / Fat: 17g / Protein: 72g / Carbs: 49g / Fiber: 7g / Sodium: 187mg

Red Wine-Braised Short Ribs with Potatoes

Serves: 4 / Prep time: 20 minutes / Cook time: 1 hour 20 minutes

- 2 pounds (907 g) bone-in beef short ribs, trimmed
- ¾ teaspoon table salt, divided
- ¼ teaspoon black pepper
- 1 tablespoon extra-virgin olive oil
- 1 onion, finely chopped   • 6 garlic cloves, minced
- 2 tablespoons tomato paste
- 1 tablespoon fresh oregano, minced (or 1 teaspoon dried)
- 1 (14½-ounce / 411-g) can whole peeled tomatoes, chopped, with ¼ cup juice reserved
- ½ cup dry red wine
- 1 pound (454 g) small red potatoes, halved
- 2 tablespoons fresh parsley, minced

1. Pat the short ribs dry with paper towels, then season them with ½ teaspoon salt and black pepper. Heat the olive oil using the highest sauté function on the Instant Pot for 5 minutes, or until just smoking. Brown the short ribs on all sides for 6 to 8 minutes, then transfer to a plate.
2. Add the onion and the remaining ¼ teaspoon salt to the fat left in the pot. Cook using the highest sauté function until the onion softens, about 3 minutes. Stir in the garlic, tomato paste, and oregano, cooking until fragrant, about 30 seconds.
3. Add the chopped tomatoes with the reserved juice and the red wine, scraping up any browned bits. Place the short ribs back into the pot, nestling them meat side down, and add any accumulated juices. Lock the lid in place, close the pressure release valve, and select high-pressure cook for 60 minutes.
4. Turn off the Instant Pot and let the pressure release naturally for 15 minutes. Quick-release any remaining

pressure, then carefully remove the lid, allowing the steam to escape away from you. Transfer the short ribs to a serving dish and tent with foil.
5. Strain the braising liquid through a fine-mesh strainer into a fat separator, transferring the solids back to the pot. After letting the liquid settle for 5 minutes, pour 1½ cups of the defatted liquid back into the pot along with any accumulated juices. Add the potatoes.
6. Lock the lid in place, close the pressure release valve, and select high-pressure cook for 4 minutes. Quick-release the pressure and carefully remove the lid.
7. Using a slotted spoon, transfer the potatoes to the serving dish. Season the sauce with salt and pepper to taste. Spoon the sauce over the short ribs and potatoes, and sprinkle with parsley. Serve.

Per Serving: Calories: 340 / Fat: 13g / Protein: 21g / Carbs: 29g / Fiber: 3g / Sodium: 700mg

Moroccan-Spiced Flank Steak with Harissa Couscous

Serves: 4 / Prep time: 5 minutes / Cook time: 15 minutes

- 1½ teaspoons coriander seeds
- 1¼ teaspoons ground ginger
- ½ teaspoon ground cumin
- ¾ teaspoon ground cinnamon
- ¼ teaspoon ground cloves
- 1½ pounds (680 g) flank steak
- 3 tablespoons olive oil   • ¾ cup chicken broth
- 1 tablespoon harissa   • 1 cup uncooked couscous
- ½ cup pitted dried dates, chopped
- Sea salt and freshly ground black pepper
- ¼ cup fresh Italian parsley, chopped

1. In a small bowl, combine the coriander, ginger, cumin, cinnamon, and cloves. Rub the steak thoroughly with the spice mixture.
2. Heat the olive oil in a large sauté pan over medium-high heat. Cook the steak for 2 to 3 minutes on each side for medium-rare. Transfer the steak to a plate and allow it to rest for 10 minutes.
3. In the same pan, mix together the meat juices with the chicken broth, harissa, and dates. Bring the mixture to a boil, then remove from heat. Add the couscous, cover, and let it stand for 5 minutes. Season with salt and pepper to taste.
4. Slice the steak thinly against the grain.
5. Serve the sliced steak with the couscous, garnished with chopped parsley.

Per Serving: Calories: 516 / Fat: 16g / Protein: 43g / Carbs: 49g / Fiber: 4g / Sodium: 137mg

Garlic Beef Meatballs in Creamy Sauce

Serves: 4 / Prep time: 15 minutes / Cook time: 6 to 8 hours

- For the Sauce:
- 1 cup low-sodium vegetable broth or chicken broth
- 1 tablespoon extra-virgin olive oil
- 2 garlic cloves, minced
- 1 tablespoon dried onion flakes
- 1 teaspoon dried rosemary
- 2 tablespoons freshly squeezed lemon juice
- Pinch of sea salt and black pepper
- For the Meatballs:
- 1 pound (454 g) ground beef   • 1 large egg
- 2 tablespoons bread crumbs
- 1 teaspoon ground cumin   • 1 teaspoon salt
- ½ teaspoon freshly ground black pepper
- To Finish:
- 2 cups plain Greek yogurt
- 2 tablespoons fresh parsley, chopped

1. Make the Sauce: In a medium bowl, whisk together the vegetable broth, olive oil, minced garlic, dried onion flakes, rosemary, lemon juice, salt, and pepper.
2. Make the Meatballs: In a large bowl, mix the ground beef, egg, bread crumbs, cumin, salt, and pepper until combined. Shape the mixture into 10 to 12 meatballs, each about 2½ inches in diameter.
3. Pour the sauce into a slow cooker.
4. Place the meatballs in the slow cooker on top of the sauce.
5. Cover and cook on Low heat for 6 to 8 hours.
6. Stir in the Greek yogurt, cover, and cook for an additional 15 to 30 minutes, or until the sauce thickens.
7. Garnish with chopped parsley before serving.

Per Serving: Calories: 345 / Fat: 20g / Protein: 29g / Carbs: 13g / Fiber: 1g / Sodium: 842mg

Balsamic-Glazed Pork Roast

Serves: 6 / Prep time: 10 minutes / Cook time: 6 to 8 hours

- 1 small onion, sliced
- 1 (3-pound / 1.4-kg) pork tenderloin
- 1 cup balsamic vinegar
- ½ cup low-sodium beef broth
- 3 garlic cloves, crushed
- 2 tablespoons capers, undrained
- 1½ teaspoons olive oil
- 1 teaspoon dried rosemary   • 1 teaspoon sea salt
- ½ teaspoon freshly ground black pepper

1. Place the sliced onion in the bottom of a slow cooker and position the pork tenderloin on top.
2. In a small bowl, whisk together the balsamic vinegar, beef broth, crushed garlic, capers, olive oil, dried rosemary, salt, and black pepper until well combined. Pour this mixture over the pork.
3. Cover and cook on Low heat for 6 to 8 hours.

Per Serving: Calories: 281 / Fat: 10g / Protein: 45g / Carbs: 7g / Fiber: 0g / Sodium: 523mg

Pork Stew with Cannellini Beans

Serves: 6 / Prep time: 15 minutes / Cook time: 1 hour

- 1 cup dried cannellini beans   • ¼ cup olive oil
- 1 medium onion, diced   • 3 cups water
- 2 pounds (907 g) pork roast, cut into 1-inch chunks
- 1 (8-ounce / 227-g) can tomato paste
- ¼ cup fresh flat-leaf parsley, chopped
- ½ teaspoon dried thyme
- Sea salt and freshly ground pepper, to taste

1. Rinse and sort the cannellini beans. Soak the beans in water overnight.
2. Heat the olive oil in a large stew pot over medium heat. Add the diced onion and cook, stirring occasionally, until it turns golden brown.
3. Add the pork chunks and cook for 5 to 8 minutes, stirring frequently, until the pork is browned. Drain and rinse the soaked beans, then add them to the pot.
4. Pour in the water and bring the mixture to a boil. Reduce the heat and simmer for 45 minutes, until the beans are tender.
5. Stir in the tomato paste, chopped parsley, and dried thyme. Simmer for an additional 15 minutes or until the sauce thickens slightly. Season with salt and pepper to taste.

Per Serving: Calories: 373 / Fat: 16g / Protein: 39g / Carbs: 19g / Fiber: 4g / Sodium: 107mg

Spiced Beef Skewers

Serves: 6 / Prep time: 15 minutes / Cook time: 10 minutes

- 2 pounds beef fillet   • 1½ teaspoons salt
- 1 teaspoon freshly ground black pepper
- ½ teaspoon ground allspice
- ½ teaspoon ground nutmeg
- ⅓ cup extra-virgin olive oil
- 1 large onion, cut into 8 wedges
- 1 large red bell pepper, cut into 1-inch cubes

1. Preheat your grill, grill pan, or lightly oiled skillet to high heat.
2. Cut the beef fillet into 1-inch cubes and place them in a large bowl.
3. In a small bowl, combine the salt, black pepper, allspice, and nutmeg.
4. Pour the olive oil over the beef cubes and toss to coat evenly. Sprinkle the seasoning mix over the beef and toss again to coat thoroughly.
5. Thread the beef onto skewers, alternating with onion and bell pepper pieces.
6. Grill the skewers, turning every 2 to 3 minutes, until all sides are cooked to your preferred doneness: about 6 minutes for medium-rare and 8 minutes for well-done. Serve warm.

Per Serving: Calories: 326 / Fat: 21g / Protein: 32g / Carbs: 4g / Fiber: 1g / Sodium: 714mg

Moroccan-Spiced Meatballs

Serves: 4 / Prep time: 10 minutes / Cook time: 20 minutes

- ¼ cup finely chopped onion (about ⅛ of an onion)
- ¼ cup coarsely chopped raisins
- 1 teaspoon ground cumin
- ½ teaspoon ground cinnamon
- ¼ teaspoon smoked paprika   • 1 large egg
- 1 pound (454 g) ground beef (93% lean) or ground lamb
- ⅓ cup panko bread crumbs
- 1 teaspoon extra-virgin olive oil
- 1 (28-ounce / 794-g) can low-sodium or no-salt-added crushed tomatoes
- Chopped fresh mint, feta cheese, and/or fresh orange or lemon wedges, for garnish (optional)

1. In a large bowl, mix together the chopped onion, raisins, cumin, cinnamon, smoked paprika, and egg. Add the ground beef (or lamb) and panko bread crumbs, combining gently with your hands. Form the mixture into 20 evenly-sized meatballs.
2. Heat the olive oil in a large skillet over medium-high heat. Add the meatballs and cook for 8 minutes, turning occasionally with tongs or a fork to brown them on most sides. (They will not be fully cooked.) Transfer the meatballs to a paper towel-lined plate. Discard excess fat from the pan, then wipe it clean with a paper towel.
3. Return the meatballs to the skillet and pour the crushed tomatoes over them. Cover and cook over medium-high heat until the sauce starts to bubble. Reduce heat to medium, partially cover, and simmer for 7 to 8 more minutes until the meatballs are cooked through. Garnish with fresh mint, feta cheese, and/or citrus wedges, if desired, and serve.

Per Serving: Calories: 351 / Fat: 18g / Protein: 28g / Carbs: 23g / Fiber: 5g / Sodium: 170mg

Pork Skewers with Onion

Serves: 3 / Prep time: 22 minutes / Cook time: 18 minutes

- 2 tablespoons tomato purée
- ½ fresh serrano pepper, minced
- ⅓ teaspoon paprika
- 1 pound (454 g) ground pork
- ½ cup finely chopped green onions
- 3 cloves garlic, minced
- 1 teaspoon ground black pepper (or to taste)
- 1 teaspoon salt (or to taste)

1. In a mixing bowl, thoroughly combine all the ingredients. Shape the mixture into sausage-like forms.
2. Cook in an air fryer at 355°F (179°C) for 18 minutes. Serve warm over a bed of salad on a serving platter. Enjoy!

Per Serving: Calories: 216 / Fat: 6g / Protein: 35g / Carbs: 4g / Fiber: 1g / Sodium: 855mg

Red Wine Mushroom Sauce Filet Mignon

Serves: 2 / Prep time: 20 minutes / Cook time: 20 minutes

- 2 (3-ounce / 85-g) pieces filet mignon
- 2 tablespoons olive oil, divided
- 8 ounces (227 g) baby bella (cremini) mushrooms, quartered
- 1 large shallot, minced (about ⅓ cup)
- 2 teaspoons flour   • 2 teaspoons tomato paste
- ½ cup red wine   • ½ teaspoon dried thyme
- 1 cup low-sodium chicken stock
- 1 sprig fresh rosemary• ¼ teaspoon salt
- 1 teaspoon herbes de Provence
- ¼ teaspoon garlic powder
- ¼ teaspoon onion powder
- Pinch freshly ground black pepper

1. Preheat the oven to 425°F (220°C) and place the oven rack in the middle position.
2. Remove the filets from the refrigerator about 30 minutes before cooking. Pat dry with paper towels and set aside.
3. Heat 1 tablespoon of olive oil in a sauté pan over medium-high heat. Add the mushrooms and minced shallot and cook for 10 minutes.
4. Stir in the flour and tomato paste, cooking for an additional 30 seconds. Pour in the red wine and scrape up any browned bits from the pan. Add the chicken stock, dried thyme, and rosemary.
5. Bring the sauce to a boil, stirring to prevent lumps from the flour, then reduce heat and cover to keep warm.
6. In a small bowl, mix the herbes de Provence, salt, garlic powder, onion powder, and pepper.
7. Rub the remaining olive oil on the beef and season both sides with the herb mixture.
8. Heat an oven-safe sauté pan over medium-high heat. Sear the beef for 2½ minutes on each side. Transfer the pan to the oven and roast for 5 minutes or until the internal temperature reaches 130°F (54°C) for medium-rare.
9. Let the meat rest for 5 minutes under foil, then serve topped with mushroom sauce.

Per Serving: Calories: 385 / Fat: 20g / Protein: 25g / Carbs: 15g / Fiber: 0g / Sodium: 330mg

Greek-Style Pork and Vegetables

Serves: 3 / Prep time: 10 minutes / Cook time: 40 minutes

- 1 pound (454 g) pork shoulder, cut into 1-inch cubes
- ¾ teaspoon fine sea salt, divided
- ½ teaspoon freshly ground black pepper, divided (plus more for serving)
- 4 tablespoons extra-virgin olive oil, divided
- 1 medium red onion, sliced
- 1 medium green bell pepper, seeded and sliced
- 1 medium carrot, peeled and julienned
- ¼ cup dry red wine   • 15 cherry tomatoes, halved

• 2 tablespoons hot water• ½ teaspoon dried oregano

1. Season the pork cubes with ¼ teaspoon sea salt and ¼ teaspoon black pepper. Flip and season with the remaining ¼ teaspoon sea salt and black pepper.
2. Heat 3 tablespoons of olive oil in a large pan over high heat. Add the pork in a single layer and brown for 2 minutes on each side without stirring.
3. Add the sliced onions and cook for 2 minutes. Add the bell peppers and carrots and cook for another 2 minutes, making sure the vegetables are well coated with oil.
4. Lower the heat to medium, cover loosely, and cook for 5 minutes, stirring occasionally.
5. Add the red wine and cook for about 4 minutes, scraping up any browned bits from the pan. Stir in 20 cherry tomato halves, drizzle with the remaining 1 tablespoon of olive oil, and add hot water.
6. Reduce heat to low and simmer for 15–20 minutes or until the liquids are mostly absorbed. Remove from heat.
7. Sprinkle with dried oregano, add the remaining cherry tomato halves, and season with the remaining ¼ teaspoon sea salt and additional black pepper to taste. Serve or store covered in the refrigerator for up to 3 days.

Per Serving: Calories: 407 / Fat: 27g / Protein: 30g / Carbs: 8g / Fiber: 2g / Sodium: 700mg

Smoky Herb Lamb Chops with Lemon-Rosemary Dressing

Serves: 6 / Prep time: 1 hour 35 minutes / Cook time: 10 minutes

• 4 large cloves garlic   • 1 cup lemon juice
• ⅓ cup fresh rosemary • 1 cup extra-virgin olive oil
• 1½ teaspoons salt
• 1 teaspoon freshly ground black pepper
• 6 (1-inch-thick) lamb chops

1. In a food processor or blender, combine garlic, lemon juice, rosemary, olive oil, salt, and black pepper. Blend for 15 seconds and set aside.
2. Place lamb chops in a large zip-top bag or container and cover with two-thirds of the rosemary dressing. Ensure all chops are coated. Marinate in the refrigerator for 1 hour.
3. When ready to cook, let the lamb chops sit at room temperature for 20 minutes. Preheat a grill, grill pan, or lightly oiled skillet to high heat.
4. Cook lamb chops for 3 minutes on each side. Drizzle with the remaining dressing before serving.

Per Serving: Calories: 484 / Fat: 42g / Protein: 24g / Carbs: 5g / Fiber: 1g / Sodium: 655mg

Goat Cheese-Stuffed Flank Steak

Serves: 6 / Prep time: 10 minutes / Cook time: 14 minutes

• 1 pound (454 g) flank steak
• 1 tablespoon avocado oil
• ½ teaspoon sea salt
• ½ teaspoon garlic powder
• ¼ teaspoon freshly ground black pepper
• 2 ounces (57 g) goat cheese, crumbled
• 1 cup baby spinach, chopped

1. Place the flank steak in a large zip-top bag or between plastic wrap. Pound the steak to a uniform ¼-inch thickness using a meat mallet or heavy skillet.
2. Brush both sides of the steak with avocado oil.
3. In a small bowl, mix sea salt, garlic powder, and black pepper. Sprinkle evenly over both sides of the steak.
4. Spread goat cheese and chopped spinach over one side of the steak.
5. Roll the steak tightly from one long side and secure with kitchen string at 3-inch intervals.
6. Preheat air fryer to 400ºF (204ºC). Place the steak roll in the air fryer basket. Cook for 7 minutes, flip, and cook for an additional 7 minutes, or until an instant-read thermometer shows 120ºF (49ºC) for medium-rare. Adjust cooking time for desired doneness.

Per Serving: Calories: 151 / Fat: 8g / Protein: 18g / Carbs: 0g / Fiber: 0g / Sodium: 281mg

Lamb Shanks with Tomatoes and Potatoes

Serves: 6 / Prep time: 10 minutes / Cook time: 8 hours

• 1 (15-ounce / 425-g) can crushed tomatoes in purée
• 3 tablespoons tomato paste
• 2 tablespoons apricot jam
• 6 cloves garlic, thinly sliced
• 3 strips orange zest
• ¾ teaspoon crushed dried rosemary
• ½ teaspoon ground ginger
• ½ teaspoon ground cinnamon
• Coarse sea salt
• Black pepper
• 3½ pounds (1.6 kg) lamb shanks, trimmed and cut into 1½-inch pieces
• 1¼ pounds (567 g) small new potatoes, halved (or quartered if large)

1. In a slow cooker, combine crushed tomatoes, tomato paste, apricot jam, garlic, orange zest, rosemary, ginger, and cinnamon. Season with salt and pepper.
2. Add the lamb shanks and potatoes, then spoon the tomato mixture over the top to coat.
3. Cover and cook on Low for 8 hours or High for 5 hours, until the lamb and potatoes are tender. Adjust seasoning with salt and pepper if needed.
4. Serve hot.

Per Serving: Calories: 438 / Fat: 10g / Protein: 62g / Carbs: 26g / Fiber: 4g / Sodium: 248mg

Chapter 5: Fish and Seafood Recipes

Mediterranean Garlic and Herb-Roasted Cod

Serves: 3 / Prep time: 10 minutes / Cook time: 15 minutes

- 4½ tablespoons extra-virgin olive oil, plus 1 teaspoon for brushing
- 1½ tablespoons dried oregano
- 1 teaspoon paprika
- 1½ teaspoons dried onion flakes
- ½ teaspoon salt
- ¼ teaspoon freshly ground black pepper
- 1½ tablespoons fresh lemon juice, plus extra for serving
- 1 garlic clove, minced
- 3 teaspoons Dijon mustard
- 1 pound (454 g) cod fillets, patted dry
- 2 tablespoons chopped fresh parsley
- Topping:
- 1½ tablespoons extra-virgin olive oil
- 4 tablespoons unseasoned breadcrumbs

1. Preheat the oven to 425ºF (220ºC). Brush a baking dish with 1 teaspoon of olive oil.
2. Mix oregano, paprika, onion flakes, salt, and black pepper in a small bowl.
3. Combine 4½ tablespoons of olive oil, lemon juice, garlic, and Dijon mustard in a medium bowl. Stir in the dry ingredients.
4. Coat each cod fillet with the mixture, then place them in the baking dish and drizzle the remaining coating over the top.
5. For the breadcrumb topping, mix breadcrumbs with 1½ tablespoons of olive oil in a small bowl. Sprinkle over the cod fillets.
6. Roast in the oven for 15 minutes or until the breadcrumbs are golden brown.
7. Serve with chopped parsley and a squeeze of lemon.

Per Serving: Calories: 410 / Fat: 29g / Protein: 29g / Carbs: 9g / Fiber: 1g / Sodium: 593mg

Cucumber and Salmon Salad

Serves: 2 / Prep time: 10 minutes / Cook time: 8 to 10 minutes

- 1 pound (454 g) salmon fillet
- 1½ tablespoons olive oil, divided
- 1 tablespoon sherry vinegar
- 1 tablespoon capers, rinsed and drained
- 1 seedless cucumber, thinly sliced
- ¼ Vidalia onion, thinly sliced
- 2 tablespoons chopped fresh parsley
- Salt and freshly ground black pepper, to taste

1. Preheat the air fryer to 400ºF (204ºC).
2. Brush the salmon with ½ tablespoon olive oil. Place it skin-side down in the air fryer basket and cook for 8 to 10 minutes, until the fish flakes easily with a fork. Transfer to a plate to cool to room temperature. Remove the skin and flake the salmon into bite-sized pieces.
3. Whisk together the remaining 1 tablespoon olive oil and sherry vinegar in a small bowl. Mix in the flaked salmon, capers, cucumber, onion, and parsley. Season with salt and black pepper. Toss gently to combine. Serve immediately or refrigerate for up to 4 hours.

Per Serving: Calories: 399 / Fat: 20g / Protein: 47g / Carbs: 4g / Fiber: 1g / Sodium: 276mg

Baked Swordfish with Herbs

Serves: 4 / Prep time: 10 minutes / Cook time: 20 minutes

- Olive oil spray
- ¼ cup fresh thyme
- 2 cloves garlic
- ¼ cup extra-virgin olive oil
- 1 cup fresh Italian parsley
- ¼ cup lemon juice
- ½ teaspoon salt
- 4 swordfish steaks (each 5 to 7 ounces / 142 to 198 g)

1. Preheat the oven to 450ºF (235ºC). Spray a large baking dish with olive oil.
2. In a food processor, blend parsley, thyme, lemon juice, garlic, olive oil, and salt until smooth.
3. Place swordfish steaks in the prepared baking dish and spoon the herb mixture over each steak.
4. Bake for 17 to 20 minutes or until cooked through.

Per Serving: Calories: 397 / Fat: 22g / Protein: 44g / Carbs: 3g / Fiber: 1g / Sodium: 495mg

Italian Tuna Roast

Serves: 8 / Prep time: 15 minutes / Cook time: 21 to 24 minutes

- Cooking spray
- 1 tablespoon Italian seasoning
- ⅛ teaspoon ground black pepper
- 1 tablespoon extra-light olive oil
- 1 teaspoon lemon juice
- 1 tuna loin (approximately 2 pounds / 907 g, 3 to 4 inches thick)

1. Spray a baking dish with cooking spray and place it in the air fryer basket. Preheat the air fryer to 390ºF (199ºC).
2. Combine Italian seasoning, pepper, olive oil, and lemon juice.
3. Use a dull knife to make small holes in the top of the tuna loin, almost to the bottom.
4. Spoon the oil mixture into the holes and push the

seasonings in as deep as possible.

5. Rub any remaining oil mixture over the outer surfaces of the tuna.
6. Place the tuna in the baking dish and roast at 390°F (199°C) for 20 minutes. Check with a meat thermometer and cook for an additional 1 to 4 minutes if needed until it reaches 145°F (63°C).
7. Let the tuna rest in the air fryer basket for 10 minutes.

Per Serving: Calories: 178 / Fat: 7g / Protein: 26g / Carbs: 0g / Fiber: 0g / Sodium: 44mg

Braised Striped Bass with Zucchini and Tomatoes

Serves: 4 / Prep time: 20 minutes / Cook time: 16 minutes

- 2 tablespoons extra-virgin olive oil, divided, plus extra for drizzling
- 3 zucchini (8 ounces / 227 g each), halved lengthwise and sliced ¼ inch thick
- 1 onion, chopped
- ¾ teaspoon table salt, divided
- 3 garlic cloves, minced
- 1 teaspoon minced fresh oregano or ¼ teaspoon dried
- ¼ teaspoon red pepper flakes
- 1 (28-ounce / 794-g) can whole peeled tomatoes, drained with juice reserved, halved
- 1½ pounds (680 g) skinless striped bass, 1½ inches thick, cut into 2-inch pieces
- ¼ teaspoon pepper
- 2 tablespoons chopped pitted kalamata olives
- 2 tablespoons shredded fresh mint

1. Set the Instant Pot to the highest sauté function and heat 1 tablespoon of oil for 5 minutes (until just smoking). Add zucchini and cook until tender, about 5 minutes; transfer to a bowl and set aside.
2. Add the remaining 1 tablespoon of oil, onion, and ¼ teaspoon salt to the pot and cook, still using the highest sauté function, until the onion is softened, about 5 minutes. Stir in garlic, oregano, and red pepper flakes and cook until fragrant, about 30 seconds. Mix in tomatoes and reserved juice.
3. Season the bass with the remaining ½ teaspoon salt and pepper. Nestle the bass pieces into the tomato mixture, spooning some of the cooking liquid over the top. Lock the lid, close the pressure release valve, and set the Instant Pot to high pressure for 0 minutes. When the pot reaches pressure, turn it off and quick-release the pressure. Carefully remove the lid, letting steam escape away from you.
4. Transfer the bass to a plate, cover with foil, and let rest while finishing the vegetables. Stir the zucchini back into the pot and heat through, about 5 minutes. Stir in olives and adjust seasoning with salt and pepper to taste. Serve the bass with the vegetables, garnished

with mint and drizzled with extra oil.

Per Serving: Calories: 302 / Fat: 12g / Protein: 34g / Carbs: 15g / Fiber: 6g / Sodium: 618mg

Italian Halibut with Grapes and Olive Oil

Serves: 4 / Prep time: 15 minutes / Cook time: 20 minutes

- ¼ cup extra-virgin olive oil
- 4 boneless halibut fillets, 4 ounces (113 g) each
- 4 cloves garlic, roughly chopped
- 1 small red chile pepper, finely chopped
- 2 cups seedless green grapes
- A handful of fresh basil leaves, roughly torn
- ½ teaspoon unrefined sea salt or salt
- Freshly ground black pepper

1. In a large skillet over medium-high heat, warm the olive oil. Add the halibut fillets, followed by garlic, chile pepper, grapes, basil, salt, and pepper. Pour in 1¾ cups water, reduce heat to medium-low, cover, and cook the fish until opaque, approximately 7 minutes per side.
2. Transfer the fish to a serving dish. Increase the heat and cook the sauce for 30 seconds to concentrate the flavors. Adjust the seasoning with salt and pepper as needed. Pour the sauce over the halibut.

Per Serving: Calories: 389 / Fat: 29g / Protein: 17g / Carbs: 15g / Fiber: 1g / Sodium: 384mg

Linguine with Clams and White Wine

Serves: 4 / Prep time: 20 minutes / Cook time: 12 minutes

- 2 tablespoons olive oil
- 4 cups sliced mushrooms
- 1 medium yellow onion, peeled and diced
- 2 tablespoons chopped fresh oregano
- 3 cloves garlic, peeled and minced
- ¼ teaspoon salt
- ¼ teaspoon ground black pepper
- ½ cup white wine   • 1½ cups water
- 8 ounces (227 g) linguine, broken in half
- 1 pound (454 g) fresh clams, rinsed and purged
- 3 tablespoons lemon juice
- ¼ cup grated Parmesan cheese
- 2 tablespoons chopped fresh parsley

1. Press the Sauté button on the Instant Pot® and heat the olive oil. Add mushrooms and onion, cooking until tender, about 5 minutes. Stir in oregano, garlic, salt, and pepper, and cook until fragrant, about 30 seconds. Add wine, water, and pasta, pressing the pasta down to ensure it is submerged. Press the Cancel button.
2. Top the pasta with clams and drizzle with lemon juice. Close the lid, set steam release to Sealing, press the Manual button, and set the timer for 5 minutes. When the timer goes off, quick-release the pressure and open

the lid. Serve in bowls, topped with Parmesan cheese and parsley.

Per Serving: Calories: 486 / Fat: 11g / Protein: 39g / Carbs: 52g / Fiber: 5g / Sodium: 301mg

Lemon Salmon with Dill

Serves: 4 / Prep time: 10 minutes / Cook time: 3 minutes

- 1 cup water
- 4 (4-ounce / 113-g) skin-on salmon fillets
- ½ teaspoon salt
- ½ teaspoon ground black pepper
- ¼ cup chopped fresh dill
- 1 small lemon, thinly sliced
- 2 tablespoons extra-virgin olive oil
- 1 tablespoon chopped fresh parsley

1. Pour water into the Instant Pot® and place the rack inside.
2. Season the salmon fillets with salt and pepper. Arrange the fillets on the rack, then top with dill and lemon slices. Close the lid, set steam release to Sealing, press the Steam button, and cook for 3 minutes.
3. When the cooking time is complete, quick-release the pressure and open the lid. Transfer the fillets to a serving plate, drizzle with olive oil, and garnish with parsley. Serve immediately.

Per Serving: Calories: 160 / Fat: 9g / Protein: 19g / Carbs: 0g / Fiber: 0g / Sodium: 545mg

Mixed Seafood Soup

Serves: 8 / Prep time: 15 minutes / Cook time: 22 minutes

- 2 tablespoons light olive oil
- 1 medium yellow onion, peeled and diced
- 1 medium red bell pepper, seeded and diced
- 3 cloves garlic, peeled and minced
- 1 tablespoon chopped fresh oregano
- ½ teaspoon Italian seasoning
- ½ teaspoon ground black pepper
- 2 tablespoons tomato paste
- ½ cup white wine
- 2 cups seafood stock
- 1 bay leaf
- ½ pound (227 g) medium shrimp, peeled and deveined
- ½ pound (227 g) fresh scallops
- ½ pound (227 g) fresh calamari rings
- 1 tablespoon lemon juice

1. Set the Instant Pot® to Sauté and heat the olive oil. Add onion and bell pepper, cooking until tender, about 5 minutes. Stir in garlic, oregano, Italian seasoning, and pepper, cooking until fragrant, about 30 seconds. Mix in the tomato paste and cook for 1 minute, then gradually add the wine, scraping the bottom of the pot. Press the Cancel button.

2. Pour in the seafood stock and add the bay leaf. Stir to combine. Close the lid, set the steam release to Sealing, press the Manual button, and set the timer for 5 minutes.
3. Once the timer sounds, quick-release the pressure and open the lid. Add shrimp, scallops, calamari rings, and lemon juice. Press the Cancel button, then press Sauté and simmer until the seafood is cooked, about 10 minutes. Discard the bay leaf and serve hot.

Per Serving: Calories: 172 / Fat: 7g / Protein: 15g / Carbs: 9g / Fiber: 1g / Sodium: 481mg

Shrimp Foil Packets

Serves: 4 / Prep time: 15 minutes / Cook time: 4 to 6 hours

- 1½ pounds (680 g) whole raw medium shrimp, peeled, deveined, and divided into 4 (6-ounce / 170-g) portions
- Sea salt
- Freshly ground black pepper
- 2 teaspoons extra-virgin olive oil, divided
- 4 teaspoons balsamic vinegar, divided
- 4 garlic cloves, minced
- 1 red onion, cut into chunks
- 1 large zucchini, sliced
- 4 Roma tomatoes, chopped
- 4 teaspoons dried oregano, divided
- Juice of 1 lemon

1. Place a large sheet of aluminum foil on a work surface. Arrange one-quarter of the shrimp in the center and season with salt and pepper. Drizzle with ½ teaspoon of olive oil and 1 teaspoon of balsamic vinegar.
2. Top with a quarter each of the garlic, onion, zucchini, tomato, and 1 teaspoon of oregano. Cover with a second sheet of foil and fold the edges to seal the packet.
3. Repeat with the remaining ingredients to make 3 additional packets. Place the packets in a slow cooker, arranging them in a single layer or stacking if necessary.
4. Cover and cook on Low for 4 to 6 hours. Use caution when opening the foil packets, as hot steam will escape. Drizzle each packet with lemon juice before serving.

Per Serving: Calories: 210 / Fat: 5g / Protein: 30g / Carbs: 17g / Fiber: 3g / Sodium: 187mg

Quick Ouzo Mussels

Serves: 4 / Prep time: 10 minutes / Cook time: 15 minutes

- 1 tablespoon olive oil
- 2 shallots, chopped
- 4 cloves garlic, sliced
- 1 pound (454 g) mussels, scrubbed and debearded
- 1 cup low-sodium chicken broth or water
- ½ cup ouzo
- Grated peel of 1 lemon
- 2 tablespoons chopped fresh flat-leaf parsley

1. Heat olive oil in a large pot over medium heat. Sauté shallots and garlic until softened, about 5 minutes. Increase heat, then add mussels, broth or water, and ouzo. Cover and bring to a boil, cooking until mussels have opened, around 8 minutes.
2. Discard any mussels that do not open. Garnish with lemon peel and parsley. Serve with the broth.

Per Serving: Calories: 238 / Fat: 6g / Protein: 16g / Carbs: 22g / Fiber: 0g / Sodium: 344mg

Delicious Spicy Steamed Chili Crab

Serves: 2 / Prep time: 10 minutes / Cook time: 3 minutes

- 2 tablespoons garlic chili sauce
- 1 tablespoon hoisin sauce
- 1 tablespoon minced fresh ginger
- 1 teaspoon fish sauce
- 2 cloves garlic, peeled and minced
- 2 small bird's eye chilies, minced
- 2 (2-pound / 907-g) Dungeness crabs
- 1 cup water

1. Combine garlic chili sauce, hoisin sauce, ginger, fish sauce, garlic, and chilies in a bowl. Coat crabs with the mixture.
2. Add water to the Instant Pot® and place the steamer basket inside. Arrange crabs in the basket. Close the lid, set steam release to Sealing, press the Manual button, and set the time to 3 minutes.
3. When cooking is complete, quick-release the pressure until the float valve drops. Press Cancel and open the lid. Transfer crabs to a serving dish. Serve hot.

Per Serving: Calories: 128 / Fat: 1g / Protein: 25g / Carbs: 1g / Fiber: 0g / Sodium: 619mg

Simple Cod Gratin

Serves: 4 / Prep time: 10 minutes / Cook time: 22 minutes

- ½ cup olive oil, divided
- 1 pound (454 g) fresh cod
- 1 cup black olives, pitted and chopped
- 4 leeks, trimmed and sliced
- 1 cup whole-wheat breadcrumbs
- ¾ cup low-salt chicken stock
- Sea salt and freshly ground pepper, to taste

1. Preheat the oven to 350°F (180°C). Brush 4 gratin dishes with a portion of the olive oil.
2. Place cod in a baking dish and bake for 5–7 minutes. Allow to cool, then cut into 1-inch pieces.
3. Heat remaining olive oil in a large skillet. Add olives and leeks, cooking over medium-low heat until leeks are tender.
4. Stir in breadcrumbs and chicken stock, mixing well. Gently fold in cod pieces. Divide the mixture among the gratin dishes, drizzle with olive oil, and season

with salt and pepper. Bake for 15 minutes or until heated through.

Per Serving: Calories: 538 / Fat: 33g / Protein: 26g / Carbs: 35g / Fiber: 4g / Sodium: 538mg

Fast and Tasty Shrimp Risotto

Serves: 4 / Prep time: 10 minutes / Cook time: 4 to 6 hours

- 1½ cups raw arborio rice
- 4½ cups low-sodium chicken broth
- ½ cup diced onion   • 2 garlic cloves, minced
- ½ teaspoon sea salt   • ½ teaspoon dried parsley
- ¼ teaspoon freshly ground black pepper
- 1 pound (454 g) whole raw medium shrimp, peeled and deveined
- ¼ cup grated Parmesan cheese

1. In a slow cooker, combine rice, chicken broth, onion, garlic, salt, parsley, and pepper. Stir to mix.
2. Cover and cook on Low for 4 to 6 hours.
3. Stir in shrimp and Parmesan cheese. Re-cover and cook on Low for an additional 15 to 30 minutes, or until shrimp are pink and cheese has melted.

Per Serving: Calories: 376 / Fat: 3g / Protein: 28g / Carbs: 59g / Fiber: 1g / Sodium: 602mg

Your Favourite Sheet Pan Fish Dinner

Serves: 4 / Prep time: 10 minutes / Cook time: 10 minutes

- Nonstick cooking spray
- 2 tablespoons extra-virgin olive oil
- 1 tablespoon balsamic vinegar
- 4 (4-ounce / 113-g) fish fillets, such as cod or tilapia (½ inch thick)
- 2½ cups green beans (about 12 ounces)
- 1 pint cherry or grape tomatoes (about 2 cups)

1. Preheat the oven to 400°F (205°C). Spray two large, rimmed baking sheets with nonstick cooking spray.
2. In a small bowl, whisk together olive oil and balsamic vinegar.
3. Arrange two fish fillets on each baking sheet.
4. In a large bowl, toss green beans and tomatoes with the oil and vinegar mixture. Distribute half of the vegetables over the fish on one baking sheet, and the rest over the fish on the other. Flip the fish to coat with the mixture and spread the vegetables evenly to allow for proper air circulation.
5. Bake for 5 to 8 minutes, or until the fish is opaque and flakes easily with a fork.

Per Serving: Calories: 190 / Fat: 8g / Protein: 22g / Carbs: 8g / Fiber: 3g / Sodium: 70mg

Steamed Clams

Serves: 4 / Prep time: 10 minutes / Cook time: 8 minutes

- 2 pounds (907 g) fresh clams, rinsed
- 1 tablespoon olive oil
- 1 small white onion, peeled and diced
- 1 clove garlic, peeled and quartered
- ½ cup Chardonnay • ½ cup water

1. Place the clams in the steamer basket of the Instant Pot® and set aside.
2. Press the Sauté button and heat olive oil. Add the onion and cook until soft, about 3 minutes. Add garlic and cook for an additional 30 seconds. Pour in Chardonnay and water. Insert the steamer basket with the clams. Press Cancel.
3. Close the lid, set the steam release to Sealing, press the Manual button, and set the time to 4 minutes. Once done, quick-release the pressure until the float valve drops. Open the lid.
4. Transfer clams to bowls and pour a generous amount of the cooking liquid over them.

Per Serving: Calories: 205 / Fat: 6g / Protein: 30g / Carbs: 7g / Fiber: 0g / Sodium: 135mg

Mussels with Potatoes

Serves: 6 / Prep time: 15 minutes / Cook time: 12 minutes

- 2 pounds (907 g) baby Yukon Gold potatoes, halved
- ½ cup water
- 2 tablespoons olive oil, divided
- 1 medium yellow onion, peeled and diced
- 1 tablespoon chopped fresh oregano
- ½ teaspoon paprika
- 4 cloves garlic, peeled and minced
- ¼ teaspoon salt
- ¼ teaspoon ground black pepper
- 1 (15-ounce / 425-g) can diced tomatoes
- 1½ cups water
- 2 pounds (907 g) mussels, cleaned and bearded
- ½ cup sliced green olives
- 2 tablespoons chopped fresh parsley

1. Add potatoes, water, and 1 tablespoon of oil to the Instant Pot®. Close the lid, set steam release to Sealing, press the Manual button, and cook for 2 minutes. When the timer goes off, quick-release the pressure and remove the lid. Drain the potatoes and set aside. Clean and dry the pot.
2. Press the Sauté button and heat the remaining oil. Sauté the onion until tender, about 4 minutes. Stir in oregano, paprika, garlic, salt, and pepper, and cook until fragrant, about 30 seconds. Add tomatoes and water, stirring well. Press Cancel.
3. Mix in mussels, olives, and potatoes. Close the lid, set steam release to Sealing, press the Manual button, and cook for 5 minutes. When the timer beeps, quick-release the pressure and open the lid. Discard any mussels that haven't opened. Garnish with parsley and serve.

Per Serving: Calories: 272 / Fat: 8g / Protein: 15g / Carbs: 35g / Fiber: 4g / Sodium: 560mg

White Wine–Sautéed Mussels

Serves: 4 / Prep time: 10 minutes / Cook time: 10 minutes

- 3 pounds (1.4 kg) live mussels, cleaned
- 4 tablespoons (½ stick) salted butter
- 2 shallots, finely chopped
- 2 tablespoons garlic, minced
- 2 cups dry white wine

1. Clean the mussels thoroughly, scrubbing the shells and removing any beards. Discard any that do not close tightly when tapped.
2. Melt butter in a large pot over medium heat. Add shallots and garlic, cooking for 2 minutes.
3. Pour in the white wine and cook for 1 minute.
4. Add the mussels to the pot, tossing to coat with the sauce. Cover and cook for 7 minutes, discarding any mussels that do not open.
5. Serve the mussels in bowls with the broth.

Per Serving: Calories: 468 / Fat: 15g / Protein: 41g / Carbs: 21g / Fiber: 0g / Sodium: 879mg

Chilean Sea Bass with Olive Relish

Serves: 2 / Prep time: 10 minutes / Cook time: 10 minutes

- Olive oil spray
- 2 (6-ounce / 170-g) Chilean sea bass fillets or other firm white fish
- 3 tablespoons extra-virgin olive oil
- ½ teaspoon ground cumin
- ½ teaspoon kosher salt
- ½ teaspoon black pepper
- ⅓ cup pitted green olives, diced
- ¼ cup finely diced onion
- 1 teaspoon chopped capers

1. Spray the air fryer basket with olive oil spray. Drizzle the sea bass fillets with olive oil, and season with cumin, salt, and pepper. Place fillets in the air fryer basket. Set the air fryer to 325°F (163°C) for 10 minutes, or until the fish flakes easily with a fork.
2. Meanwhile, combine the diced olives, onion, and capers in a small bowl.
3. Serve the sea bass topped with the olive relish.

Per Serving: Calories: 379 / Fat: 26g / Protein: 32g / Carbs: 3g / Fiber: 1g / Sodium: 581mg

Rosemary Salmon

Serves: 4 / Prep time: 5 minutes / Cook time: 5 minutes

- 1 cup water
- 4 (4-ounce / 113-g) salmon fillets
- ½ teaspoon salt

- ½ teaspoon ground black pepper
- 1 sprig rosemary, leaves finely chopped
- 2 tablespoons chopped fresh thyme
- 2 tablespoons extra-virgin olive oil
- 4 lemon wedges

1. Pour water into the Instant Pot® and place the rack inside.
2. Season the salmon fillets with salt and pepper. Cut four pieces of foil large enough to wrap the fillets. Place the fillets on the foil, sprinkle with rosemary and thyme, and drizzle with olive oil. Wrap the foil around the fillets loosely.
3. Place the foil packets on the rack. Close the lid, set steam release to Sealing, press the Steam button, and cook for 5 minutes.
4. When the timer ends, quick-release the pressure until the float valve drops. Open the lid carefully and remove the packets. Serve immediately with lemon wedges.

Per Serving: Calories: 160 / Fat: 8g / Protein: 24g / Carbs: 0g / Fiber: 0g / Sodium: 445mg

Saffron Rice with Cod

Serves: 4 / Prep time: 10 minutes / Cook time: 35 minutes

- 4½ cups water
- 2 cups long-grain rice, rinsed
- 1 teaspoon saffron threads
- 1½ teaspoons salt
- 1 teaspoon turmeric
- 1 large onion, chopped
- 3 cod fillets, rinsed and patted dry
- 4 tablespoons extra-virgin olive oil, divided

1. Heat 2 tablespoons of olive oil in a large pot over medium heat. Sauté the onions for 5 minutes.
2. While the onions are cooking, heat another large pan over high heat. Add the remaining 2 tablespoons of olive oil and cook the cod fillets for 2 minutes on each side. Remove the cod from the pan and set aside.
3. Once the onions are ready, add the water, saffron, salt, turmeric, and rice to the pot. Stir well, cover, and cook for 12 minutes.
4. Cut the cod into 1-inch pieces and stir them into the rice. Cover and cook for an additional 10 minutes.
5. Fluff the rice with a fork, cover, and let it sit for 5 minutes before serving warm.

Per Serving: Calories: 564 / Fat: 15g / Protein: 26g / Carbs: 78g / Fiber: 2g / Sodium: 945mg

Crispy Oregano Tilapia

Serves: 4 / Prep time: 15 minutes / Cook time: 9 minutes

- 1 pound (454 g) tilapia fillet
- ½ cup coconut flour
- 2 eggs, beaten
- ½ teaspoon ground paprika
- 1 teaspoon dried oregano
- 1 teaspoon avocado oil

1. Cut the tilapia fillets into finger-sized pieces and

season with paprika and oregano.
2. Dip each piece in beaten eggs, then coat with coconut flour.
3. Sprinkle the fish fingers with avocado oil and cook in an air fryer at 370°F (188°C) for 9 minutes.

Per Serving: Calories: 187 / Fat: 9g / Protein: 26g / Carbs: 2g / Fiber: 1g / Sodium: 92mg

Seafood Fideo Bake

Serves: 6 to 8 / Prep time: 15 minutes / Cook time: 20 minutes

- 2 tablespoons extra-virgin olive oil, plus ½ cup, divided
- 6 cups zucchini noodles, roughly chopped (2 to 3 medium zucchini)
- 1 pound (454 g) shrimp, peeled, deveined, and chopped
- 6 to 8 ounces (170 to 227 g) canned chopped clams, drained
- 4 ounces (113 g) crabmeat
- ½ cup crumbled goat cheese
- ½ cup crumbled feta cheese
- 1 (28-ounce / 794-g) can chopped tomatoes, with their juices
- 1 teaspoon salt
- 1 teaspoon garlic powder
- ½ teaspoon smoked paprika
- ½ cup shredded Parmesan cheese
- ¼ cup chopped fresh flat-leaf Italian parsley, for garnish

1. Preheat the oven to 375°F (190°C).
2. Pour 2 tablespoons of olive oil into the bottom of a 9-by-13-inch baking dish and swirl to coat.
3. In a large bowl, mix the zucchini noodles, shrimp, clams, and crabmeat.
4. In another bowl, combine goat cheese, feta, and ¼ cup of olive oil. Add canned tomatoes with their juices, salt, garlic powder, and paprika, mixing well. Combine this mixture with the zucchini and seafood.
5. Transfer the mixture to the prepared baking dish, spreading evenly. Top with shredded Parmesan and drizzle with the remaining ¼ cup of olive oil. Bake for 20 to 25 minutes, until bubbly. Garnish with chopped parsley before serving warm.

Per Serving: Calories: 302 / Fat: 21g / Protein: 22g / Carbs: 9g / Fiber: 3g / Sodium: 535mg

Burgundy-Style Salmon

Serves: 4 / Prep time: 10 minutes / Cook time: 26 minutes

- 4 salmon steaks
- Sea salt and freshly ground pepper, to taste
- 1 tablespoon olive oil
- 1 shallot, minced
- 2 cups high-quality Burgundy wine
- ½ cup beef stock
- 2 tablespoons tomato paste
- 1 teaspoon fresh thyme, chopped

1. Preheat the oven to 350°F (180°C).

2. Season the salmon steaks with sea salt and pepper. Wrap them in aluminum foil and bake for 10–13 minutes.
3. Meanwhile, heat olive oil in a deep skillet over medium heat. Cook the shallot for 3 minutes until tender.
4. Add the wine, beef stock, and tomato paste to the skillet, and simmer for 10 minutes, or until the sauce thickens and reduces by one-third.
5. Place the salmon on a serving platter and pour the sauce over it. Garnish with fresh thyme and serve.

Per Serving: Calories: 546 / Fat: 17g / Protein: 66g / Carbs: 6g / Fiber: 0g / Sodium: 303mg

Olive Oil Poached Tuna

Serves: 4 / Prep time: 5 minutes / Cook time: 45 minutes

- 1 cup extra-virgin olive oil, plus additional if needed
- 4 (3- to 4-inch) sprigs fresh rosemary
- 8 (3- to 4-inch) sprigs fresh thyme
- 2 large garlic cloves, thinly sliced
- 2 (2-inch) strips lemon zest
- 1 teaspoon salt
- ½ teaspoon freshly ground black pepper
- 1 pound (454 g) fresh tuna steaks (about 1 inch thick)

1. Choose a thick pot large enough to fit the tuna in a single layer. Combine olive oil, rosemary, thyme, garlic, lemon zest, salt, and pepper in the pot. Heat over medium-low until warm and fragrant, 20 to 25 minutes, adjusting the heat if it begins to smoke.
2. Remove from heat and let cool for 25 to 30 minutes until warm but not hot.
3. Add the tuna steaks to the pot, adding more oil if necessary to fully submerge the tuna. Return to medium-low heat and cook for 5 to 10 minutes, or until the oil is warm and fragrant but not smoking.
4. Take the pot off the heat and let the tuna sit in the warm oil for 4 to 5 minutes, depending on your preferred level of doneness. For rare tuna, cook for 2 to 3 minutes.
5. Remove the tuna from the oil and serve warm, drizzling 2 to 3 tablespoons of the seasoned oil over it. For storage, place the tuna in a covered container and pour the cooled oil over it. Refrigerate for up to 1 week. Allow to reach room temperature and liquify the oil before serving.

Per Serving: Calories: 606 / Fat: 55g / Protein: 28g / Carbs: 1g / Fiber: 0g / Sodium: 631mg

Moroccan Halibut with Cinnamon and Capers

Serves: 4 / Prep time: 5 minutes / Cook time: 20 minutes

- ¼ cup olive oil
- 4 halibut fillets (about 6 ounces or 170 g each, 1 inch thick)
- ¾ teaspoon ground cumin
- 1½ tablespoons capers, drained
- 1 (15-ounce / 425-g) can diced tomatoes, drained
- ½ teaspoon cinnamon
- ½ teaspoon salt, divided
- ½ teaspoon freshly ground black pepper, divided

1. Heat olive oil in a large skillet over medium heat. Add the cumin and cook, stirring, for 1 minute. Mix in the tomatoes, capers, cinnamon, ¼ teaspoon of salt, and ¼ teaspoon of pepper. Cook for about 10 minutes, or until the sauce thickens.
2. Pat the fish dry with paper towels and season with the remaining ¼ teaspoon of salt and ¼ teaspoon of pepper. Place the fish into the sauce, cover, and simmer for 8 to 10 minutes, until the fish is fully cooked. Serve immediately.

Per Serving: Calories: 309 / Fat: 14g / Protein: 40g / Carbs: 5g / Fiber: 2g / Sodium: 525mg

Spicy Crab Patties

Serves:3 / Prep time: 30 minutes / Cook time: 14 minutes

- 10 ounces (283 g) crab meat
- 1 tablespoon olive oil
- 2 eggs, beaten
- 1 teaspoon smoked paprika
- 1 teaspoon yellow mustard
- 1 teaspoon chopped fresh cilantro
- 1 shallot, chopped
- 2 garlic cloves, crushed
- ½ teaspoon ground black pepper
- Sea salt, to taste
- ¾ cup grated Parmesan cheese

1. In a bowl, mix together the eggs, shallot, garlic, olive oil, mustard, cilantro, crab meat, paprika, black pepper, and salt until well combined.
2. Shape the mixture into 6 patties and coat them in grated Parmesan cheese. Refrigerate for 2 hours.
3. Lightly coat the crab patties with cooking oil. Cook in an air fryer preheated to 360ºF (182ºC) for 14 minutes. Serve on dinner rolls if desired. Enjoy!

Per Serving: Calories: 288 / Fat: 16g / Protein: 32g / Carbs: 4g / Fiber: 1g / Sodium: 355mg

Parsley-Covered Trout

Serves: 4 / Prep time: 10 minutes / Cook time: 3 minutes

- 4 river trout (½-pound / 227-g each), rinsed and patted dry
- ¾ teaspoon salt, divided
- 4 cups torn lettuce leaves, divided
- 1 teaspoon white wine vinegar
- ½ cup water

- ½ cup chopped fresh flat-leaf parsley
- 1 small shallot, peeled and minced
- 2 tablespoons olive oil mayonnaise
- ½ teaspoon lemon juice
- ¼ teaspoon sugar
- 2 tablespoons toasted sliced almonds

1. Season the trout with ½ teaspoon of salt both inside and out. Place 3 cups of lettuce in the bottom of the Instant Pot®. Arrange the trout on top of the lettuce and add the remaining lettuce on top. Mix the vinegar into the water and pour it into the pot.
2. Close the lid, set the steam release to Sealing, press the Manual button, and set the timer for 3 minutes. When the timer goes off, quick-release the pressure until the float valve drops, then open the lid.
3. Transfer the trout to a serving plate. Discard the skin and fish heads if desired.
4. In a small bowl, combine the parsley, shallot, mayonnaise, lemon juice, sugar, and the remaining ¼ teaspoon of salt. Spread this mixture evenly over the trout and sprinkle with toasted almonds. Serve immediately.

Per Serving: Calories: 159 / Fat: 9g / Protein: 15g / Carbs: 4g / Fiber: 1g / Sodium: 860mg

Baked Flounder with Tomatoes and Basil

Serves: 4 / Prep time: 10 minutes / Cook time: 20 minutes

- 1 pound (454 g) cherry tomatoes
- 2 tablespoons extra-virgin olive oil
- 2 tablespoons lemon juice
- 4 garlic cloves, sliced
- 2 tablespoons fresh basil, cut into ribbons
- ½ teaspoon kosher salt
- ¼ teaspoon freshly ground black pepper
- 4 flounder fillets (5 to 6 ounces or 142 to 170 g each)

1. Preheat the oven to 425°F (220°C).
2. In a baking dish, combine the tomatoes, garlic, olive oil, lemon juice, basil, salt, and black pepper. Mix well and bake for 5 minutes.
3. Remove the dish from the oven and place the flounder fillets on top of the tomato mixture. Return to the oven and bake for an additional 10 to 15 minutes, or until the fish is opaque and flakes easily with a fork.

Per Serving: Calories: 215 / Fat: 9g / Protein: 28g / Carbs: 6g / Fiber: 2g / Sodium: 261mg

Seared Scallops with Dandelion Greens

Serves: 4 / Prep time: 5 minutes / Cook time: 15 minutes

- 3 tablespoons olive oil, divided
- 2 cloves garlic, thinly sliced
- 1 pound (454 g) dandelion greens

- 1 cup low-sodium chicken broth or water
- ½ teaspoon kosher salt, divided
- ¼ teaspoon ground black pepper, divided
- 1 cup chopped fresh mint
- 1 cup chopped fresh flat-leaf parsley
- 1 pound (454 g) scallops, muscle tabs removed
- Lemon wedges, for serving

1. Heat 1 tablespoon of olive oil in a large skillet over medium-high heat. Cook the garlic until softened, about 2 minutes. Add the dandelion greens and broth or water, bringing to a boil. Cover and cook until the greens are wilted, about 2 minutes. Season with ¼ teaspoon of salt and ⅛ teaspoon of pepper, and continue cooking until the greens are tender, 5 to 10 minutes. Stir in the mint and parsley.
2. Meanwhile, pat the scallops dry and season with the remaining ¼ teaspoon salt and ⅛ teaspoon pepper. Heat 1 tablespoon of olive oil in a large nonstick skillet over medium heat. Cook the scallops in a single layer without moving them, until browned, 1 to 2 minutes. Add the remaining tablespoon of oil, flip the scallops, and cook until browned on the other side, 1 to 2 minutes. Serve the scallops over the braised greens with lemon wedges.

Per Serving: Calories: 235 / Fat: 12g / Protein: 18g / Carbs: 17g / Fiber: 5g / Sodium: 850mg

Lemon-Infused Pesto Salmon

Serves: 2 / Prep time: 5 minutes / Cook time: 10 minutes

- 10 ounces (283 g) salmon fillet (one large piece or two smaller pieces)
- Salt
- Freshly ground black pepper
- 2 tablespoons pesto sauce
- 1 large lemon, sliced

1. Preheat the grill to medium-high heat and oil the grill grates. Alternatively, preheat your oven to 350°F (180°C) for roasting.
2. Season the salmon fillet with salt and freshly ground black pepper, then spread the pesto sauce evenly over the top.
3. Arrange lemon slices on the grill or a baking sheet, creating a bed for the salmon. Place the salmon on top of the lemon slices and add more lemon slices on top of the fish.
4. Grill the salmon for 6 to 10 minutes until it turns opaque and flakes easily. For roasting, cook for about 20 minutes. There's no need to flip the salmon.

Per Serving: Calories: 315 / Fat: 21g / Protein: 29g / Carbs: 1g / Fiber: 0g / Sodium: 176mg

Chapter 6: Easy Snacks and Appetizers

Feta and Artichoke Marinade

Prep time: 10 minutes / Cook time: 0 minutes / Makes: 1½ cups

- 4 ounces (113 g) Greek feta cheese, cut into ½-inch cubes
- 4 ounces (113 g) artichoke hearts, drained and quartered
- ⅓ cup extra-virgin olive oil
- Zest and juice from 1 lemon
- 2 tablespoons chopped fresh rosemary
- 2 tablespoons chopped fresh parsley
- ½ teaspoon black peppercorns

1. Combine the feta cheese and artichoke hearts in a glass bowl or large jar. Add the olive oil, lemon zest and juice, rosemary, parsley, and peppercorns. Gently toss to mix, being careful not to crumble the feta.
2. Cover and refrigerate for at least 4 hours, or up to 4 days. Remove from the fridge 30 minutes before serving.

Per Serving: Calories: 108 / Fat: 9g / Protein: 3g / Carbs: 4g / Fiber: 1g / Sodium: 294mg

North African-Spiced Grilled Sweet Potatoes

Serves: 8 / Prep time: 5 minutes / Cook time: 20 minutes

- ¼ cup olive oil
- 3 garlic cloves, crushed into a paste
- 1 teaspoon kosher salt
- 1 teaspoon ground cumin
- ½ teaspoon ground coriander
- ¼ teaspoon ground cinnamon
- Pinch of cayenne pepper
- 2 pounds (907 g) sweet potatoes, scrubbed and cut into ½-inch wedges
- ¼ cup chopped fresh parsley
- ¼ cup sliced kalamata olives

1. Preheat the grill to medium-high heat and oil the grill rack or pan.
2. In a large bowl, mix together the olive oil, garlic, salt, cumin, coriander, cinnamon, and cayenne pepper. Add the sweet potato wedges and toss until well-coated.
3. Grill the sweet potatoes, turning occasionally, until they have grill marks and are tender, about 3 to 6 minutes per side.
4. Transfer the grilled sweet potatoes to a serving dish. Drizzle with any remaining oil from the bowl and top with parsley and olives.

Per Serving: Calories: 179 / Fat: 10g / Protein: 2g / Carbs: 22g / Fiber: 4g / Sodium: 466mg

Muhammara from Lebanon

Serves: 6 / Prep time: 15 minutes / Cook time: 15 minutes

- 2 large red bell peppers
- ¼ cup plus 2 tablespoons extra-virgin olive oil
- 1 cup walnut halves
- 1 tablespoon agave syrup or honey
- 1 teaspoon fresh lemon juice
- 1 teaspoon ground cumin
- 1 teaspoon kosher salt
- 1 teaspoon red pepper flakes
- Raw vegetables or toasted pita chips, for serving

1. Drizzle the bell peppers with 2 tablespoons of olive oil and place them in the air fryer basket. Set the air fryer to 400°F (204°C) and cook for 10 minutes.
2. Add the walnuts to the basket and cook for an additional 5 minutes at 400°F (204°C).
3. Remove the peppers, seal them in a plastic bag, and let them rest for 5 to 10 minutes. Transfer the walnuts to a plate to cool.
4. Peel the softened peppers and place them in a food processor with the walnuts, agave syrup, lemon juice, cumin, salt, and ½ teaspoon of the red pepper flakes. Blend until smooth.
5. Transfer the mixture to a serving bowl, make a small well in the center, and pour the remaining ¼ cup olive oil into the well. Sprinkle the remaining ½ teaspoon of red pepper flakes on top. Serve with raw veggies or pita chips.

Per Serving: Calories: 219 / Fat: 20g / Protein: 3g / Carbs: 9g / Fiber: 2g / Sodium: 391mg

Crispy Roasted Chickpeas

Prep time: 5 minutes / Cook time: 15 minutes / Makes: About 1 cup

- 1 (15-ounce / 425-g) can chickpeas, drained
- 2 teaspoons curry powder
- ¼ teaspoon salt
- 1 tablespoon olive oil

1. Thoroughly drain the chickpeas and spread them on paper towels. Cover with another towel and gently press to remove excess moisture.
2. Combine the curry powder and salt.
3. Place the chickpeas in a bowl and toss with the seasoning mixture.

4. Add the olive oil and stir to coat the chickpeas evenly.
5. Air fry at 390ºF (199ºC) for 15 minutes, shaking the basket halfway through.
6. Let cool completely before storing in an airtight container.

Per Serving (¼ cup): Calories: 181 / Fat: 6g / Protein: 8g / Carbs: 24g / Fiber: 7g / Sodium: 407mg

Zesty Lemon Garlic Hummus

Serves: 6 / Prep time: 5 minutes / Cook time: 0 minutes

- 1 (15-ounce / 425-g) can chickpeas, drained (reserve liquid)
- 3 tablespoons freshly squeezed lemon juice (from about 1 large lemon)
- 2 tablespoons peanut butter
- 3 tablespoons extra-virgin olive oil, divided
- 2 garlic cloves
- ¼ teaspoon kosher or sea salt (optional)
- Raw veggies or whole-grain crackers, for serving (optional)

1. In a food processor, combine the chickpeas with 2 tablespoons of the reserved liquid, lemon juice, peanut butter, 2 tablespoons of olive oil, and garlic. Blend for 1 minute, then scrape down the sides and blend for another minute until smooth.
2. Transfer to a serving bowl, drizzle with the remaining 1 tablespoon of olive oil, and sprinkle with salt if desired. Serve with veggies or crackers if preferred.

Per Serving: Calories: 192 / Fat: 11g / Protein: 6g / Carbs: 18g / Fiber: 5g / Sodium: 258mg

Ricotta and Orange-Raisin Flatbread

Serves: 4 to 6 / Prep time: 5 minutes / Cook time: 8 minutes

- ¾ cup golden raisins, chopped
- 1 shallot, finely minced
- 1 tablespoon olive oil
- 1 tablespoon red wine vinegar
- 1 tablespoon honey
- 1 tablespoon chopped parsley
- 1 tablespoon fresh orange zest
- Pinch of salt
- 1 oval pre-baked whole-wheat flatbread (e.g., naan or pocketless pita)
- 8 ounces (227 g) ricotta cheese
- ½ cup baby arugula

1. Preheat the oven to 450°F (235°C).
2. In a small bowl, mix the raisins, shallot, olive oil, vinegar, honey, parsley, orange zest, and salt.
3. Place the flatbread on a baking sheet and toast in the oven for about 8 minutes, or until the edges are slightly browned.
4. Spread the ricotta cheese over the warm flatbread

using the back of a spoon. Top with arugula. Cut the flatbread into triangles and add a spoonful of the relish to each piece. Serve immediately.

Per Serving: Calories: 195 / Fat: 9g / Protein: 6g / Carbs: 25g / Fiber: 1g / Sodium: 135mg

Lemon-Pepper Air-Fried Chicken Legs

Serves: 2 / Prep time: 30 minutes / Cook time: 30 minutes

- 2 teaspoons freshly ground black pepper
- 1 teaspoon baking powder
- ½ teaspoon garlic powder
- 4 chicken drumsticks (4 ounces / 113 g each)
- Kosher salt, to taste
- 1 lemon

1. In a small bowl, combine the pepper, baking powder, and garlic powder. Rub the mixture evenly over the chicken drumsticks. Refrigerate for at least 1 hour or overnight.
2. Season the drumsticks with salt, then arrange them in the air fryer basket, standing them bone-end up. Air fry at 375ºF (191ºC) for about 30 minutes, or until the chicken is cooked through and crispy.
3. Transfer the drumsticks to a serving plate, grate lemon zest over them while still hot, and cut the lemon into wedges to serve alongside.

Per Serving: Calories: 438 / Fat: 24g / Protein: 48g / Carbs: 6g / Fiber: 2g / Sodium: 279mg

Herb-Marinated Olives and Mushrooms

Serves: 8 / Prep time: 10 minutes / Cook time: 0 minutes

- 1 pound (454 g) white button mushrooms
- 1 pound (454 g) assorted high-quality olives
- 2 tablespoons fresh thyme leaves
- 1 tablespoon white wine vinegar
- ½ tablespoon crushed fennel seeds
- Pinch of chili flakes
- Olive oil, to cover
- Sea salt and freshly ground black pepper, to taste

1. Rinse and clean the mushrooms under cold water and pat them dry.
2. Mix the mushrooms and olives in a glass jar or airtight container. Add thyme, white wine vinegar, fennel seeds, and chili flakes. Cover with olive oil and season with sea salt and pepper.
3. Shake the jar to mix ingredients and let it marinate for at least 1 hour. Serve at room temperature.

Per Serving: Calories: 61 / Fat: 4g / Protein: 2g / Carbs: 5g / Fiber: 2g / Sodium: 420mg

Smoky Eggplant Dip

Serves: 6 / Prep time: 50 minutes / Cook time: 40 minutes

- 2 large eggplants, cleaned
- ¼ cup lemon juice
- 1 teaspoon minced garlic
- 1 teaspoon salt
- ½ cup tahini paste
- 3 tablespoons extra-virgin olive oil

1. Grill the eggplants over a low flame, turning every 5 minutes, until evenly cooked, about 40 minutes.
2. Place the grilled eggplants in a bowl or on a plate, cover with plastic wrap, and let them steam for 5 to 10 minutes.
3. Peel the charred skin off the eggplants and remove the stem.
4. Place the eggplant flesh in a food processor with lemon juice, garlic, salt, and tahini. Pulse 5 to 7 times until well combined.
5. Transfer to a serving plate, drizzle with olive oil, and serve chilled or at room temperature.

Per Serving: Calories: 230 / Fat: 18g / Protein: 5g / Carbs: 16g / Fiber: 7g / Sodium: 416mg

Crispy Baked Potato Sticks

Serves:2 / Prep time: 10 minutes / Cook time: 15 minutes per batch

- 2 to 3 russet potatoes, peeled and cut into ¼-inch sticks
- 2 to 3 teaspoons olive or vegetable oil
- Salt, to taste

1. Cut the potatoes into ¼-inch sticks (a mandolin with a julienne blade works well). Rinse the potato sticks under cold water several times and soak in cold water for at least 10 minutes or overnight.
2. Preheat the air fryer to 380ºF (193ºC).
3. Drain and dry the potato sticks thoroughly with a clean kitchen towel. Toss with oil in a bowl, then air fry in batches at 380ºF (193ºC) for 15 minutes, shaking the basket occasionally.
4. Combine the cooked fries with the second batch in the air fryer to warm through for a few minutes. Season with salt and serve warm with ketchup or your favorite dip.

Per Serving: Calories: 207 / Fat: 5g / Protein: 5g / Carbs: 38g / Fiber: 3g / Sodium: 11mg

Spanish-Inspired Pan-Seared Cod

Serves: 4 / Prep time: 15 minutes / Cook time: 25 minutes

- 4 tablespoons olive oil
- 8 garlic cloves, minced
- ½ small onion, finely chopped
- ½ pound (227 g) small red or new potatoes, quartered
- 1 (14½-ounce / 411-g) can low-sodium diced tomatoes, with their juices
- 16 pimiento-stuffed low-salt Spanish olives, sliced

(about ⅓ cup)
- 4 tablespoons finely chopped fresh parsley
- 4 (4-ounce / 113-g) cod fillets, about 1 inch thick
- Salt and freshly ground black pepper (optional)

1. In a 10-inch skillet, heat 2 tablespoons of olive oil and the minced garlic over medium heat. Cook until fragrant, about 1 to 2 minutes, taking care not to let the garlic burn.
2. Increase the heat to medium-high, then add the onion, potatoes, diced tomatoes with their juices, olives, and 3 tablespoons of parsley. Bring to a boil, then reduce the heat and simmer, covered, for 15 to 18 minutes, or until the potatoes are tender. Transfer the mixture to a large bowl and keep warm. Wipe out the skillet and return it to the heat.
3. Heat the remaining 2 tablespoons of olive oil in the skillet over medium-high heat. Season the cod with salt and pepper if using, and add to the skillet. Cook for 2 to 3 minutes per side, or until the fish flakes easily with a fork.
4. Divide the tomato mixture among four plates and top each with a cod fillet. Sprinkle with the remaining 1 tablespoon of parsley and serve.

Per Serving: Calories: 297 / Fat: 20g / Protein: 9g / Carbs: 20g / Fiber: 4g / Sodium: 557mg

Greek-Inspired Mini Tacos

Prep time: 10 minutes / Cook time: 3 minutes / Makes: 8 small tacos

- 8 small flour tortillas (4-inch diameter)
- 8 tablespoons hummus
- 4 tablespoons crumbled feta cheese
- 4 tablespoons chopped kalamata olives (optional)
- Olive oil for misting

1. Spread 1 tablespoon of hummus or tapenade in the center of each tortilla. Top with 1 teaspoon of crumbled feta and 1 teaspoon of chopped olives, if desired.
2. Moisten the edges of each tortilla with water using your finger or a small spoon.
3. Fold the tortilla into a half-moon shape, pressing the center gently and the edges firmly to seal.
4. Mist both sides of each taco with olive oil.
5. Place the tacos in the air fryer basket close together but not overlapping.
6. Air fry at 390ºF (199ºC) for 3 minutes, until lightly browned and crispy.

Per Serving: Calories: 127 / Fat: 4g / Protein: 4g / Carbs: 19g / Fiber: 1g / Sodium: 292mg

Cinnamon-Dusted Apple Crisps

Serves: 4 / Prep time: 10 minutes / Cook time: 32 minutes

- Oil for spraying
- 2 Red Delicious or Honeycrisp apples
- ¼ teaspoon ground cinnamon, divided

1. Line the air fryer basket with parchment paper and lightly spray with oil.
2. Trim the ends off the apples and slice them thinly using a mandoline or sharp knife. Discard the cores.
3. Arrange half of the apple slices in a single layer in the prepared basket and sprinkle with half of the cinnamon.
4. Place a metal air fryer trivet over the apples to keep them from moving during cooking.
5. Air fry at 300ºF (149ºC) for 16 minutes, flipping every 5 minutes for even cooking. Repeat with the remaining apple slices and cinnamon.
6. Allow the chips to cool to room temperature before serving; they will become crispier as they cool.

Per Serving: Calories: 63 / Fat: 0g / Protein: 0g / Carbs: 15g / Fiber: 3g / Sodium: 1mg

Herb-Infused Italian Chickpea Crepes

Serves: 6 / Prep time: 15 minutes / Cook time: 20 minutes per crepe

- 2 cups cold water
- 1 cup chickpea flour
- ½ teaspoon kosher salt
- ¼ teaspoon freshly ground black pepper
- 3½ tablespoons extra-virgin olive oil, divided
- ½ onion, julienned
- ½ cup fresh herbs, chopped (such as thyme, sage, and rosemary)

1. In a large bowl, whisk together the water, chickpea flour, salt, and black pepper. Add 2 tablespoons of olive oil and whisk until combined. Let the batter rest at room temperature for at least 30 minutes.
2. Preheat the oven to 450ºF (235ºC). Place a 12-inch cast-iron or oven-safe skillet in the oven to warm.
3. Carefully remove the hot pan from the oven, add ½ tablespoon of olive oil and one-third of the onion, stir, and return the pan to the oven. Cook, stirring occasionally, until the onions are golden brown, about 5 to 8 minutes.
4. Remove the pan from the oven and pour in one-third of the batter (approximately 1 cup). Sprinkle with one-third of the herbs and return to the oven. Bake for 10 minutes, or until firm and edges are set.
5. Increase the oven setting to broil and cook for an additional 3 to 5 minutes, or until golden brown. Transfer the crepe to a cutting board, and repeat twice more. Cut each crepe into wedges and serve warm or at room temperature.

Per Serving: Calories: 135 / Fat: 9g / Protein: 4g / Carbs: 11g / Fiber: 2g / Sodium: 105mg

Arabic-Spiced Baked Chickpeas

Serves: 2 / Prep time: 15 minutes / Cook time: 35 minutes

- For the Spice Mix:
- ¾ teaspoon cumin
- ½ teaspoon coriander
- ½ teaspoon salt
- ¼ teaspoon freshly ground black pepper
- ¼ teaspoon paprika
- ¼ teaspoon cardamom
- ¼ teaspoon cinnamon
- ¼ teaspoon allspice
- For the Chickpeas:
- 1 (15-ounce / 425-g) can chickpeas, drained and rinsed
- 1 tablespoon olive oil
- ¼ teaspoon salt

1. Combine all the spices for the seasoning mix in a small bowl and set aside.
2. Preheat the oven to 400ºF (205ºC) and line a baking sheet with parchment paper.
3. Pat the chickpeas dry with paper towels or a clean kitchen towel.
4. Toss the chickpeas with olive oil and ¼ teaspoon salt in a bowl.
5. Spread the chickpeas on the prepared baking sheet and roast for 25 to 35 minutes, turning them once or twice, until light brown and slightly crisp.
6. Return the roasted chickpeas to the bowl, add the seasoning mix, and toss to coat evenly. Adjust salt to taste and serve warm.

Per Serving: Calories: 268 / Fat: 11g / Protein: 11g / Carbs: 35g / Fiber: 10g / Sodium: 301mg

Burrata and Tomato Delight

Serves: 4 / Prep time: 5 minutes / Cook time: 0 minutes

- 1 large heirloom tomato
- ½ teaspoon salt
- ¼ teaspoon freshly ground black pepper
- 1 (4 ounces / 113 g) ball of burrata cheese
- 8 fresh basil leaves, thinly sliced
- 2 tablespoons extra-virgin olive oil
- 1 tablespoon red wine or balsamic vinegar

1. Cut the tomato into 4 thick slices, removing any tough center core. Season with salt and pepper and arrange on a plate with the seasoned side facing up.
2. Slice the burrata into 4 thick pieces and place one slice on each tomato slice. Top each with one-quarter of the basil and pour any leftover burrata cream from the plate over them.
3. Drizzle with olive oil and vinegar. Serve with a fork and knife.

Per Serving: Calories: 109 / Fat: 7g / Protein: 9g / Carbs: 3g / Fiber: 1g / Sodium: 504mg

Citrus-Infused Melon Salad

Serves: 4 / Prep time: 5 minutes / Cook time: 0 minutes

- 2 cups cubed melon (such as Crenshaw, Sharlyn, or honeydew)
- 2 cups cubed cantaloupe
- ½ cup freshly squeezed orange juice
- ¼ cup freshly squeezed lime juice
- 1 tablespoon orange zest

1. Combine the cubed melons in a large bowl. In a separate small bowl, whisk together the orange juice, lime juice, and orange zest. Pour over the melon.
2. Cover and chill for at least 4 hours, stirring occasionally. Serve cold.

Per Serving: Calories: 80 / Fat: 0g / Protein: 2g / Carbs: 20g / Fiber: 2g / Sodium: 30mg

Lemon-Feta Olive Medley

Serves: 8 / Prep time: 10 minutes / Cook time: 0 minutes

- 1 (1-pound / 454-g) block of Greek feta cheese
- 3 cups mixed olives (Kalamata and green), drained and pitted
- ¼ cup extra-virgin olive oil
- 3 tablespoons lemon juice
- 1 teaspoon grated lemon zest
- 1 teaspoon dried oregano
- Pita bread for serving

1. Cut the feta cheese into ½-inch cubes and place them in a large bowl. Add the olives.
2. In a small bowl, mix together the olive oil, lemon juice, lemon zest, and oregano.
3. Pour the dressing over the feta and olives, and gently toss to coat.
4. Serve with pita bread.

Per Serving: Calories: 269 / Fat: 24g / Protein: 9g / Carbs: 6g / Fiber: 2g / Sodium: 891mg

Herb-Infused Steamed Artichokes

Serves: 6 / Prep time: 10 minutes / Cook time: 10 minutes

- 3 medium artichokes, stems trimmed
- 1 medium lemon, halved
- 1 cup water
- ¼ cup lemon juice
- ⅓ cup extra-virgin olive oil
- 1 clove garlic, minced
- ¼ teaspoon salt
- 1 teaspoon chopped fresh oregano
- 1 teaspoon chopped fresh rosemary
- 1 teaspoon chopped fresh parsley
- 1 teaspoon fresh thyme leaves

1. Rinse the artichokes under running water, ensuring water gets between the leaves to remove any debris. Cut off the top third of each artichoke and remove any tough outer leaves. Rub cut surfaces with lemon.
2. In the Instant Pot®, combine water and lemon juice, then place the rack inside. Set the artichokes upside down on the rack. Close the lid, set the steam release to Sealing, press the Manual button, and cook for 10 minutes. Allow pressure to release naturally for about 20 minutes.
3. Release the lid, remove the artichokes, and slice them in half. Arrange on a serving platter.
4. Mix together the olive oil, garlic, salt, oregano, rosemary, parsley, and thyme. Drizzle half of this mixture over the artichokes and serve the rest in a small bowl for dipping. Serve warm.

Per Serving: Calories: 137 / Fat: 13g / Protein: 2g / Carbs: 7g / Fiber: 4g / Sodium: 158mg

Crispy Sweet Potato Sticks

Serves: 4 / Prep time: 15 minutes / Cook time: 40 minutes

- 4 large sweet potatoes, peeled and cut into stick shapes
- 2 tablespoons extra-virgin olive oil
- ½ teaspoon salt
- ½ teaspoon freshly ground black pepper

1. Preheat the oven to 350°F (180°C). Line a baking sheet with aluminum foil. Toss the sweet potato sticks with olive oil, salt, and pepper in a large bowl.
2. Spread the potatoes in a single layer on the baking sheet and bake until the edges are browned, about 40 minutes. Serve hot.

Per Serving: Calories: 171 / Fat: 7g / Protein: 2g / Carbs: 26g / Fiber: 4g / Sodium: 362mg

Chapter 7: Delicious Veggies and Sides

Spicy Air-Fried Bok Choy

Serves: 4 / Prep time: 10 minutes / Cook time: 7 to 10 minutes

- 2 tablespoons olive oil
- 2 tablespoons reduced-sodium coconut aminos
- 2 teaspoons sesame oil
- 2 teaspoons chili-garlic sauce
- 2 cloves garlic, minced
- 1 head bok choy (about 1 pound / 454 g), cut into quarters lengthwise
- 2 teaspoons black sesame seeds

1. Preheat the air fryer to 400°F (204°C).
2. In a large bowl, mix the olive oil, coconut aminos, sesame oil, chili-garlic sauce, and garlic. Add the bok choy and toss, ensuring all leaves are coated.
3. Place the bok choy in the air fryer basket. Air fry for 7 to 10 minutes, shaking the basket halfway through, until the bok choy is tender and the leaves start to crisp.
4. Remove from the basket and let cool briefly before chopping coarsely. Garnish with sesame seeds before serving.

Per Serving: Calories: 145 / Fat: 13g / Protein: 4g / Carbs: 6g / Fiber: 3g / Sodium: 176mg

Flaxseed Tortillas

Serves: 6 / Prep time: 5 minutes / Cook time: 10 minutes

- 1 cup flax meal
- ⅓ cup coconut flour
- ¼ cup ground chia seeds
- 2 tablespoons whole psyllium husks
- 1 teaspoon salt, or to taste
- 1 cup lukewarm water
- 2 tablespoons extra-virgin avocado oil or ghee

1. Combine the flax meal, coconut flour, chia seeds, psyllium husks, and salt in a bowl. Add the water and mix until well combined. Chill the dough in the refrigerator for about 30 minutes.
2. Divide the dough into 4 equal portions. Roll each portion between two pieces of parchment paper until very thin. Alternatively, use a silicone roller and mat.
3. Use an 8-inch (20 cm) lid or cut a circle from parchment paper to shape the tortillas.
4. Heat a pan with avocado oil and cook each tortilla for 2 to 3 minutes per side over medium heat until lightly browned. Avoid overcooking to keep them flexible.
5. Store the cooled tortillas in a sealed container for up to a week. Reheat in a dry pan if needed.

Per Serving: Calories: 182 / Fat: 16g / Protein: 4g / Carbs: 8g / Fiber: 7g / Sodium: 396mg

Kohlrabi Sticks

Serves: 4 / Prep time: 10 minutes / Cook time: 20 to 30 minutes

- 2 pounds (907 g) kohlrabi, peeled and cut into ¼ to ½-inch sticks
- 2 tablespoons olive oil
- Salt and freshly ground black pepper, to taste

1. Preheat the air fryer to 400°F (204°C).
2. Toss the kohlrabi with olive oil, salt, and pepper in a large bowl until well coated.
3. Arrange the kohlrabi in a single layer in the air fryer basket. Air fry for 20 to 30 minutes, shaking the basket halfway through, until the kohlrabi sticks are browned and crispy.

Per Serving: Calories: 121 / Fat: 7g / Protein: 4g / Carbs: 14g / Fiber: 8g / Sodium: 45mg

Ginger-Sesame Broccoli

Serves: 4 / Prep time: 10 minutes / Cook time: 15 minutes

- 3 tablespoons toasted sesame oil
- 2 teaspoons sesame seeds
- 1 tablespoon chili-garlic sauce
- 2 teaspoons minced fresh ginger
- ½ teaspoon kosher salt
- ½ teaspoon black pepper
- 1 (16-ounce / 454-g) package frozen broccoli florets (do not thaw)

1. Combine the sesame oil, sesame seeds, chili-garlic sauce, ginger, salt, and pepper in a large bowl. Add the frozen broccoli and toss until well coated.
2. Place the broccoli in the air fryer basket and set to 325°F (163°C) for 15 minutes. Toss halfway through cooking for even crispness and browning.

Per Serving: Calories: 143 / Fat: 11g / Protein: 4g / Carbs: 9g / Fiber: 4g / Sodium: 385mg

Pine Nut-Garlic Green Beans

Serves: 4 to 6 / Prep time: 10 minutes / Cook time: 20 minutes

- 1 pound (454 g) green beans, trimmed
- 1 head garlic (10 to 12 cloves), smashed
- 2 tablespoons extra-virgin olive oil
- ½ teaspoon kosher salt
- ¼ teaspoon red pepper flakes
- 1 tablespoon white wine vinegar
- ¼ cup toasted pine nuts

1. Preheat the oven to 425ºF (220ºC). Line a baking sheet with parchment paper or foil.
2. Toss the green beans and garlic with olive oil, salt, and red pepper flakes in a large bowl. Spread them in a single layer on the baking sheet.
3. Roast for 10 minutes, stir, then roast for an additional 10 minutes, or until golden brown.
4. Toss the roasted green beans with vinegar and sprinkle with pine nuts before serving.

Per Serving: Calories: 165 / Fat: 13g / Protein: 4g / Carbs: 12g / Fiber: 4g / Sodium: 150mg

Watercress Salad with Orange and Beet

Serves: 4 / Prep time: 20 minutes / Cook time: 8 minutes

• 2 pounds (907 g) beets, peeled, trimmed, and cut into ¾-inch cubes
• ½ cup water
• 1 teaspoon caraway seeds
• ½ teaspoon table salt
• 1 cup plain Greek yogurt
• 1 small garlic clove, minced into a paste
• 5 ounces (142 g) watercress, torn into bite-sized pieces
• 1 tablespoon extra-virgin olive oil, divided, plus extra for drizzling
• 1 tablespoon white wine vinegar, divided
• 1 teaspoon grated orange zest
• 2 tablespoons orange juice
• ¼ cup toasted hazelnuts, chopped
• ¼ cup fresh dill, chopped
• Coarse sea salt

1. Place beets, water, caraway seeds, and table salt in an Instant Pot. Seal the lid and close the pressure release valve. Set to high pressure and cook for 8 minutes. Turn off the Instant Pot and quick-release the pressure. Carefully remove the lid, allowing steam to escape away from you.
2. Using a slotted spoon, transfer the beets to a plate and let them cool slightly. In a bowl, mix yogurt, garlic, and 3 tablespoons of the beet cooking liquid. Discard the rest of the cooking liquid. In a large bowl, toss watercress with 2 teaspoons of olive oil and 1 teaspoon of vinegar. Season with table salt and pepper to taste.
3. Spread the yogurt mixture on a serving dish. Top with the watercress, leaving a 1-inch border of yogurt around the edge. Toss the beets with orange zest, orange juice, remaining 2 teaspoons of vinegar, and remaining 1 teaspoon of olive oil. Season with table salt and pepper to taste. Place the beets over the watercress. Drizzle with extra olive oil and sprinkle with hazelnuts, dill, and sea salt. Serve.

Per Serving: Calories: 240 / Fat: 15g / Protein: 9g / Carbs: 19g / Fiber: 5g / Sodium: 440mg

Maple-Baked Cherry Tomatoes

Serves: 2 / Prep time: 15 minutes / Cook time: 20 minutes

• 10 ounces (283 g) cherry tomatoes, halved
• Kosher salt, to taste
• 2 tablespoons maple syrup
• 1 tablespoon vegetable oil
• 2 sprigs fresh thyme, stems removed
• 1 garlic clove, minced
• Freshly ground black pepper

1. Sprinkle the tomatoes with salt in a colander and let them drain for 10 minutes.
2. Arrange the tomatoes cut-side up in a baking pan. Drizzle with maple syrup and vegetable oil. Sprinkle with thyme leaves and garlic, and season with pepper. Roast in the air fryer at 325ºF (163ºC) for about 20 minutes until tomatoes are soft, collapsed, and slightly caramelized.
3. Serve directly from the pan or transfer to a plate and drizzle with the pan juices.

Per Serving: Calories: 139 / Fat: 7g / Protein: 1g / Carbs: 20g / Fiber: 2g / Sodium: 10mg

Roasted Tomato Salsa

Prep time: 15 minutes / Cook time: 30 minutes / Makes: 2 cups

• 2 large San Marzano tomatoes, cored and cut into large chunks
• ½ medium white onion, peeled and diced
• ½ medium jalapeño, seeded and diced
• 2 cloves garlic, peeled and chopped
• ½ teaspoon salt
• 1 tablespoon coconut oil
• ¼ cup fresh lime juice

1. Place tomatoes, onion, and jalapeño in an ungreased round nonstick baking dish. Add garlic, sprinkle with salt, and drizzle with coconut oil.
2. Bake in the air fryer basket at 300ºF (149ºC) for 30 minutes until vegetables are dark brown around the edges and tender.
3. Transfer the mixture to a food processor or blender, add lime juice, and blend on low speed for 30 seconds until mostly smooth with a few chunks remaining.
4. Refrigerate in a sealed container for at least 1 hour before serving chilled.

Per Serving: Calories: 115 / Fat: 7g / Protein: 2g / Carbs: 13g / Fiber: 3g / Sodium: 593mg

Provençal Artichokes

Serves: 4 / Prep time: 15 minutes / Cook time: 10 minutes

• 4 large artichokes
• 1 medium lemon, halved
• 2 tablespoons olive oil
• ½ medium white onion, peeled and sliced
• 4 cloves garlic, peeled and chopped
• 2 tablespoons fresh oregano, chopped

- 2 tablespoons fresh basil, chopped
- 2 sprigs fresh thyme   • ¼ teaspoon salt
- 2 medium tomatoes, seeded and chopped
- ¼ cup Kalamata olives, chopped
- ¼ cup red wine   • ¼ cup water
- ¼ teaspoon ground black pepper

1. Rinse artichokes under running water, ensuring the water gets between the leaves to remove debris. Trim the top third of each artichoke, trim the stem, and remove any tough outer leaves. Rub cut surfaces with lemon.
2. Set the Instant Pot® to Sauté and heat the olive oil. Cook the onion until tender, about 2 minutes. Add garlic, oregano, basil, and thyme, cooking until fragrant, about 30 seconds. Stir in tomatoes and olives, then add wine and water, cooking for 30 seconds. Press Cancel, then add artichokes cut side down to the Instant Pot®.
3. Close the lid, set the steam release to Sealing, press Manual, and set the time to 5 minutes. When done, quick-release the pressure. Open the lid and transfer artichokes to a serving platter. Spoon sauce over the artichokes and season with salt and pepper. Serve warm.

Per Serving: Calories: 449 / Fat: 16g / Protein: 20g / Carbs: 40g / Fiber: 12g / Sodium: 762mg

Charred Zucchini with Kimchi Herb Sauce

Serves: 2 / Prep time: 10 minutes / Cook time: 15 minutes

- 2 medium zucchini, ends trimmed (about 6 ounces / 170 g each)
- 2 tablespoons olive oil
- ½ cup kimchi, finely chopped
- ¼ cup fresh cilantro, finely chopped
- ¼ cup fresh flat-leaf parsley, finely chopped, plus extra for garnish
- 2 tablespoons rice vinegar
- 2 teaspoons Asian chili-garlic sauce
- 1 teaspoon fresh ginger, grated
- Kosher salt and freshly ground black pepper, to taste

1. Brush zucchini with half of the olive oil and place in the air fryer. Cook at 400°F (204°C), turning halfway through, until lightly charred and tender, about 15 minutes.
2. In a small bowl, mix the remaining olive oil, kimchi, cilantro, parsley, vinegar, chili-garlic sauce, and ginger.
3. Once the zucchini is cooked, transfer to a colander and let cool for 5 minutes. Tear into bite-sized pieces and season with salt and pepper. Toss well and let sit for another 5 minutes to drain excess liquid. Serve zucchini on top of the kimchi sauce and garnish with extra parsley.

Per Serving: Calories: 172 / Fat: 15g / Protein: 4g / Carbs: 8g / Fiber: 3g / Sodium: 102mg

Cauliflower with Lemon-Tahini Drizzle

Serves: 2 / Prep time: 10 minutes / Cook time: 20 minutes

- ½ large head cauliflower, cut into florets (about 3 cups)
- 1 tablespoon olive oil   • 2 tablespoons tahini
- 2 tablespoons fresh lemon juice
- 1 teaspoon harissa paste   • Pinch of salt

1. Preheat the oven to 400°F (205°C) and place the rack in the lowest position. Line a baking sheet with parchment paper or foil.
2. In a large bowl, toss the cauliflower florets with olive oil and then spread them out on the prepared baking sheet. Reserve the bowl for the tahini sauce.
3. Roast the cauliflower for 15 minutes, turning once or twice, until it starts to become golden.
4. In the reserved bowl, mix tahini, lemon juice, harissa paste, and a pinch of salt.
5. Once the cauliflower is tender, remove it from the oven and coat with the tahini mixture. Return to the sheet pan and roast for an additional 5 minutes.

Per Serving: Calories: 205 / Fat: 15g / Protein: 7g / Carbs: 15g / Fiber: 7g / Sodium: 161mg

Sicilian Roasted Cauliflower with Capers, Currants, and Crispy Crumbs

Serves: 4 / Prep time: 10 minutes / Cook time: 55 minutes

- 1 large head cauliflower (2 pounds / 907 g), cut into 2-inch florets
- 6 tablespoons olive oil, divided
- 1 teaspoon salt
- ½ teaspoon freshly ground black pepper
- 3 garlic cloves, thinly sliced
- 2 tablespoons salt-packed capers, soaked, rinsed, and patted dry
- ¾ cup whole-wheat breadcrumbs
- ½ cup chicken broth
- 1 teaspoon anchovy paste
- ⅓ cup golden raisins
- 1 tablespoon white wine vinegar
- 2 tablespoons chopped fresh parsley

1. Preheat the oven to 425°F (220°C).
2. Toss the cauliflower florets in 3 tablespoons of olive oil along with salt and pepper. Spread in a single layer on a large, rimmed baking sheet and roast for about 45 minutes, stirring occasionally, until golden brown and crispy at the edges.
3. While the cauliflower roasts, heat the remaining 3 tablespoons of olive oil in a small saucepan over medium-low heat. Add garlic and cook, stirring, for about 5 minutes until it turns golden. Add capers and cook for an additional 3 minutes. Stir in breadcrumbs and cook until golden and crisp. Use a slotted spoon to transfer the breadcrumbs to a bowl or plate.

4. In the same saucepan, combine the chicken broth and anchovy paste and bring to a boil over medium-high heat. Add raisins and vinegar and cook, stirring occasionally, for 5 minutes until most of the liquid is absorbed.
5. Transfer the roasted cauliflower to a large bowl, mix in the raisin mixture, and toss. Top with the crispy breadcrumbs and serve immediately, garnished with parsley.

Per Serving: Calories: 364 / Fat: 22g / Protein: 8g / Carbs: 37g / Fiber: 6g / Sodium: 657mg

Garlicky Broccoli Rabe with Artichokes

Serves: 4 / Prep time: 5 minutes / Cook time: 10 minutes

- 2 pounds (907 g) fresh broccoli rabe
- ½ cup extra-virgin olive oil, divided
- 3 garlic cloves, finely minced
- 1 teaspoon salt
- 1 teaspoon red pepper flakes
- 1 (13¾-ounce / 390-g) can artichoke hearts, drained and quartered
- 1 tablespoon water
- 2 tablespoons red wine vinegar
- Freshly ground black pepper

1. Remove any thick stems and yellow leaves from the broccoli rabe. Cut into individual florets with a few inches of thin stem attached.
2. Heat ¼ cup olive oil in a large skillet over medium-high heat. Add the broccoli rabe, garlic, salt, and red pepper flakes and sauté for 5 minutes, until the broccoli starts to soften. Add artichoke hearts and sauté for another 2 minutes.
3. Add water and reduce heat to low. Cover and simmer until the broccoli stems are tender, about 3 to 5 minutes.
4. In a small bowl, whisk together the remaining ¼ cup olive oil and red wine vinegar. Drizzle over the broccoli and artichokes. Season with black pepper if desired.

Per Serving: Calories: 341 / Fat: 28g / Protein: 11g / Carbs: 18g / Fiber: 12g / Sodium: 750mg

Vegetable and Brown Rice Pilaf

Prep time: 20 minutes / Cook time: 5 hours / Makes: 9 (¾-cup) servings

- 1 onion, minced
- 1 cup sliced cremini mushrooms
- 2 carrots, sliced
- 2 garlic cloves, minced
- 1½ cups long-grain brown rice
- 2½ cups vegetable broth
- ½ teaspoon salt
- ½ teaspoon dried marjoram leaves
- ⅛ teaspoon freshly ground black pepper
- ⅓ cup grated Parmesan cheese

1. In a slow cooker, combine onion, mushrooms, carrots, garlic, and rice.
2. Add vegetable broth, salt, marjoram, and pepper. Stir to combine.
3. Cover and cook on low for 5 hours, or until rice is tender and liquid is absorbed.
4. Stir in Parmesan cheese and serve.

Per Serving: Calories: 68 / Fat: 1g / Protein: 2g / Carbs: 12g / Fiber: 1g / Sodium: 207mg

Cucumber and Avocado Stuffed

Serves: 2 / Prep time: 10 minutes / Cook time: 0 minutes

- 1 English cucumber
- 1 avocado, diced
- 1 tomato, diced
- Dash of lime juice
- Sea salt and freshly ground pepper, to taste
- Small bunch cilantro, chopped

1. Slice the cucumber in half lengthwise and scoop out the flesh and seeds into a small bowl.
2. Combine the cucumber flesh with tomato, avocado, and lime juice without mashing too much.
3. Season with sea salt and freshly ground pepper to taste.
4. Spoon the mixture back into the cucumber halves and cut each half into smaller pieces. Garnish with cilantro and serve.

Per Serving: Calories: 189 / Fat: 15g / Protein: 3g / Carbs: 15g / Fiber: 8g / Sodium: 13mg

Dill-Infused Rice Pilaf

Serves: 6 / Prep time: 15 minutes / Cook time: 25 minutes

- 2 tablespoons olive oil
- 1 carrot, finely diced (about ¾ cup)
- 2 leeks, halved lengthwise, cleaned, and sliced into half-moons
- ½ teaspoon salt
- ¼ teaspoon freshly ground black pepper
- 2 tablespoons chopped fresh dill
- 1 cup low-sodium vegetable broth or water
- ½ cup basmati rice

1. Heat the olive oil in a 2- or 3-quart saucepan over medium heat. Add the carrot, leeks, salt, pepper, and 1 tablespoon of dill. Cover and cook for 6 to 8 minutes, stirring occasionally, until the vegetables are softened but not browned.
2. Pour in the broth or water and bring to a boil. Add the rice, reduce the heat to maintain a simmer, cover, and cook for 15 minutes. Remove from heat and let it sit, covered, for 10 minutes.
3. Fluff the rice with a fork and mix in the remaining 1 tablespoon of dill. Serve.

Per Serving: 1 cup: Calories: 100 / Fat: 7g / Protein: 2g / Carbs: 11g / Fiber: 4g / Sodium: 209mg

Potatoes and Green Beans with Basil

Serves: 4 / Prep time: 20 minutes / Cook time: 10 minutes

- 2 tablespoons extra-virgin olive oil, plus additional for drizzling
- 1 onion, finely chopped
- 2 tablespoons minced fresh oregano or 2 teaspoons dried
- 2 tablespoons tomato paste
- 4 garlic cloves, minced
- 1 (14½-ounce / 411-g) can whole peeled tomatoes, drained and chopped, with juice reserved
- 1 cup water
- 1 teaspoon salt
- ¼ teaspoon black pepper
- 1½ pounds (680 g) green beans, trimmed and cut into 2-inch pieces
- 1 pound (454 g) Yukon Gold potatoes, peeled and cut into 1-inch cubes
- 3 tablespoons chopped fresh basil or parsley
- 2 tablespoons toasted pine nuts
- Shaved Parmesan cheese

1. Set the Instant Pot to the highest sauté setting and heat the oil until it shimmers. Add the onion and cook until softened, about 5 minutes. Stir in oregano, tomato paste, and garlic, cooking until fragrant, about 30 seconds.
2. Add the chopped tomatoes and their juice, water, salt, and pepper. Stir in the green beans and potatoes. Lock the lid in place and close the pressure release valve. Select the high-pressure cook setting and cook for 5 minutes.
3. Turn off the Instant Pot and use the quick-release method to release the pressure. Carefully remove the lid, allowing steam to escape away from you. Season with additional salt and pepper if needed. Garnish individual servings with basil, pine nuts, and Parmesan, and drizzle with extra olive oil. Serve.

Per Serving: Calories: 280 / Fat: 10g / Protein: 7g / Carbs: 42g / Fiber: 8g / Sodium: 880mg

Cheese and Herb Flatbread

Serves: 2 / Prep time: 5 minutes / Cook time: 7 minutes

- 1 cup shredded Mozzarella cheese
- ¼ cup blanched almond flour
- 1 ounce (28 g) full-fat cream cheese, softened

1. In a large microwave-safe bowl, melt the Mozzarella cheese in the microwave for 30 seconds. Stir in the almond flour until the mixture is smooth, then add the cream cheese. Continue mixing until a dough forms, kneading gently with wet hands if necessary.
2. Divide the dough into two portions and roll each out to ¼-inch thickness between two sheets of parchment paper. Cut another piece of parchment to fit your air fryer basket.

3. Place one piece of flatbread on the parchment and into the air fryer, cooking in two batches if needed. Set the air fryer to 320°F (160°C) and air fry for 7 minutes.
4. Flip the flatbread halfway through the cooking time. Serve warm.

Per Serving: Calories: 235 / Fat: 14g / Protein: 23g / Carbs: 6g / Fiber: 3g / Sodium: 475mg

Goat Cheese and Mushroom Delight

Serves: 4 / Prep time: 10 minutes / Cook time: 10 minutes

- 3 tablespoons vegetable oil
- 1 pound (454 g) mixed mushrooms, cleaned and sliced
- 1 clove garlic, minced   • ¼ teaspoon dried thyme
- ½ teaspoon black pepper
- 4 ounces (113 g) goat cheese, diced
- 2 teaspoons chopped fresh thyme leaves (optional)

1. In a baking pan, combine the vegetable oil, mushrooms, garlic, dried thyme, and black pepper. Mix in the goat cheese. Place the pan in the air fryer basket. Set the air fryer to 400°F (204°C) and cook for 10 minutes, stirring halfway through.
2. If desired, sprinkle with fresh thyme before serving.

Per Serving: Calories: 218 / Fat: 19g / Protein: 10g / Carbs: 4g / Fiber: 1g / Sodium: 124mg

Mediterranean Stuffed Zucchini

Serves: 4 / Prep time: 5 minutes / Cook time: 10 minutes

- 1 large zucchini, halved lengthwise and ends removed
- 6 grape tomatoes, quartered   • ¼ teaspoon salt
- ¼ cup feta cheese   • 1 tablespoon olive oil
- 1 tablespoon balsamic vinegar

1. Scoop out 2 tablespoons from the center of each zucchini half to create space for the filling.
2. Fill the centers of the zucchini halves with the tomatoes and sprinkle with salt. Place them into an ungreased air fryer basket. Set the temperature to 350°F (177°C) and cook for 10 minutes, or until the zucchini is tender.
3. Transfer the zucchini boats to a serving plate. Sprinkle with feta cheese and drizzle with balsamic vinegar and olive oil. Serve warm.

Per Serving: Calories: 92 / Fat: 6g / Protein: 3g / Carbs: 8g / Fiber: 2g / Sodium: 242mg

Sweet Potato Mash Bites

Prep time: 10 minutes / Cook time: 12 to 13 minutes per batch / Makes: 18 to 24 bites

- 1 cup cooked mashed sweet potatoes
- 1 egg white, beaten
- ⅛ teaspoon ground cinnamon
- A dash of nutmeg

- 2 tablespoons chopped pecans
- 1½ teaspoons honey
- Salt, to taste
- ½ cup panko bread crumbs
- Oil for misting or cooking spray

1. Preheat the air fryer to 390°F (199°C).
2. In a large bowl, combine the mashed sweet potatoes, egg white, cinnamon, nutmeg, pecans, honey, and salt.
3. Spread the panko bread crumbs on a sheet of wax paper.
4. For each bite, use approximately 2 teaspoons of the sweet potato mixture. Shape each portion by placing it onto the panko crumbs, pressing the crumbs around the edges, and then turning it over to coat the other side.
5. Mist the bites with oil or cooking spray and arrange them in a single layer in the air fryer basket.
6. Air fry at 390°F (199°C) for 12 to 13 minutes, or until they are golden and crispy.
7. Repeat the cooking process with the remaining mixture.

Per Serving: Calories: 51 / Fat: 1g / Protein: 1g / Carbs: 9g / Fiber: 1g / Sodium: 45mg

Spicy Lemon Potatoes

Prep time: 10 minutes / Cook time: 8 hours / Makes: 7 (1-cup) servings

- 2 pounds (907 g) creamer potatoes
- 1 onion, chopped
- 3 garlic cloves, minced
- 1 chipotle chile in adobo sauce, minced
- 2 tablespoons fresh lemon juice
- 2 tablespoons water
- 1 tablespoon chili powder
- ½ teaspoon ground cumin
- ½ teaspoon salt
- ⅛ teaspoon freshly ground black pepper

1. Place all the ingredients into the slow cooker and stir well.
2. Cover and cook on low for 7 to 8 hours, or until the potatoes are tender.

Per Serving: Calories: 113 / Fat: 0g / Protein: 3g / Carbs: 25g / Fiber: 4g / Sodium: 208mg

Baked Tomato and Mozzarella Salad

Serves: 4 / Prep time: 15 minutes / Cook time: 30 minutes

- 2 pints (about 20 ounces / 567 g) cherry tomatoes
- 6 thyme sprigs
- 6 garlic cloves, smashed
- 2 tablespoons extra-virgin olive oil
- ½ teaspoon kosher salt
- 8 ounces (227 g) fresh Mozzarella cheese, cut into bite-sized pieces

- ¼ cup fresh basil, chopped or torn into ribbons
- Loaf of crusty whole-wheat bread, for serving

1. Preheat the oven to 350°F (180°C) and line a baking sheet with parchment paper or foil.
2. In a large bowl, combine the tomatoes, thyme, garlic, olive oil, and salt. Spread the mixture evenly on the prepared baking sheet. Roast for 30 minutes, or until the tomatoes are juicy and bursting.
3. Transfer the Mozzarella cheese to a serving dish. Pour the roasted tomato mixture over the cheese, including the juices. Top with basil.
4. Serve with slices of crusty bread.

Per Serving: Calories: 250 / Fat: 17g / Protein: 17g / Carbs: 9g / Fiber: 2g / Sodium: 157mg

Rosemary and Sage White Beans

Serves: 2 / Prep time: 10 minutes / Cook time: 10 minutes

- 1 tablespoon olive oil
- 2 garlic cloves, minced
- 1 (15-ounce / 425-g) can white cannellini beans, drained and rinsed
- ¼ teaspoon dried sage
- 1 teaspoon minced fresh rosemary (from 1 sprig) plus 1 whole fresh rosemary sprig
- ½ cup low-sodium chicken stock
- Salt to taste

1. Heat olive oil in a sauté pan over medium-high heat. Add minced garlic and cook for 30 seconds.
2. Add beans, dried sage, minced rosemary, whole rosemary sprig, and chicken stock. Bring to a boil.
3. Reduce heat to medium and simmer for 10 minutes, or until most of the liquid is absorbed. For a thicker consistency, mash some beans with a fork if desired.
4. Season with salt. Remove the rosemary sprig before serving.

Per Serving: Calories: 155 / Fat: 7g / Protein: 6g / Carbs: 17g / Fiber: 8g / Sodium: 153mg

Sweet Potato Glaze Bites

Serves: 4 / Prep time: 10 minutes / Cook time: 25 minutes

- Oil, for spraying
- 3 medium sweet potatoes, peeled and cut into 1-inch cubes
- 2 tablespoons honey
- 1 tablespoon olive oil
- 2 teaspoons ground cinnamon

1. Line the air fryer basket with parchment paper and lightly spray with oil.
2. Toss the sweet potato cubes with honey, olive oil, and cinnamon in a large bowl until well coated.
3. Place the sweet potatoes in the prepared basket.
4. Air fry at 400°F (204°C) for 20 to 25 minutes, or until

they are crispy and can be easily pierced with a fork.

Per Serving: Calories: 149 / Fat: 3g / Protein: 2g / Carbs: 29g / Fiber: 4g / Sodium: 54mg

Cabbage Rolls with Barley, Pine Nuts, and Currants

Serves: 4 / Prep time: 15 minutes / Cook time: 2 hours

- 1 large head green cabbage, core removed
- 1 tablespoon olive oil
- 1 large yellow onion, diced
- 3 cups cooked pearl barley
- 3 ounces (85 g) crumbled feta cheese
- ½ cup dried currants
- 2 tablespoons toasted pine nuts
- 2 tablespoons fresh flat-leaf parsley, chopped
- ½ teaspoon sea salt
- ½ teaspoon black pepper
- ½ cup apple juice
- 1 tablespoon apple cider vinegar
- 1 (15-ounce / 425-g) can crushed tomatoes, with juice

1. Steam the cabbage head in a large pot over boiling water for 8 minutes. Transfer to a cutting board and allow to cool slightly.
2. Carefully separate 16 leaves from the cabbage head (reserve the remaining cabbage for another use). Trim the thick part of the center vein from each leaf (do not remove completely).
3. Heat the olive oil in a large nonstick skillet over medium heat. Add the onion, cover, and cook for 6 minutes, or until tender. Transfer to a large bowl.
4. Mix the barley, feta cheese, currants, pine nuts, and parsley into the cooked onion. Season with ¼ teaspoon salt and ¼ teaspoon pepper.
5. Place each cabbage leaf on a flat surface. Spoon about ⅓ cup of the barley mixture into the center of each leaf. Fold in the edges and roll up the leaf to encase the filling, similar to making a burrito. Repeat with the remaining leaves and filling.
6. Arrange the stuffed cabbage rolls in the slow cooker.
7. In a bowl, combine the remaining ¼ teaspoon salt, ¼ teaspoon pepper, apple juice, apple cider vinegar, and crushed tomatoes. Pour this mixture evenly over the cabbage rolls.
8. Cover and cook on high for 2 hours or on low for 6 to 8 hours. Serve warm.

Per Serving: Calories: 394 / Fat: 12g / Protein: 12g / Carbs: 66g / Fiber: 16g / Sodium: 560mg

Caramelized Fennel Wedges

Serves: 4 / Prep time: 10 minutes / Cook time: 50 minutes

- 2 large fennel bulbs
- ¼ cup extra-virgin avocado oil or ghee, divided
- 1 small shallot or red onion
- 1 clove garlic, thinly sliced
- 4 to 6 thyme sprigs
- 1 small bunch fresh parsley, leaves and stalks separated
- 1 cup water
- 3 tablespoons fresh lemon juice
- Salt and black pepper, to taste
- ¼ cup extra-virgin olive oil, for drizzling

1. Remove the fennel stalks from the bulbs and set them aside. Halve the fennel bulbs, trim the tough bottom part, and cut into wedges.
2. In a saucepan, heat 2 tablespoons of avocado oil over medium-high heat. Sauté the shallot, garlic, thyme sprigs, fennel stalks, and parsley stalks for about 5 minutes. Add water, bring to a boil, then reduce to a simmer for 10 minutes. Remove from heat, let sit for 10 minutes, then strain out the solids.
3. Preheat the oven to 350°F (180°C) for fan-assisted or 400°F (205°C) for conventional.
4. Heat an ovenproof skillet with the remaining 2 tablespoons of avocado oil over medium-high heat. Add the fennel wedges and sear until caramelized, about 5 minutes, turning once. Pour the strained stock and lemon juice over the fennel, then season with salt and pepper. Cover loosely with aluminum foil and bake for approximately 30 minutes, or until tender.
5. Remove from the oven, sprinkle with chopped parsley, and drizzle with olive oil. Cool and refrigerate any leftovers for up to 5 days.

Per Serving: Calories: 225 / Fat: 20g / Protein: 2g / Carbs: 12g / Fiber: 5g / Sodium: 187mg

Herb-Infused Shiitake Mushrooms

Serves: 4 / Prep time: 10 minutes / Cook time: 5 minutes

- 8 ounces (227 g) shiitake mushrooms, stems removed and caps roughly chopped
- 1 tablespoon olive oil
- ½ teaspoon salt
- Freshly ground black pepper, to taste
- 1 teaspoon fresh thyme leaves, chopped
- 1 teaspoon fresh oregano, chopped
- 1 tablespoon fresh parsley, chopped

1. Preheat the air fryer to 400°F (204°C).
2. Toss the shiitake mushrooms with olive oil, salt, pepper, thyme, and oregano. Air fry for 5 minutes, shaking the basket once or twice during cooking. The mushrooms will have a slightly chewy texture; cook longer if a softer texture is preferred.
3. Once cooked, mix in the parsley and adjust seasoning if needed. Serve immediately.

Per Serving: Calories: 50 / Fat: 4g / Protein: 1g / Carbs: 4g / Fiber: 2g / Sodium: 296mg

Chapter 8: Yummy Vegetarian Mains

Ricotta-Stuffed Portobello Mushrooms

Serves: 4 / Prep time: 10 minutes / Cook time: 30 minutes

- 6 tablespoons extra-virgin olive oil, divided
- 4 portobello mushroom caps, cleaned and gills removed
- 1 cup whole-milk ricotta cheese
- ⅓ cup chopped fresh herbs (such as basil, parsley, rosemary, oregano, or thyme)
- 2 garlic cloves, finely minced
- ½ teaspoon salt
- ¼ teaspoon freshly ground black pepper

1. Preheat the oven to 400°F (205°C).
2. Line a baking sheet with parchment paper or foil and evenly drizzle with 2 tablespoons of olive oil. Arrange the mushroom caps on the sheet, gill-side up.
3. In a medium bowl, combine the ricotta, herbs, 2 tablespoons of olive oil, garlic, salt, and pepper. Spoon a quarter of the cheese mixture into each mushroom cap, pressing gently. Drizzle with the remaining 2 tablespoons of olive oil and bake for 30 to 35 minutes, or until golden and mushrooms are tender.

Per Serving: Calories: 308 / Fat: 29g / Protein: 9g / Carbs: 6g / Fiber: 1g / Sodium: 351mg

Oven-Baked Falafel Sliders

Prep time: 10 minutes / Cook time: 30 minutes / Makes: 6 sliders

- Olive oil cooking spray
- 1 (15-ounce / 425-g) can no-salt-added or low-sodium chickpeas, drained and rinsed
- 1 onion, roughly chopped
- 2 garlic cloves, peeled
- 2 tablespoons fresh parsley, chopped
- 2 tablespoons whole-wheat flour
- ½ teaspoon ground coriander
- ½ teaspoon ground cumin
- ½ teaspoon baking powder
- ½ teaspoon kosher salt
- ¼ teaspoon freshly ground black pepper

1. Preheat the oven to 350°F (180°C). Line a baking sheet with parchment paper or foil and lightly spray with olive oil.
2. In a food processor, combine the chickpeas, onion, garlic, parsley, flour, coriander, cumin, baking powder, salt, and pepper. Process until smooth, stopping to scrape down the sides as needed.
3. Form the mixture into 6 slider patties, each about

a heaping ¼ cup, and place on the prepared baking sheet. Bake for 30 minutes, turning halfway through.

Per Serving: 1 slider: Calories: 90 / Fat: 1g / Protein: 4g / Carbs: 17g / Fiber: 3g / Sodium: 110mg

Grilled Eggplant Towers

Serves: 2 / Prep time: 20 minutes / Cook time: 10 minutes

- 1 medium eggplant, cut into 8 crosswise slices
- ¼ teaspoon salt
- 1 teaspoon Italian herb seasoning mix
- 2 tablespoons olive oil
- 1 large tomato, cut into 4 slices
- 4 (1-ounce / 28-g) slices of buffalo mozzarella
- Fresh basil, for garnish

1. Arrange the eggplant slices in a colander and sprinkle with salt. Let sit for 15 minutes.
2. Preheat the grill to medium-high heat (about 350°F / 180°C).
3. Pat the eggplant dry and toss with the Italian herb seasoning mix and olive oil in a mixing bowl.
4. Grill the eggplant slices for 5 minutes per side, or until marked and tender.
5. Place a slice of tomato and mozzarella on four of the grilled eggplant slices. Top with the remaining eggplant slices to form stacks.
6. Reduce the grill heat to low, cover, and check after 30 seconds. Remove when the cheese is melted.
7. Garnish with fresh basil before serving.

Per Serving: Calories: 354 / Fat: 29g / Protein: 13g / Carbs: 19g / Fiber: 9g / Sodium: 340mg

Zucchini Boats with Cheese

Serves: 4 / Prep time: 20 minutes / Cook time: 8 minutes

- 1 large zucchini, cut into four pieces
- 2 tablespoons olive oil
- 1 cup ricotta cheese, at room temperature
- 2 tablespoons chopped scallions
- 1 heaping tablespoon fresh parsley, chopped
- 1 heaping tablespoon minced coriander
- 2 ounces (57 g) freshly grated Cheddar cheese
- 1 teaspoon celery seeds
- ½ teaspoon salt
- ½ teaspoon garlic pepper

1. Cook the zucchini pieces in the air fryer basket at 350°F (177°C) for about 10 minutes, checking for doneness. Cook an additional 2-3 minutes if necessary.

2. Meanwhile, prepare the stuffing by combining the ricotta, scallions, parsley, coriander, Cheddar cheese, celery seeds, salt, and garlic pepper.
3. Once the zucchini is tender, open up each piece and fill with the cheese mixture. Bake for an additional 5 minutes.

Per Serving: Calories: 242 / Fat: 20g / Protein: 12g / Carbs: 5g / Fiber: 1g / Sodium: 443mg

Mediterranean Tempeh with Tomatoes and Garlic

Serves: 4 / Prep time: 25 minutes / Cook time: 35 minutes

- For the Tempeh:
- 12 ounces (340 g) tempeh   • ¼ cup white wine
- 2 tablespoons extra-virgin olive oil
- 2 tablespoons lemon juice   • Zest of 1 lemon
- ¼ teaspoon kosher salt
- ¼ teaspoon freshly ground black pepper
- For the Tomatoes and Garlic Sauce:
- 1 tablespoon extra-virgin olive oil
- 1 onion, diced
- 3 garlic cloves, minced
- 1 (14½-ounce / 411-g) can no-salt-added crushed tomatoes
- 1 beefsteak tomato, diced   • 1 dried bay leaf
- 1 teaspoon white wine vinegar
- 1 teaspoon lemon juice
- 1 teaspoon dried oregano
- 1 teaspoon dried thyme
- ¾ teaspoon kosher salt
- ¼ cup basil, cut into ribbons
- Prepare the Tempeh:

1. Place tempeh in a medium saucepan and cover with water by 1 to 2 inches. Bring to a boil over medium-high heat, cover, and reduce to a simmer. Cook for 10 to 15 minutes. Remove tempeh, pat dry, cool, and cut into 1-inch cubes.
2. In a large bowl, mix white wine, olive oil, lemon juice, lemon zest, salt, and pepper. Add tempeh, cover, and refrigerate for 4 hours or overnight.
3. Preheat the oven to 375ºF (190ºC). Place marinated tempeh and marinade in a baking dish and bake for 15 minutes.

Prepare the Tomatoes and Garlic Sauce:
4. Heat olive oil in a large skillet over medium heat. Add onion and sauté until translucent, 3 to 5 minutes. Add garlic and sauté for 30 seconds. Stir in crushed tomatoes, beefsteak tomato, bay leaf, vinegar, lemon juice, oregano, thyme, and salt. Simmer for 15 minutes.
5. Gently fold the baked tempeh into the tomato mixture. Garnish with basil before serving.

Per Serving: Calories: 330 / Fat: 20g / Protein: 18g / Carbs: 22g / Fiber: 4g / Sodium: 305mg

Walnut and Feta Stuffed Eggplant

Serves: 6 / Prep time: 10 minutes / Cook time: 55 minutes

- 3 medium eggplants, sliced lengthwise
- 2 teaspoons salt, divided
- ¼ cup olive oil, plus 2 tablespoons, divided
- 2 medium onions, diced
- 1½ pints cherry or grape tomatoes, halved
- ¾ cup roughly chopped walnuts
- 2¼ teaspoons ground cinnamon
- 1½ teaspoons dried oregano
- ½ teaspoon freshly ground black pepper
- ¼ cup whole-wheat breadcrumbs
- ⅔ cup (about 3 ounces / 85 g) crumbled feta cheese

1. Scoop out the insides of the eggplants, leaving a ½-inch border around the edges. Dice the removed flesh and place it in a colander over the sink. Sprinkle 1½ teaspoons of salt over the diced eggplant and inside the eggplant shells, letting them sit for 30 minutes. Rinse and pat dry both the shells and diced flesh.
2. Heat ¼ cup of olive oil in a large skillet over medium heat. Place the eggplant shells cut-side down and cook for about 4 minutes, until they are browned and softened. Flip and cook the other side until golden brown and tender, about another 4 minutes. Transfer to a paper towel-lined plate to drain.
3. Discard all but 1 to 2 tablespoons of oil from the skillet and heat over medium-high. Add the onions and cook, stirring, until they start to soften, about 3 minutes. Add the diced eggplant, tomatoes, walnuts, cinnamon, oregano, ¼ cup water, the remaining ½ teaspoon of salt, and the pepper. Cook, stirring occasionally, until the vegetables are golden and tender, about 8 minutes.
4. Preheat the broiler to high.
5. In a small bowl, combine the breadcrumbs with 1 tablespoon of olive oil.
6. Place the eggplant shells cut-side up on a large baking sheet. Brush each shell with about ½ teaspoon of olive oil. Broil until tender and starting to brown, about 5 minutes. Remove from the broiler and reduce the oven temperature to 375ºF (190ºC).
7. Fill the eggplant shells with the vegetable mixture, dividing it evenly. Sprinkle the tops with the breadcrumb mixture and then the crumbled feta cheese. Bake for about 35 minutes, until the filling is hot and the topping is golden and crisp.

Per Serving: Calories: 274 / Fat: 15g / Protein: 7g / Carbs: 34g / Fiber: 13g / Sodium: 973mg

Moroccan-Style Poached Eggs in Tomato Sauce

Serves: 4 / Prep time: 10 minutes / Cook time: 35 minutes

- 1 tablespoon olive oil

- 1 medium yellow onion, diced
- 2 red bell peppers, seeded and diced
- 1¾ teaspoons sweet paprika
- 1 teaspoon ras al hanout
- ½ teaspoon cayenne pepper
- 1 teaspoon salt
- ¼ cup tomato paste
- 1 (28-ounce / 794-g) can diced tomatoes, drained
- 8 eggs
- ¼ cup chopped cilantro

1. Heat the olive oil in a skillet over medium-high heat. Add the onion and bell peppers, cooking and stirring until they are softened, about 5 minutes. Stir in the paprika, ras al hanout, cayenne, salt, and tomato paste. Cook, stirring occasionally, for 5 minutes.
2. Mix in the diced tomatoes, reduce heat to medium-low, and let simmer for about 15 minutes, until the tomatoes break down and the sauce thickens.
3. Create 8 wells in the sauce and gently crack an egg into each well. Cover and cook for about 10 minutes, until the whites are set but the yolks remain runny.
4. Serve the eggs and sauce hot, garnished with chopped cilantro.

Per Serving: Calories: 238 / Fat: 13g / Protein: 15g / Carbs: 18g / Fiber: 5g / Sodium: 735mg

Caprese-Inspired Eggplant Layers

Serves: 4 / Prep time: 5 minutes / Cook time: 12 minutes

- 1 medium eggplant, sliced into ¼-inch rounds
- 2 large tomatoes, sliced into ¼-inch rounds
- 4 ounces (113 g) fresh mozzarella, sliced into ½-ounce / 14-g rounds
- 2 tablespoons olive oil
- ¼ cup fresh basil, sliced

1. In a baking dish, layer four slices of eggplant at the bottom. Top each with a slice of tomato, then a slice of mozzarella, and repeat the layering as needed.
2. Drizzle with olive oil. Cover the dish with foil and place it in the air fryer basket.
3. Set the air fryer to 350°F (177°C) and cook for 12 minutes, checking halfway through to avoid burning. The eggplant should be tender and the top golden brown when done.
4. Garnish with fresh basil before serving.

Per Serving: Calories: 97 / Fat: 7g / Protein: 2g / Carbs: 8g / Fiber: 4g / Sodium: 11mg

Hearty Vegetable and Brown Rice Bowl

Serves: 4 / Prep time: 15 minutes / Cook time: 20 minutes

- Nonstick cooking spray
- 2 cups broccoli florets
- 2 cups cauliflower florets

- 1 (15-ounce / 425-g) can chickpeas, drained and rinsed
- 1 cup carrots, sliced 1 inch thick
- 2 to 3 tablespoons extra-virgin olive oil, divided
- Salt
- Freshly ground black pepper
- 2 to 3 tablespoons sesame seeds, for garnish
- 2 cups cooked brown rice
- For the Dressing:
- 3 to 4 tablespoons tahini
- 2 tablespoons honey
- Juice of 1 lemon
- 1 garlic clove, minced
- Salt
- Freshly ground black pepper

1. Preheat the oven to 400°F (205°C). Spray two baking sheets with cooking spray.
2. Spread the broccoli and cauliflower on one baking sheet and the chickpeas and carrots on the other. Toss each with half of the olive oil and season with salt and pepper.
3. Roast the carrots and chickpeas for 10 minutes, keeping the carrots slightly crisp, and the broccoli and cauliflower for 20 minutes, until tender. Stir each tray halfway through roasting.
4. For the dressing, mix tahini, honey, lemon juice, and minced garlic in a small bowl. Season with salt and pepper to taste.
5. Serve the rice in individual bowls, topped with the roasted vegetables and a drizzle of dressing.

Per Serving: Calories: 454 / Fat: 18g / Protein: 12g / Carbs: 62g / Fiber: 11g / Sodium: 61mg

Mediterranean Air-Fryer Pizza

Serves: 2 / Prep time: 5 minutes / Cook time: 8 minutes

- 1 cup shredded mozzarella cheese
- ¼ medium red bell pepper, seeded and chopped
- ½ cup chopped fresh spinach
- 2 tablespoons chopped black olives
- 2 tablespoons crumbled feta cheese

1. Spread the mozzarella evenly in an ungreased round nonstick baking dish. Top with the red bell pepper, spinach, black olives, and feta cheese.
2. Place the dish in the air fryer basket. Set the temperature to 350°F (177°C) and cook for 8 minutes, checking halfway through to prevent burning. The pizza should be golden and the cheese melted when done.
3. Allow to cool for 5 minutes before slicing and serving.

Per Serving: Calories: 108 / Fat: 1g / Protein: 20g / Carbs: 5g / Fiber: 3g / Sodium: 521mg

Creamy Stuffed Portobello Caps

Serves: 4 / Prep time: 10 minutes / Cook time: 8 minutes

- 3 ounces (85 g) cream cheese, softened
- ½ medium zucchini, diced
- ¼ cup red bell pepper, seeded and diced
- 1½ cups fresh spinach leaves, chopped
- 4 large portobello mushrooms, stems removed
- 2 tablespoons melted coconut oil
- ½ teaspoon salt

1. In a medium bowl, combine the cream cheese, zucchini, red bell pepper, and spinach.
2. Brush the mushrooms with melted coconut oil and season with salt. Spoon ¼ of the zucchini mixture into each mushroom cap.
3. Arrange the mushrooms in an ungreased air fryer basket. Set the temperature to 400ºF (204ºC) and air fry for 8 minutes. The portobellos should be tender and the tops slightly browned. Serve warm.

Per Serving: Calories: 151 / Fat: 13g / Protein: 4g / Carbs: 6g / Fiber: 2g / Sodium: 427mg

Pistachio and Mint Pasta

Serves: 4 / Prep time: 10 minutes / Cook time: 10 minutes

- 8 ounces (227 g) whole-wheat pasta
- 1 cup fresh mint
- ½ cup fresh basil
- ⅓ cup unsalted pistachios, shelled
- 1 garlic clove, peeled
- ½ teaspoon kosher salt
- Juice of ½ lime
- ⅓ cup extra-virgin olive oil

1. Cook the pasta according to package instructions. Drain and reserve ½ cup of the cooking water.
2. In a food processor, combine the mint, basil, pistachios, garlic, salt, and lime juice. Process until the pistachios are roughly chopped. Gradually add the olive oil while processing until well mixed.
3. Toss the cooked pasta with the pistachio mint pesto. If a thinner sauce is preferred, mix in some of the reserved pasta water until the desired consistency is achieved.

Per Serving: Calories: 420 / Fat: 3g / Protein: 11g / Carbs: 48g / Fiber: 2g / Sodium: 150mg

Orzo-Stuffed Heirloom Tomatoes

Serves: 2 / Prep time: 15 minutes / Cook time: 30 minutes

- 1 tablespoon olive oil
- 1 small zucchini, finely chopped
- ½ medium onion, finely chopped
- 1 garlic clove, minced
- ⅔ cup cooked orzo (from ¼ cup dry orzo, cooked as per package instructions)
- ½ teaspoon salt
- 2 teaspoons dried oregano

- 6 medium round tomatoes (not Roma)

1. Preheat the oven to 350ºF (180ºC).
2. Heat olive oil in a large skillet over medium-high heat. Add zucchini, onion, and garlic, and sauté for about 15 minutes until golden.
3. Stir in the cooked orzo, salt, and oregano, and cook until heated through. Remove from heat and set aside.
4. Cut the tops off the tomatoes and scoop out about half of the flesh with a paring knife. Reserve the flesh for another use or salad.
5. Fill each tomato with the orzo mixture. Place the tomatoes in a baking dish or muffin tin if they fit. Roast for about 15 minutes until the tomatoes are tender but not overcooked. Alternatively, serve the stuffed tomatoes without roasting.

Per Serving: Calories: 241 / Fat: 8g / Protein: 7g / Carbs: 38g / Fiber: 6g / Sodium: 301mg

Mascarpone Mushroom Pappardelle

Serves: 2 / Prep time: 10 minutes / Cook time: 20 minutes

- 2 tablespoons olive oil
- 1 large shallot, minced
- 8 ounces (227 g) baby bella (cremini) mushrooms, sliced
- ¼ cup dry sherry
- 1 teaspoon dried thyme
- 2 cups low-sodium vegetable stock
- 6 ounces (170 g) dry pappardelle pasta
- 2 tablespoons mascarpone cheese
- Salt
- Freshly ground black pepper

1. Heat olive oil in a large skillet over medium-high heat. Add shallot and mushrooms, and sauté for about 10 minutes until the mushrooms release their moisture.
2. Pour in the sherry, thyme, and vegetable stock. Bring the mixture to a boil.
3. Add the pappardelle, breaking it as needed to fit into the pan. Return to a boil, then cover and reduce heat to medium-low. Cook for about 10 minutes or until pasta is al dente, stirring occasionally to prevent sticking. Add water or additional stock if needed.
4. Stir in the mascarpone cheese and season with salt and pepper. The sauce will thicken slightly when removed from heat.

Per Serving: Calories: 517 / Fat: 18g / Protein: 16g / Carbs: 69g / Fiber: 3g / Sodium: 141mg

Spinach and Artichoke Stuffed Caps

Serves: 4 / Prep time: 10 minutes / Cook time: 10 to 14 minutes

- 2 tablespoons olive oil
- 4 large portobello mushrooms, stems removed and gills

scraped
- ½ teaspoon salt
- ¼ teaspoon freshly ground black pepper
- 4 ounces (113 g) goat cheese, crumbled
- ½ cup chopped marinated artichoke hearts
- 1 cup frozen spinach, thawed and squeezed dry
- ½ cup grated Parmesan cheese
- 2 tablespoons chopped fresh parsley

1. Preheat the air fryer to 400°F (204°C).
2. Coat the portobello mushrooms with olive oil and season with salt and pepper. Place them top-side down on a clean surface.
3. In a small bowl, mix goat cheese, artichoke hearts, and spinach. Mash together until well combined. Spoon the mixture onto each mushroom and sprinkle with Parmesan cheese.
4. Air fry for 10 to 14 minutes, until mushrooms are tender and the cheese starts to brown. Garnish with fresh parsley just before serving.

Per Serving: Calories: 284 / Fat: 21g / Protein: 16g / Carbs: 10g / Fiber: 4g / Sodium: 686mg

Savory Fava Bean and Chicory Mash

Serves: 4 / Prep time: 5 minutes / Cook time: 2 hours 10 minutes

- ½ pound (227 g) dried fava beans, soaked overnight and drained
- 1 pound (454 g) chicory leaves
- ¼ cup olive oil
- 1 small onion, diced
- 1 clove garlic, minced
- Salt

1. In a pot, cover the fava beans with at least an inch of water. Bring to a boil over medium-high heat. Lower the heat, cover, and simmer until the beans are very tender, about 2 hours. Check periodically to ensure there's enough water, adding more if necessary.
2. Drain the beans and mash them using a potato masher.
3. Meanwhile, bring a large pot of salted water to a boil. Cook the chicory for about 3 minutes until tender. Drain well.
4. Heat olive oil in a medium skillet over medium-high heat. Add the onion and a pinch of salt. Cook, stirring often, until the onion is soft and starting to brown, about 5 minutes. Add garlic and cook for another minute.
5. Mix half of the onion mixture and oil into the mashed beans. Season with salt to taste.
6. Serve the fava bean mash topped with the remaining onion mixture and oil, with the chicory leaves on the side.

Per Serving: Calories: 336 / Fat: 14g / Protein: 17g / Carbs: 40g / Fiber: 19g / Sodium: 59mg

Greek-Style Egg Bake with Tomato and Olive Salad

Serves: 4 to 6 / Prep time: 10 minutes / Cook time: 25 minutes

- Egg Bake:
- 2 tablespoons olive oil
- 6 scallions, sliced thin
- 4 cups (about 5 ounces / 142 g) baby spinach leaves
- 8 eggs
- ¼ cup whole-wheat breadcrumbs, divided
- 1 cup (about 3 ounces / 85 g) crumbled feta cheese
- ¾ teaspoon salt
- ¼ teaspoon freshly ground black pepper
- Tomato and Olive Salad:
- 2 tablespoons olive oil
- 1 tablespoon lemon juice
- ¼ teaspoon dried oregano
- ½ teaspoon salt
- ¼ teaspoon freshly ground black pepper
- 1 pint cherry, grape, or small tomatoes, halved
- 3 pepperoncini, chopped
- ½ cup coarsely chopped Kalamata olives

1. Preheat the oven to 450°F (235°C).
2. Heat olive oil in an ovenproof skillet over medium-high heat. Sauté scallions and spinach, stirring frequently, until the spinach is wilted, about 4 minutes.
3. In a bowl, whisk together eggs, 2 tablespoons breadcrumbs, feta cheese, ¾ cup water, salt, and pepper. Pour this mixture into the skillet with the spinach and scallions. Sprinkle the remaining 2 tablespoons of breadcrumbs on top. Bake for about 20 minutes, until the egg is set and the top is golden brown.
4. While the egg bake is in the oven, prepare the salad. In a medium bowl, whisk together olive oil, lemon juice, oregano, salt, and pepper. Add tomatoes, pepperoncini, and olives; toss to combine.
5. Once the frittata is done, invert it onto a serving platter and cut into wedges. Serve warm or at room temperature with the tomato and olive salad.

Per Serving: Calories: 246 / Fat: 19g / Protein: 11g / Carbs: 8g / Fiber: 1g / Sodium: 832mg

Moroccan Poached Eggs in Tomato Sauce

Serves: 4 / Prep time: 10 minutes / Cook time: 35 minutes

- 1 tablespoon olive oil
- 1 medium yellow onion, diced
- 2 red bell peppers, diced
- 1¾ teaspoons sweet paprika
- 1 teaspoon ras el hanout
- ½ teaspoon cayenne pepper
- 1 teaspoon salt
- ¼ cup tomato paste

- 1 (28-ounce / 794-g) can diced tomatoes, drained
- 8 eggs
- ¼ cup chopped cilantro

1. Heat olive oil in a skillet over medium-high heat. Sauté onion and bell peppers until softened, about 5 minutes. Stir in paprika, ras el hanout, cayenne, salt, and tomato paste. Cook, stirring occasionally, for 5 minutes.
2. Add the diced tomatoes, reduce heat to medium-low, and simmer for about 15 minutes, until the sauce thickens and tomatoes break down.
3. Create 8 wells in the sauce and crack an egg into each well. Cover the skillet and cook for about 10 minutes, until the egg whites are set but yolks remain runny.
4. Serve the eggs and sauce in bowls, garnished with cilantro.

Per Serving: Calories: 238 / Fat: 13g / Protein: 15g / Carbs: 18g / Fiber: 5g / Sodium: 735mg

Crispy Roasted Veggie Medley

Serves: 2 / Prep time: 10 minutes / Cook time: 15 minutes

- 1 cup broccoli florets
- 1 cup Brussels sprouts, quartered
- ½ cup cauliflower florets
- ¼ medium white onion, sliced into ¼-inch rounds
- ½ medium green bell pepper, sliced into ¼-inch rounds
- 1 tablespoon coconut oil
- 2 teaspoons chili powder
- ½ teaspoon garlic powder
- ½ teaspoon cumin

1. Combine all vegetables in a large bowl with coconut oil and seasonings, tossing until evenly coated.
2. Place vegetables in the air fryer basket.
3. Set the temperature to 360ºF (182ºC) and roast for 15 minutes, shaking the basket two or three times during cooking. Serve warm.

Per Serving: Calories: 112 / Fat: 8g / Protein: 4g / Carbs: 11g / Sugars: 3g / Fiber: 5g / Sodium: 106mg

Eggplant Parmesan Bites

Serves: 4 / Prep time: 15 minutes / Cook time: 17 minutes

- 1 medium eggplant, sliced into ½-inch rounds
- ¼ teaspoon salt

- 2 tablespoons coconut oil
- ½ cup grated Parmesan cheese
- 1 ounce (28 g) 100% cheese crisps, crushed
- ½ cup low-carb marinara sauce
- ½ cup shredded Mozzarella cheese

1. Sprinkle salt on both sides of the eggplant rounds and wrap them in a kitchen towel for 30 minutes. Press to remove excess moisture, then brush both sides with coconut oil.
2. Mix Parmesan and crushed cheese crisps in a bowl. Coat each eggplant slice with this mixture.
3. Arrange the eggplant slices in an ungreased air fryer basket. Set the temperature to 350ºF (177ºC) and air fry for 15 minutes, flipping halfway through, until edges are crispy.
4. Top with marinara sauce and sprinkle with Mozzarella. Continue to air fry at 350ºF (177ºC) for 2 more minutes until the cheese melts. Serve warm.

Per Serving: Calories: 208 / Fat: 13g / Protein: 12g / Carbs: 13g / Fiber: 5g / Sodium: 531mg

Portobello Mushroom Pizzas with Mozzarella and Sun-Dried Tomatoes

Serves: 4 / Prep time: 10 minutes / Cook time: 10 minutes

- 4 large portobello mushroom caps
- 3 tablespoons extra-virgin olive oil
- Salt
- Freshly ground black pepper
- 4 sun-dried tomatoes
- 1 cup shredded mozzarella cheese, divided
- ½ to ¾ cup low-sodium tomato sauce

1. Set the broiler to high.
2. Arrange the mushroom caps on a baking sheet. Brush with olive oil and season with salt and pepper. Broil the mushrooms for 5 minutes on each side, flipping them once, until they become tender.
3. Place 1 sun-dried tomato, 2 tablespoons of mozzarella, and 2 to 3 tablespoons of tomato sauce in each mushroom cap. Top with an additional 2 tablespoons of mozzarella on each. Return the mushrooms to the broiler for 2 to 3 more minutes until the cheese is melted. Cut the mushrooms into quarters and serve.

Per Serving: Calories: 218 / Fat: 16g / Protein: 11g / Carbs: 12g / Fiber: 2g / Sodium: 244mg

Chapter 9: Simple Salads

Classic Greek Salad

Serves: 4 to 6 / Prep time: 10 minutes / Cook time: 0 minutes

- 1 head iceberg lettuce
- 1 pint (2 cups) cherry tomatoes
- 1 large cucumber
- 1 medium onion
- ½ cup extra-virgin olive oil
- ¼ cup lemon juice
- 1 teaspoon salt
- 1 clove garlic, minced
- 1 cup Kalamata olives, pitted
- 1 (6-ounce / 170-g) package crumbled feta cheese

1. Tear the lettuce into 1-inch pieces and place them in a large salad bowl.
2. Halve the cherry tomatoes and add them to the bowl.
3. Cut the cucumber into bite-sized pieces and add them to the bowl.
4. Thinly slice the onion and incorporate it into the salad.
5. In a separate bowl, whisk together the olive oil, lemon juice, salt, and garlic. Pour the dressing over the salad and gently toss to combine.
6. Top the salad with Kalamata olives and crumbled feta cheese before serving.

Per Serving: Calories: 297 / Fat: 27g / Protein: 6g / Carbs: 11g / Fiber: 3g / Sodium: 661mg

Tuscan Kale and Anchovy Salad

Serves: 4 / Prep time: 15 minutes / Cook time: 0 minutes

- 1 large bunch lacinato or dinosaur kale
- ¼ cup toasted pine nuts
- 1 cup fresh Parmesan cheese, shaved or coarsely shredded
- ¼ cup extra-virgin olive oil
- 8 anchovy fillets, coarsely chopped
- 2 to 3 tablespoons freshly squeezed lemon juice (from 1 large lemon)
- 2 teaspoons red pepper flakes (optional)

1. Remove the tough stems from the kale and roughly tear the leaves into 4-by-1-inch strips. Place the kale in a large bowl and add the pine nuts and Parmesan cheese.
2. In a small bowl, whisk together the olive oil, anchovies, lemon juice, and red pepper flakes (if using). Drizzle the dressing over the salad and toss to coat thoroughly. Allow the salad to sit at room temperature for 30 minutes before serving, tossing again just before serving.

Per Serving: Calories: 333 / Fat: 27g / Protein: 16g / Carbs: 12g / Fiber: 4g / Sodium: 676mg

Watermelon and Burrata Cheese Salad

Serves: 4 / Prep time: 10 minutes / Cook time: 0 minutes

- 2 cups watermelon cubes or chunks
- 1½ cups small burrata cheese balls, cut into medium chunks
- 1 small red onion or 2 shallots, thinly sliced into half-moons
- ¼ cup olive oil
- ¼ cup balsamic vinegar
- 4 fresh basil leaves, sliced into thin strips
- 1 tablespoon lemon zest
- Salt and freshly ground black pepper, to taste

1. Combine all ingredients in a large bowl. Refrigerate until chilled before serving.

Per Serving (1 cup):Calories: 224 / Fat: 14g / Protein: 14g / Carbs: 12g / Fiber: 1g / Sodium: 560mg

Salt Cod and Black-Eyed Pea Salad

Serves: 4 / Prep time: 10 minutes / Cook time: 10 minutes

- 1 pound (454 g) salt cod fillets
- ¼ cup olive oil, plus 1 tablespoon, divided
- 3 tablespoons white wine vinegar
- 1 teaspoon salt
- ¼ teaspoon freshly ground black pepper
- 1 (15-ounce / 425-g) can black-eyed peas, drained and rinsed
- 1 small yellow onion, halved and thinly sliced
- 1 small clove garlic, minced
- ¼ cup chopped fresh parsley, divided

1. Rinse the salt cod under cold water to remove surface salt. Place the cod in a large pot, cover with water, and refrigerate for 24 hours, changing the water several times.
2. Drain the water, refill the pot with fresh water, and gently boil the cod until it flakes easily with a fork, about 7 to 10 minutes (or longer, depending on thickness). Drain and let cool.
3. In a small bowl, whisk together the olive oil, vinegar, salt, and pepper to make the dressing.
4. In a large bowl, mix the black-eyed peas, onion, garlic, and ¾ of the parsley. Add the dressing and mix well. Fold in the cod, cover, and refrigerate for at least 2 hours to let the flavors combine. Let sit at room temperature for 30 minutes before serving.
5. Garnish with the remaining parsley before serving.

Per Serving: Calories: 349 / Fat: 18g / Protein: 32g / Carbs: 16g / Fiber: 4g / Sodium: 8mg

Pear and Fennel Salad with Pomegranate

Serves: 6 / Prep time: 15 minutes / Cook time: 5 minutes

- Dressing:
- 2 tablespoons red wine vinegar
- 1½ tablespoons pomegranate molasses
- 2 teaspoons finely chopped shallot
- ½ teaspoon Dijon mustard
- ½ teaspoon kosher salt
- ¼ teaspoon ground black pepper
- ¼ cup extra-virgin olive oil
- Salad:
- ¼ cup walnuts, coarsely chopped, or pine nuts
- 2 red pears, halved, cored, and very thinly sliced
- 1 bulb fennel, halved, cored, and very thinly sliced, with fronds reserved
- 1 tablespoon fresh lemon juice
- 4 cups baby arugula
- ½ cup pomegranate seeds
- ⅓ cup crumbled feta cheese or shaved Parmigiano-Reggiano cheese

1. To make the dressing, combine vinegar, pomegranate molasses, shallot, mustard, salt, and pepper in a small bowl or jar. Add the olive oil and whisk or shake until emulsified.
2. Toast the nuts in a small skillet over medium heat until golden and fragrant, about 4 to 5 minutes. Allow to cool.
3. In a large bowl, combine the pear slices and fennel. Drizzle with lemon juice and toss gently.
4. Add the arugula and toss again to combine. Pour 3 to 4 tablespoons of dressing over the salad and toss to coat. Add the pomegranate seeds, cheese, and nuts, then toss again. Adjust dressing as needed or store the remainder in the refrigerator for up to 1 week. Garnish with reserved fennel fronds before serving.

Per Serving: Calories: 165 / Fat: 10g / Protein: 3g / Carbs: 18g / Fiber: 4g / Sodium: 215mg

Kale Tabouleh Without Grains

Serves: 8 / Prep time: 15 minutes / Cook time: 0 minutes

- 2 plum tomatoes, seeded and diced
- ½ cup finely chopped fresh parsley
- 4 scallions (green onions), finely chopped
- 1 head kale, finely chopped (about 2 cups)
- 1 cup finely chopped fresh mint
- 1 small Persian cucumber, peeled, seeded, and diced
- 3 tablespoons extra-virgin olive oil
- 2 tablespoons fresh lemon juice

- Coarsely ground black pepper (optional)

1. Set the tomatoes in a strainer over a bowl to drain off excess liquid.
2. In a large bowl, mix together the parsley, scallions, kale, and mint.
3. After shaking off any remaining liquid from the tomatoes, add them to the kale mixture along with the cucumber.
4. Stir in the olive oil and lemon juice, and toss to combine. Season with black pepper if desired.

Per Serving (1 cup): Calories: 65 / Fat: 5g / Protein: 1g / Carbs: 4g / Fiber: 1g / Sodium: 21mg

Arugula Salad with Grapes, Goat Cheese, and Za'atar Croutons

Serves: 4 / Prep time: 10 minutes / Cook time: 10 minutes

- Croutons:
- 2 slices whole wheat bread, cut into cubes
- 2 teaspoons olive oil, divided
- 1 teaspoon za'atar
- Vinaigrette:
- 2 tablespoons olive oil
- 1 tablespoon red wine vinegar
- ½ teaspoon chopped fresh rosemary
- ¼ teaspoon kosher salt
- ⅛ teaspoon ground black pepper
- Salad:
- 4 cups baby arugula
- 1 cup grapes, halved
- ½ red onion, thinly sliced
- 2 ounces (57 g) goat cheese, crumbled

1. For the croutons: Toss the bread cubes with 1 teaspoon of olive oil and za'atar. Heat the remaining olive oil in a medium skillet over medium heat. Cook the bread cubes, stirring often, until they are golden and crispy, about 8 to 10 minutes.
2. For the vinaigrette: Whisk together olive oil, red wine vinegar, rosemary, salt, and pepper in a small bowl.
3. For the salad: Toss the arugula, grapes, and red onion in a large bowl with the vinaigrette. Top with goat cheese and croutons.

Per Serving: Calories: 204 / Fat: 14g / Protein: 6g / Carbs: 15g / Fiber: 2g / Sodium: 283mg

Roasted Red Pepper, Pomegranate, and Walnut Salad

Serves: 4 / Prep time: 5 minutes / Cook time: 40 minutes

- 2 red bell peppers, halved and seeded
- 1 teaspoon plus 2 tablespoons olive oil
- 4 teaspoons pomegranate molasses, divided
- 2 teaspoons fresh lemon juice

- ¼ teaspoon kosher salt
- ⅛ teaspoon ground black pepper
- 4 plum tomatoes, halved, seeded, and chopped
- ¼ cup walnut halves, chopped
- ¼ cup chopped fresh parsley

1. Preheat the oven to 450°F (235°C). Brush the red bell peppers with 1 teaspoon of olive oil and place them cut side up on a large rimmed baking sheet. Drizzle 2 teaspoons of pomegranate molasses into the cavities of the peppers. Roast until the peppers are tender and the skins are charred, turning once, about 30 to 40 minutes. Cool to room temperature, then peel off the skins and coarsely chop the peppers.
2. In a large bowl, whisk together the lemon juice, salt, black pepper, remaining 2 tablespoons of olive oil, and remaining 2 teaspoons of pomegranate molasses. Add the roasted peppers, tomatoes, walnuts, and parsley, and toss gently to combine. Serve at room temperature.

Per Serving: Calories: 166 / Fat: 13g / Protein: 2g / Carbs: 11g / Fiber: 3g / Sodium: 153mg

Mediterranean Potato Salad

Serves: 6 / Prep time: 15 minutes / Cook time: 15 to 18 minutes

- 1½ pounds (680 g) small red or new potatoes
- ½ cup olive oil
- ⅓ cup red wine vinegar
- 1 teaspoon fresh Greek oregano
- 4 ounces (113 g) crumbled feta cheese, or 4 ounces (113 g) grated Swiss cheese (for a less salty option)
- 1 green bell pepper, seeded and chopped (1¼ cups)
- 1 small red onion, halved and thinly sliced (generous 1 cup)
- ½ cup Kalamata olives, pitted and halved

1. Place the potatoes in a large saucepan and cover with water. Bring to a boil and cook until tender, about 15 to 18 minutes. Drain and let cool until manageable.
2. In a large bowl, whisk together olive oil, red wine vinegar, and oregano.
3. Cut the cooled potatoes into 1-inch pieces and toss them with the dressing in the bowl. Add the cheese, bell pepper, onion, and olives, and gently mix. Let the salad sit for 30 minutes before serving.

Per Serving: Calories: 315 / Fat: 23g / Protein: 5g / Carbs: 21g / Fiber: 3g / Sodium: 360mg

Cretan Salad (Dakos)

Serves: 1 / Prep time: 7 minutes / Cook time: 0 minutes

- 1 medium ripe tomato (any variety)
- 2 whole-grain crispbreads or rusks (or 1 slice toasted whole-grain bread)
- 1 tablespoon plus 1 teaspoon extra virgin olive oil
- Pinch of kosher salt

- 1½ ounces (43 g) crumbled feta cheese
- 2 teaspoons capers, drained
- 2 Kalamata olives, pitted
- Pinch of dried oregano

1. Cut a thin slice off the bottom of the tomato. Grate the tomato over a plate using the large holes of a grater until only the skin remains. Discard the skin and drain the liquid from the grated tomato using a fine mesh strainer.
2. Arrange the crispbreads or toasted bread on a plate and lightly sprinkle with water. Drizzle 1 tablespoon of olive oil over them and spread the grated tomato on top.
3. Sprinkle with kosher salt, then layer the crumbled feta, capers, and olives over the tomato. Add a pinch of dried oregano and drizzle with the remaining teaspoon of olive oil. Serve immediately. (This salad is best enjoyed fresh.)

Per Serving: Calories: 346 / Fat: 24g / Protein: 12g / Carbs: 21g / Fiber: 4g / Sodium: 626mg

Herb-Infused Wild Greens Salad

Serves: 6 to 8Serves: 6 to 8Prep time: 10 minutes / Cook time: 20 minutes /

- ¼ cup olive oil
- 2 pounds (907 g) dandelion greens, stems removed and coarsely chopped
- 1 small bunch chicory, trimmed and coarsely chopped
- 1 cup chopped fresh parsley, divided
- 1 cup chopped fresh mint, divided
- ½ cup water
- 2 tablespoons red wine vinegar or apple cider vinegar
- 1 tablespoon fresh thyme, chopped
- 2 cloves garlic, minced
- ½ teaspoon kosher salt
- ½ teaspoon ground black pepper
- ¼ cup coarsely chopped almonds or walnuts
- 2 tablespoons chopped fresh chives or scallion greens
- 1 tablespoon chopped fresh dill

1. Heat the oil in a large pot over medium heat. Add the greens, half of the parsley, half of the mint, water, vinegar, thyme, garlic, salt, and pepper. Reduce heat to simmer and cook until the greens are very tender, about 20 minutes.
2. Meanwhile, toast the nuts in a small skillet over medium heat until golden and fragrant, about 5 to 8 minutes. Remove from heat.
3. If serving immediately, stir in the chives or scallion greens, dill, and the remaining parsley and mint. If serving cold, let the salad reach room temperature or chill before adding the fresh herbs. Top with toasted nuts before serving.

Per Serving: Calories: 190 / Fat: 13g / Protein: 6g / Carbs: 17g / Fiber: 7g / Sodium: 279mg

Greek Salad with Oregano and Goat Cheese

Serves: 4 / Prep time: 10 minutes / Cook time: 0 minutes

- ½ cup white wine vinegar
- 1 small garlic clove, minced
- 1 teaspoon crumbled dried Greek oregano
- ½ teaspoon salt
- ¼ teaspoon freshly ground black pepper
- 2 Persian cucumbers, thinly sliced
- 4 to 6 long, slender red or yellow banana peppers or other mild peppers
- 1 medium red onion, sliced into rings
- 1 pint mixed small heirloom tomatoes, halved
- 2 ounces (57 g) crumbled goat cheese or feta

1. In a large non-reactive bowl, whisk together vinegar, garlic, oregano, salt, and pepper. Add cucumbers, peppers, and onion and toss to combine. Cover and chill for at least 1 hour.
2. Add tomatoes to the bowl and toss to coat. Serve garnished with crumbled cheese.

Per Serving: Calories: 98 / Fat: 4g / Protein: 4g / Carbs: 13g / Fiber: 3g / Sodium: 460mg

Mediterranean Tossed Green Salad

Serves: 4 / Prep time: 15 minutes / Cook time: 0 minutes

- 1 medium head romaine lettuce, washed, dried, and chopped into bite-sized pieces
- 2 medium cucumbers, peeled and sliced
- 3 spring onions (white parts only), sliced
- ½ cup finely chopped fresh dill
- ⅓ cup extra virgin olive oil
- 2 tablespoons fresh lemon juice
- ¼ teaspoon fine sea salt
- 4 ounces (113 g) crumbled feta
- 7 Kalamata olives, pitted

1. Combine lettuce, cucumber, spring onions, and dill in a large bowl and toss.
2. In a small bowl, whisk together olive oil and lemon juice. Drizzle the dressing over the salad, toss well, and then sprinkle sea salt on top.
3. Add feta and olives, toss gently once more, and serve immediately. (Best enjoyed fresh.)

Per Serving: Calories: 284 / Fat: 25g / Protein: 7g / Carbs: 10g / Fiber: 5g / Sodium: 496mg

Warm Spinach, Fennel, and Cherry Tomato Salad

Serves: 2 / Prep time: 15 minutes / Cook time: 0 minutes

- 4 tablespoons chicken broth
- 4 cups baby spinach leaves
- 10 cherry tomatoes, halved
- Sea salt and freshly ground pepper, to taste
- 1 fennel bulb, sliced
- ¼ cup olive oil
- Juice of 2 lemons

1. Heat the chicken broth in a large sauté pan over medium heat. Add spinach and tomatoes and cook until spinach wilts. Season with sea salt and pepper.
2. Remove from heat and mix in fennel slices. Let the fennel warm through, then transfer the mixture to a large bowl.
3. Drizzle with olive oil and lemon juice, and serve immediately.

Per Serving: Calories: 319 / Fat: 28g / Protein: 5g / Carbs: 18g / Fiber: 6g / Sodium: 123mg

Valencia Citrus Salad

Serves: 4 / Prep time: 5 minutes / Cook time: 0 minutes

- 2 small oranges, peeled, thinly sliced, and pitted
- 1 small blood orange, peeled, thinly sliced, and pitted
- 1 (7-ounce / 198-g) bag butter lettuce
- ½ English cucumber, sliced into rounds
- 1 (6-ounce / 170-g) can pitted black olives, halved
- 1 small shallot, thinly sliced (optional)
- ¼ cup raw hulled pumpkin seeds
- 8 slices Manchego cheese, roughly broken
- 2 to 3 tablespoons extra-virgin olive oil
- Juice of 1 orange

1. Toss oranges, lettuce, cucumber, olives, shallot (if using), pumpkin seeds, and cheese together in a large bowl. Divide the mixture among four plates.
2. Drizzle with olive oil and orange juice before serving.

Per Serving: Calories: 419 / Fat: 31g / Protein: 17g / Carbs: 22g / Fiber: 5g / Sodium: 513mg

Spinach Salad with Dual Apples

Serves: 4 / Prep time: 15 minutes / Cook time: 0 minutes

- 8 cups baby spinach
- 1 medium Granny Smith apple, diced
- 1 medium red apple, diced
- ½ cup toasted walnuts
- 2 ounces (57 g) sharp white cheddar cheese, cubed
- 3 tablespoons olive oil
- 1 tablespoon red wine vinegar or apple cider vinegar

1. Combine the spinach, apples, walnuts, and cheese in a bowl. Drizzle with olive oil and vinegar and toss lightly before serving.

Per Serving: Calories: 275 / Fat: 22g / Protein: 7g / Carbs: 16g / Fiber: 4g / Sodium: 140mg

Arugula and Fennel Salad with Basil

Serves: 4 / Prep time: 5 minutes / Cook time: 0 minutes

- 3 tablespoons olive oil
- 3 tablespoons lemon juice
- 1 teaspoon honey
- ½ teaspoon salt
- 1 medium fennel bulb, thinly sliced
- 1 small cucumber, thinly sliced
- 2 cups arugula
- ¼ cup toasted pine nuts
- ½ cup crumbled feta cheese
- ¼ cup fresh basil leaves, julienned

1. In a medium bowl, mix together olive oil, lemon juice, honey, and salt. Add fennel and cucumber, tossing to coat. Let sit for about 10 minutes.
2. Place arugula in a large salad bowl. Add the marinated fennel and cucumber along with the dressing and toss well. Garnish with pine nuts, feta cheese, and basil before serving.

Per Serving: Calories: 237 / Fat: 21g / Protein: 6g / Carbs: 11g / Fiber: 3g / Sodium: 537mg

Bell Pepper and White Bean Italian Salad

Serves: 4 / Prep time: 15 minutes / Cook time: 0 minutes

- 2 tablespoons extra-virgin olive oil
- 2 tablespoons white wine vinegar
- ½ shallot, minced
- ½ teaspoon kosher salt
- ¼ teaspoon freshly ground black pepper
- 3 cups cooked cannellini beans, or 2 (15-ounce / 425-g) cans no-salt-added or low-sodium cannellini beans, drained and rinsed
- 2 celery stalks, diced
- ½ red bell pepper, diced
- ¼ cup chopped fresh parsley
- ¼ cup chopped fresh mint

1. In a large bowl, whisk together olive oil, vinegar, shallot, salt, and black pepper.
2. Add beans, celery, red bell pepper, parsley, and mint to the bowl. Toss to combine.

Per Serving: Calories: 300 / Fat: 8g / Protein: 15g / Carbs: 46g / Fiber: 11g / Sodium: 175mg

Tuscan Bread and Tomato Salad (Panzanella)

Serves: 6 / Prep time: 10 minutes / Cook time: 20 minutes

- 4 ounces (113 g) sourdough bread, cut into 1-inch slices
- 3 tablespoons extra-virgin olive oil, divided
- 2 tablespoons red wine vinegar
- 2 cloves garlic, mashed into a paste
- 1 teaspoon finely chopped fresh oregano or ½ teaspoon dried
- 1 teaspoon fresh thyme leaves
- ½ teaspoon Dijon mustard
- Pinch of kosher salt
- Few grinds of black pepper
- 2 pounds (907 g) ripe tomatoes, assorted colors
- 6 ounces (170 g) fresh mozzarella pearls

- 1 cucumber, sliced into ½-inch thick half-moons
- 1 small red onion, thinly sliced
- 1 cup baby arugula
- ½ cup torn fresh basil

1. Preheat a grill rack or pan to medium-high heat, brushing with olive oil.
2. Brush 1 tablespoon of olive oil on both sides of the bread slices and grill until marked, about 2 minutes per side. Cut bread into 1-inch cubes.
3. In a large bowl, whisk together red wine vinegar, garlic, oregano, thyme, Dijon mustard, salt, pepper, and the remaining 2 tablespoons of olive oil until combined.
4. Add grilled bread, tomatoes, mozzarella, cucumber, red onion, arugula, and basil. Toss to mix and let sit for 10 minutes to absorb flavors.

Per Serving: Calories: 219 / Fat: 12g / Protein: 10g / Carbs: 19g / Fiber: 3g / Sodium: 222mg

Tuna and Olive Salad with Italian Flair

Serves: 4 / Prep time: 5 minutes / Cook time: 0 minutes

- ¼ cup olive oil
- 3 tablespoons white wine vinegar
- 1 teaspoon salt
- 1 cup pitted green olives
- 1 medium red bell pepper, seeded and diced
- 1 small garlic clove, minced
- 2 (6-ounce / 170-g) cans or jars tuna in olive oil, well drained
- Several leaves of curly green or red lettuce

1. Whisk olive oil, vinegar, and salt together in a large bowl.
2. Add olives, bell pepper, and garlic to the bowl and toss to coat. Stir in the tuna, cover, and refrigerate for at least 1 hour to let flavors meld.
3. Serve over a bed of lettuce leaves.

Per Serving: Calories: 339 / Fat: 24g / Protein: 25g / Carbs: 4g / Fiber: 2g / Sodium: 626mg

Mediterranean Chopped Salad

Serves: 4 / Prep time: 10 minutes / Cook time: 0 minutes

- 5 large tomatoes, cut into medium chunks
- 2 red onions, cut into medium chunks or sliced
- 1 English cucumber, peeled and cut into medium chunks
- 2 green bell peppers, cut into medium chunks
- ¼ cup extra-virgin olive oil, plus additional for drizzling
- 1 cup Kalamata olives
- ¼ teaspoon dried oregano, plus extra for garnish
- ¼ lemon
- 4 ounces (113 g) Greek feta cheese, sliced

1. Combine tomatoes, onions, cucumber, bell peppers, olive oil, olives, and oregano in a large bowl.

2. Distribute the salad evenly into four bowls. Squeeze lemon juice over each serving and top with a slice of feta cheese. Drizzle with extra olive oil, garnish with additional oregano, and serve.

Per Serving: Calories: 315 / Fat: 24g / Protein: 8g / Carbs: 21g / Fiber: 6g / Sodium: 524mg

Lentil Salad with Herbs and Citrus

Serves: 6 / Prep time: 20 minutes / Cook time: 25 minutes

- For the Lentils:
- 1 cup French lentils   • 1 garlic clove, crushed
- 1 dried bay leaf
- For the Salad:
- 2 tablespoons extra-virgin olive oil
- 2 tablespoons red wine vinegar
- ½ teaspoon ground cumin   • ½ teaspoon kosher salt
- ¼ teaspoon freshly ground black pepper
- 2 celery stalks, finely diced
- 1 bell pepper, finely diced
- ½ red onion, finely diced
- ¼ cup chopped fresh parsley
- ¼ cup chopped fresh mint

1. To prepare the lentils, place them, garlic, and bay leaf in a large saucepan. Cover with water by about 3 inches and bring to a boil. Reduce heat, cover, and simmer until tender, about 20 to 30 minutes.
2. Drain the lentils and discard the garlic and bay leaf.
3. In a large bowl, whisk together olive oil, vinegar, cumin, salt, and pepper. Add celery, bell pepper, onion, parsley, and mint; toss to combine.
4. Stir in the cooked lentils and mix thoroughly.

Per Serving: Calories: 200 / Fat: 8g / Protein: 10g / Carbs: 26g / Fiber: 10g / Sodium: 165mg

Summer Peach and Tomato Salad

Serves: 2 / Prep time: 15 minutes / Cook time: 0 minutes

- 2 ripe peaches, pitted and cut into wedges
- 2 ripe tomatoes, cut into wedges
- ½ red onion, thinly sliced
- Sea salt and freshly ground black pepper, to taste
- 3 tablespoons olive oil   • 1 tablespoon lemon juice

1. In a large bowl, combine peaches, tomatoes, and red onion. Season with sea salt and pepper.
2. Drizzle with olive oil and lemon juice, then gently toss. Serve at room temperature.

Per Serving: Calories: 272 / Fat: 21g / Protein: 3g / Carbs: 22g / Fiber: 4g / Sodium: 8mg

Spinach Salad with Lentils, Pomegranate, and Pistachios

Serves: 4 / Prep time: 10 minutes / Cook time: 30 minutes

- 1 tablespoon extra-virgin olive oil
- 1 shallot, finely chopped
- 1 small red chile pepper, such as Fresno, finely chopped (wear gloves)
- ½ teaspoon ground cumin
- ¼ teaspoon ground coriander
- ¼ teaspoon ground cinnamon
- Pinch of kosher salt
- 1 cup French green lentils, rinsed
- 3 cups water   • 6 cups baby spinach
- ½ cup pomegranate seeds
- ¼ cup chopped fresh cilantro
- ¼ cup chopped fresh parsley
- ¼ cup chopped pistachios
- 2 tablespoons fresh lemon juice
- 1 teaspoon finely grated lemon peel
- Ground black pepper, to taste

1. Heat oil in a medium saucepan over medium heat until shimmering. Cook shallot and chile pepper, stirring until shallot is translucent, about 8 minutes. Add cumin, coriander, cinnamon, and salt, and cook until fragrant, about 1 minute. Add lentils and water, bring to a boil. Cover and reduce heat to simmer until lentils are tender and water is absorbed, about 30 minutes.
2. In a large bowl, combine cooked lentils with spinach, pomegranate seeds, cilantro, parsley, pistachios, lemon juice, lemon peel, and black pepper to taste.

Per Serving: Calories: 279 / Fat: 7g / Protein: 15g / Carbs: 39g / Fiber: 10g / Sodium: 198mg

Moroccan Chickpea and Green Bean Salad with Spices

Serves: 6 to 8 / Prep time: 10 minutes / Cook time: 10 minutes

- 1 pound (454 g) green beans, trimmed
- 2 tablespoons olive oil
- 2 tablespoons red wine vinegar
- 1 garlic clove, minced   • 2 teaspoons ras el hanout
- 1 (15½-ounce / 439-g) can no-salt-added chickpeas, drained and rinsed
- 1 shallot, finely chopped
- 3 tablespoons chopped fresh parsley

1. Bring a large pot of water to a boil. Cook green beans until crisp-tender, then drain and rinse under cold water to stop cooking.
2. In a large bowl, whisk together olive oil, vinegar, garlic, and ras el hanout.
3. Add chickpeas, green beans, shallot, and parsley, and toss to mix. Serve.

Per Serving: 1 cup: Calories: 68 / Fat: 4g / Protein: 2g / Carbs: 7g / Fiber: 3g / Sodium: 16mg

Chapter 10: Classic Pasta Recipes

Tomato Basil Pasta Dish

Serves: 4 / Prep time: 10 minutes / Cook time: 15 minutes

- 8 ounces (227 g) whole-grain linguine
- 1 tablespoon extra-virgin olive oil
- 2 garlic cloves, minced
- ¼ cup chopped yellow onion
- 1 teaspoon chopped fresh oregano
- ½ teaspoon salt
- ¼ teaspoon freshly ground black pepper
- 1 teaspoon tomato paste
- 8 ounces (227 g) cherry tomatoes, halved
- ½ cup grated Parmesan cheese
- 1 tablespoon chopped fresh parsley

1. Boil a large pot of water and cook the linguine according to the package instructions until al dente. Drain, saving ½ cup of pasta water. Do not rinse the pasta.
2. In a large skillet, heat olive oil over medium-high heat. Sauté garlic, onion, and oregano until the onion becomes translucent, about 5 minutes.
3. Mix in salt, pepper, tomato paste, and ¼ cup reserved pasta water. Cook for 1 minute.
4. Add cherry tomatoes and cooked pasta, tossing to coat. Adjust with more pasta water if needed.
5. Serve the pasta in shallow bowls, topped with Parmesan cheese and parsley.

Per Serving: Calories: 310 / Fat: 9g / Protein: 10g / Carbs: 49g / Fiber: 7g / Sodium: 305mg

Broccoli and Anchovy Penne

Serves: 4 / Prep time: 10 minutes / Cook time: 10 minutes

- ¼ cup olive oil
- 1 pound (454 g) whole-wheat penne
- ½ pound (227 g) broccoli or broccoli rabe, cut into 1-inch florets
- 3 to 4 anchovy fillets, packed in olive oil
- 2 cloves garlic, sliced
- Pinch red pepper flakes
- ¼ cup freshly grated low-fat Parmesan
- Sea salt and freshly ground black pepper, to taste

1. Heat olive oil in a deep skillet over medium heat.
2. Meanwhile, cook the penne al dente according to package directions.
3. Sauté broccoli, anchovies, and garlic in the oil until the broccoli is nearly tender and garlic is lightly browned, about 5 minutes.
4. Drain and rinse the pasta, then add it to the skillet. Stir to coat the pasta with the garlic oil.

5. Transfer to a serving dish, sprinkle with red pepper flakes and Parmesan, and season to taste.

Per Serving: Calories: 568 / Fat: 17g / Protein: 21g / Carbs: 89g / Fiber: 11g / Sodium: 203mg

Walnut and Ricotta Spaghetti

Serves: 6 / Prep time: 10 minutes / Cook time: 20 minutes

- 1 pound (454 g) whole-wheat spaghetti
- ½ cup olive oil
- 4 cloves garlic, minced
- ¾ cup walnuts, toasted and finely chopped
- 2 tablespoons low-fat ricotta cheese
- ½ cup freshly grated low-fat Parmesan cheese
- ¼ cup chopped flat-leaf parsley
- Sea salt and freshly ground black pepper, to taste

1. Cook spaghetti in boiling water according to package instructions, reserving 1 cup of pasta water.
2. Heat olive oil in a large skillet over medium-low heat. Add garlic and sauté for 1–2 minutes.
3. Add ½ cup of reserved pasta water to the skillet and simmer for 5–10 minutes.
4. Mix in walnuts and ricotta cheese.
5. Combine the spaghetti with the walnut sauce in a large bowl. Top with Parmesan cheese and parsley. Season and serve.

Per Serving: Calories: 551 / Fat: 31g / Protein: 16g / Carbs: 60g / Fiber: 7g / Sodium: 141mg

Orzo with Shrimp and Feta

Serves: 4 to 6 / Prep time: 10 minutes / Cook time: 15 minutes

- 1 pound (454 g) large shrimp (26 to 30 per pound), peeled and deveined
- 1 tablespoon grated lemon zest plus 1 tablespoon lemon juice
- ¼ teaspoon table salt
- ¼ teaspoon black pepper
- 2 tablespoons extra-virgin olive oil, plus extra for drizzling
- 1 onion, finely chopped
- 2 garlic cloves, minced
- 2 cups orzo
- 2 cups chicken broth, plus more if needed
- 1¼ cups water
- ½ cup pitted Kalamata olives, coarsely chopped
- 1 ounce (28 g) feta cheese, crumbled (¼ cup), plus extra for serving

- 1 tablespoon chopped fresh dill

1. Season shrimp with lemon zest, salt, and pepper. Refrigerate until ready to use.
2. In the Instant Pot, heat oil on the highest sauté setting. Cook onion until softened, about 5 minutes. Add garlic and cook until fragrant, about 30 seconds.
3. Stir in orzo and cook, stirring frequently, until lightly browned, about 5 minutes. Add broth and water, scraping up any browned bits.
4. Lock lid in place, set to high pressure, and cook for 2 minutes. Quick-release the pressure and carefully remove the lid.
5. Stir in shrimp, olives, and feta. Cover and let sit until shrimp are opaque, 5 to 7 minutes. Adjust consistency with extra hot broth if needed. Mix in dill and lemon juice. Season with salt and pepper. Garnish with extra feta and a drizzle of oil before serving.

Per Serving: Calories: 320 / Fat: 8g / Protein: 18g / Carbs: 46g / Fiber: 2g / Sodium: 670mg

Rotini Salad with Tomato, Arugula, and Feta

Serves: 8 / Prep time: 10 minutes / Cook time: 4 minutes

- 1 pound (454 g) rotini
- 4 cups water
- 3 tablespoons extra-virgin olive oil, divided
- 2 medium Roma tomatoes, diced
- 2 cloves garlic, minced
- 1 medium red bell pepper, seeded and diced
- 2 tablespoons white wine vinegar
- 5 ounces (142 g) baby arugula
- 1 cup crumbled feta cheese
- ½ teaspoon salt
- ½ teaspoon ground black pepper

1. Add rotini, water, and 1 tablespoon of oil to the Instant Pot®. Close lid, set steam release to Sealing, press Manual, and set the timer for 4 minutes. When the timer ends, quick-release the pressure, open the lid, and drain the pasta. Rinse with cold water and set aside.
2. In a large bowl, mix remaining 2 tablespoons of oil, tomatoes, garlic, bell pepper, vinegar, arugula, and feta cheese. Stir in pasta and season with salt and pepper. Cover and refrigerate for 2 hours before serving.

Per Serving: Calories: 332 / Fat: 12g / Protein: 12g / Carbs: 44g / Fiber: 3g / Sodium: 480mg

Rotini with Chickpeas and Cabbage

Serves: 8 / Prep time: 20 minutes / Cook time: 30 minutes

- 1 pound (454 g) rotini pasta
- 8 cups water, divided
- 2 tablespoons olive oil, divided
- 1 stalk celery, thinly sliced
- 1 medium red onion, peeled and sliced
- 1 small head savoy cabbage, cored and shredded
- ⅔ cup dried chickpeas, soaked overnight and drained
- 8 ounces (227 g) button mushrooms, sliced
- ½ teaspoon salt
- ¾ teaspoon ground black pepper
- ½ cup grated Pecorino Romano cheese

1. Combine pasta, 4 cups of water, and 1 tablespoon of olive oil in the Instant Pot®. Close the lid, set steam release to Sealing, press the Manual button, and set the time to 4 minutes. Once the timer goes off, quick-release the pressure until the float valve drops, then open the lid and drain the pasta. Press the Cancel button and set aside.
2. Press the Sauté button and heat the remaining 1 tablespoon of oil. Add celery and onion, cooking until tender, about 4 minutes. Stir in cabbage and cook until wilted, about 2 minutes. Add chickpeas, mushrooms, and the remaining 4 cups of water. Stir thoroughly and press the Cancel button.
3. Close the lid, set steam release to Sealing, press the Manual button, and set the time to 20 minutes. After cooking, let the pressure release naturally for about 25 minutes.
4. Open the lid and stir well. Season with salt and pepper. Use a fork to mash some of the chickpeas to thicken the sauce. Pour the sauce over the pasta and sprinkle with cheese. Serve hot.

Per Serving: Calories: 301 / Fat: 5g / Protein: 9g / Carbs: 49g / Fiber: 3g / Sodium: 207mg

Greek-Inspired Spaghetti with Meat Sauce

Serves: 6 / Prep time: 10 minutes / Cook time: 17 minutes

- 1 pound (454 g) spaghetti
- 4 cups water
- 3 tablespoons olive oil, divided
- 1 medium white onion, peeled and diced
- ½ pound (227 g) lean ground veal
- ½ teaspoon salt
- ¼ teaspoon ground black pepper
- ¼ cup white wine
- ½ cup tomato sauce
- 1 cinnamon stick
- 2 bay leaves
- 1 clove garlic, peeled
- ¼ cup grated aged Myzithra or Parmesan cheese

1. Combine pasta, water, and 1 tablespoon of olive oil in the Instant Pot®. Close the lid, set steam release to Sealing, press the Manual button, and set the time to 4 minutes. Once the timer beeps, quick-release the pressure until the float valve drops, then open the lid

and drain the pasta. Press the Cancel button and set aside.

2. Press the Sauté button and heat the remaining 2 tablespoons of oil. Add onion and cook until soft, about 3 minutes. Add veal and crumble well, cooking until browned, about 5 minutes. Stir in salt, pepper, wine, and tomato sauce.
3. Add cinnamon stick, bay leaves, and garlic. Press the Cancel button. Close the lid, set steam release to Sealing, press the Manual button, and set the time to 5 minutes. When the timer goes off, quick-release the pressure until the float valve drops and open the lid. Discard the cinnamon stick and bay leaves.
4. Place pasta in a large bowl. Top with meat sauce and sprinkle with cheese. Serve immediately.

Per Serving: Calories: 447 / Fat: 15g / Protein: 18g / Carbs: 60g / Fiber: 4g / Sodium: 394mg

Penne with Tuna and Green Olives

Serves: 4 / Prep time: 5 minutes / Cook time: 5 minutes

- 2 tablespoons olive oil
- 3 garlic cloves, minced
- ½ cup green olives
- ½ teaspoon salt
- ¼ teaspoon freshly ground black pepper
- 2 (6-ounce / 170-g) cans tuna in olive oil (do not drain)
- ½ teaspoon wine vinegar
- 12 ounces (340 g) penne pasta, cooked according to package instructions
- 2 tablespoons chopped flat-leaf parsley

1. Heat olive oil in a medium skillet over medium heat. Add garlic and cook, stirring, for 2 to 3 minutes, until garlic begins to brown. Add olives, salt, pepper, and tuna with its oil. Stir for a minute or two to heat through. Remove from heat and stir in the vinegar.
2. Combine the cooked pasta with the sauce in the skillet and toss to mix. Serve immediately, garnished with parsley.

Per Serving: Calories: 511 / Fat: 22g / Protein: 31g / Carbs: 52g / Fiber: 1g / Sodium: 826mg

Vegetable Couscous Delight

Serves: 8 / Prep time: 20 minutes / Cook time: 10 minutes

- 1 tablespoon light olive oil
- 1 medium zucchini, chopped
- 1 medium yellow squash, chopped
- 1 large red bell pepper, chopped
- 1 large orange bell pepper, chopped
- 2 tablespoons chopped fresh oregano
- 2 cups Israeli couscous

- 3 cups vegetable broth
- ½ cup crumbled feta cheese
- ¼ cup red wine vinegar
- ¼ cup extra-virgin olive oil
- ½ teaspoon ground black pepper
- ¼ cup chopped fresh basil

1. Press the Sauté button on the Instant Pot® and heat light olive oil. Add zucchini, squash, bell peppers, and oregano, and sauté for 8 minutes. Press the Cancel button. Transfer vegetables to a serving bowl and let cool.
2. Add couscous and vegetable broth to the Instant Pot® and stir. Close the lid, set steam release to Sealing, press the Manual button, and set the time to 2 minutes. Once the timer beeps, allow pressure to release naturally for 5 minutes, then quick-release the remaining pressure and open the lid.
3. Fluff couscous with a fork and mix in cooked vegetables, feta cheese, vinegar, extra-virgin olive oil, black pepper, and basil. Serve warm.

Per Serving: Calories: 355 / Fat: 9g / Protein: 14g / Carbs: 61g / Fiber: 7g / Sodium: 588mg

Savory Baked Penne

Serves: 8 / Prep time: 10 minutes / Cook time: 40 minutes

- 1 pound (454 g) penne pasta
- 1 pound (454 g) ground beef
- 1 teaspoon salt
- 1 (25-ounce / 709 g) jar marinara sauce
- 1 (1 pound / 454 g) bag baby spinach, washed
- 3 cups shredded mozzarella cheese, divided

1. Boil a large pot of salted water, cook penne for 7 minutes, reserving 2 cups of pasta water. Drain the pasta.
2. Preheat the oven to 350°F (180°C).
3. In a large saucepan over medium heat, cook ground beef with salt, browning for about 5 minutes.
4. Stir in marinara sauce and 2 cups of reserved pasta water. Simmer for 5 minutes.
5. Gradually add spinach to the sauce, cooking for an additional 3 minutes.
6. In a 9-by-13-inch baking dish, combine pasta with the sauce. Stir in 1½ cups of mozzarella cheese. Cover with foil and bake for 20 minutes.
7. Remove the foil, sprinkle with the remaining mozzarella cheese, and bake for another 10 minutes. Serve warm.

Per Serving: Calories: 454 / Fat: 13g / Protein: 31g / Carbs: 55g / Fiber: 9g / Sodium: 408mg

Chapter 11: Your Favourite Pizzas, Wraps, and Sandwiches

Avocado and Asparagus Tortilla Wraps

Serves: 6 / Prep time: 10 minutes / Cook time: 10 minutes

- 12 spears asparagus
- 1 ripe avocado, slightly mashed
- Juice of 1 lime
- 2 cloves garlic, minced
- 2 cups cooked and chilled brown rice
- 3 tablespoons Greek yogurt
- Sea salt and freshly ground pepper, to taste
- 3 (8-inch) whole-grain tortillas
- ½ cup diced cilantro
- 2 tablespoons diced red onion

1. Steam the asparagus using a microwave or stovetop steamer until tender. In a medium bowl, combine the mashed avocado, lime juice, and garlic. In another bowl, mix the rice with Greek yogurt.
2. Season both the avocado mixture and the rice mixture with sea salt and freshly ground pepper. Warm the tortillas in a dry nonstick skillet.
3. Spread the avocado mixture on each tortilla, then add the rice, cilantro, and red onion, followed by the asparagus.
4. Fold in the sides of the tortilla and roll it tightly. Cut the wraps in half diagonally before serving.

Per Serving: Calories: 361 / Fat: 9g / Protein: 9g / Carbs: 63g / Fiber: 7g / Sodium: 117mg

Herbed Tuna Bocadillo with Piquillo Peppers

Serves: 4 / Prep time: 5 minutes / Cook time: 20 minutes

- 2 tablespoons olive oil, plus extra for brushing
- 1 medium onion, finely chopped
- 2 leeks, white and tender green parts only, finely chopped
- 1 teaspoon chopped thyme
- ½ teaspoon dried marjoram
- ½ teaspoon salt
- ¼ teaspoon freshly ground black pepper
- 3 tablespoons sherry vinegar
- 1 carrot, finely diced
- 2 (8-ounce / 227-g) jars Spanish tuna in olive oil
- 4 crusty whole-wheat rolls, split
- 1 ripe tomato, grated
- 4 piquillo peppers, cut into thin strips

1. Heat 2 tablespoons of olive oil in a medium skillet over medium heat. Add onion, leeks, thyme, marjoram, salt, and pepper, stirring frequently until onions soften,

about 10 minutes. Mix in the vinegar and carrot, cooking until the liquid evaporates, about 5 minutes. Cool the mixture to room temperature or refrigerate for about 15 minutes.
2. In a medium bowl, mix the tuna with its oil and the cooled onion mixture, breaking the tuna into chunks with a fork.
3. Lightly brush the rolls with oil and toast them under the broiler until lightly browned, about 2 minutes. Spread the tomato pulp on the bottom half of each roll, then top with the tuna mixture and piquillo pepper slices. Serve immediately.

Per Serving: Calories: 416 / Fat: 18g / Protein: 35g / Carbs: 30g / Fiber: 5g / Sodium: 520mg

Goat Cheese and Chicken Flatbread Pizza

Serves: 4 / Prep time: 10 minutes / Cook time: 10 minutes

- All-purpose flour, for dusting
- 1 pound (454 g) premade pizza dough
- 2 tablespoons olive oil
- 1 cup shredded cooked chicken
- 3 ounces (85 g) crumbled goat cheese
- Sea salt
- Freshly ground black pepper

1. Preheat the oven to 475°F (245°C).
2. On a floured surface, roll out the dough into a 12-inch round and place it on a lightly floured pizza pan or baking sheet. Drizzle with olive oil and spread it evenly. Top with shredded chicken and crumbled goat cheese.
3. Bake for 8 to 10 minutes, or until the crust is golden and cooked through.
4. Season with salt and pepper and serve hot.

Per Serving: Calories: 555 / Fat: 23g / Protein: 24g / Carbs: 60g / Fiber: 2g / Sodium: 660mg

Mediterranean Tuna Salad Sandwiches

Serves: 2 / Prep time: 10 minutes / Cook time: 5 minutes

- 1 can white tuna, packed in water or olive oil, drained
- 1 roasted red pepper, diced
- ½ small red onion, diced
- 10 low-salt olives, pitted and finely chopped
- ¼ cup plain Greek yogurt
- 1 tablespoon chopped flat-leaf parsley
- Juice of 1 lemon

- Sea salt and freshly ground pepper, to taste
- 4 slices whole-grain bread

1. Combine all ingredients except the bread in a small bowl and mix well.
2. Season to taste with sea salt and freshly ground pepper. Toast or warm the bread in a pan.
3. Assemble the sandwiches and serve immediately.

Per Serving: Calories: 307 / Fat: 7g / Protein: 30g / Carbs: 31g / Fiber: 5g / Sodium: 564mg

Greek-Style Salad Wraps

Serves: 4 / Prep time: 15 minutes / Cook time: 0 minutes

- 1½ cups peeled and chopped seedless cucumber (about 1 large cucumber)
- 1 cup chopped tomato (about 1 large tomato)
- ½ cup finely chopped fresh mint
- 1 (2¼ ounces / 64 g) can sliced black olives (about ½ cup), drained
- ¼ cup diced red onion (about ¼ onion)
- 2 tablespoons extra-virgin olive oil
- 1 tablespoon red wine vinegar
- ¼ teaspoon freshly ground black pepper
- ¼ teaspoon kosher or sea salt
- ½ cup crumbled goat cheese (about 2 ounces / 57 g)
- 4 whole-wheat flatbread wraps or soft whole-wheat tortillas

1. In a large bowl, combine cucumber, tomato, mint, olives, and red onion.
2. In a small bowl, whisk together olive oil, red wine vinegar, black pepper, and salt. Drizzle the dressing over the salad and mix gently.
3. Spread crumbled goat cheese evenly over each wrap. Spoon a quarter of the salad mixture down the center of each wrap.
4. Fold the bottom of the wrap up, then fold each side over and roll tightly. Repeat with the remaining wraps and serve.

Per Serving: Calories: 217 / Fat: 14g / Protein: 7g / Carbs: 17g / Fiber: 3g / Sodium: 329mg

Grilled Feta and Eggplant Sandwiches

Serves: 2 / Prep time: 10 minutes / Cook time: 8 minutes

- 1 medium eggplant, cut into ½-inch-thick slices
- 2 tablespoons olive oil
- Sea salt and freshly ground pepper, to taste
- 5 to 6 tablespoons hummus
- 4 slices toasted whole-wheat bread
- 1 cup baby spinach leaves
- 2 ounces (57 g) feta cheese, softened

1. Heat a gas or charcoal grill to medium-high. Sprinkle salt on both sides of the eggplant slices and let them sit

for 20 minutes to remove the bitterness.
2. Rinse the eggplant slices and pat them dry with a paper towel. Brush with olive oil and season with sea salt and pepper.
3. Grill the eggplant slices for about 3–4 minutes on each side, until lightly charred but still firm.
4. Spread hummus on the toasted bread. Layer with spinach, feta, and grilled eggplant. Top with another slice of bread and serve warm.

Per Serving: Calories: 516 / Fat: 27g / Protein: 14g / Carbs: 59g / Fiber: 14g / Sodium: 597mg

Roasted Pepper and Turkey Provolone Panini

Serves: 4 / Prep time: 15 minutes / Cook time: 1 hour 5 minutes

- For the peppers and onions:
- 2 red bell peppers, seeded and quartered
- 2 red onions, peeled and quartered
- 2 tablespoons olive oil
- ½ teaspoon salt
- ½ teaspoon freshly ground black pepper
- For the panini:
- 2 tablespoons olive oil
- 8 slices whole-wheat bread
- 8 ounces (227 g) thinly sliced provolone cheese
- 8 ounces (227 g) sliced roasted turkey or chicken breast

1. Preheat the oven to 375°F (190°C). Toss the peppers and onions with olive oil, salt, and pepper on a large baking sheet. Bake for 45 to 60 minutes, turning occasionally, until tender and beginning to brown. Let cool, then peel the peppers and slice them thinly. Slice the onions.
2. Heat a skillet or grill pan over medium-high heat.
3. Brush one side of each bread slice with olive oil. Place 4 slices, oiled side down, on a work surface. Layer with ¼ of the cheese, ¼ of the turkey, and some roasted peppers and onions. Top with the remaining 4 slices of bread, oiled side up.
4. Cook the sandwiches in the skillet or grill pan (in batches if needed), covered, until the bread is golden and the cheese starts to melt, about 2 minutes per side. Cut each sandwich in half and serve hot.

Per Serving: Calories: 603 / Fat: 32g / Protein: 41g / Carbs: 37g / Fiber: 6g / Sodium: 792mg

Spicy Beef and Bean Pita Pizzas

Serves: 4 / Prep time: 10 minutes / Cook time: 7 to 9 minutes

- ¾ cup refried beans (from a 16-ounce / 454-g can)
- ½ cup salsa
- 10 thawed and sliced precooked beef meatballs

- 1 jalapeño pepper, sliced
- 4 whole-wheat pita breads
- 1 cup shredded pepper Jack cheese
- ½ cup shredded Colby cheese
- ⅓ cup sour cream

1. Mix the refried beans, salsa, meatballs, and jalapeño pepper in a medium bowl.
2. Preheat the air fryer for 3 to 4 minutes.
3. Spread the bean mixture over the pitas and top with cheeses.
4. Air fry at 370ºF (188ºC) for 7 to 9 minutes, or until crispy and the cheese is melted and starting to brown.
5. Add a dollop of sour cream on each pizza and serve warm.

Per Serving: Calories: 484 / Fat: 30g / Protein: 24g / Carbs: 32g / Fiber: 7g / Sodium: 612mg

Open-Face Margherita Sandwiches

Serves: 4 / Prep time: 10 minutes / Cook time: 5 minutes

- 2 whole-wheat submarine or hoagie rolls (6 to 7 inches), sliced open horizontally
- 1 tablespoon extra-virgin olive oil
- 1 garlic clove, halved
- 1 large ripe tomato, cut into 8 slices
- ¼ teaspoon dried oregano
- 1 cup fresh mozzarella (about 4 ounces / 113 g), patted dry and sliced
- ¼ cup fresh basil leaves, torn
- ¼ teaspoon freshly ground black pepper

1. Preheat the broiler with the rack 4 inches from the heat. Place the bread on a baking sheet and broil for 1 minute, until lightly toasted.
2. Remove the bread from the oven and brush with olive oil, rubbing with the garlic half.
3. Return the bread to the oven and top each slice with tomato, oregano, and mozzarella. Broil for 1½ to 2 minutes, until the cheese is melted and edges are browned.
4. Top with basil and black pepper before serving.

Per Serving: Calories: 176 / Fat: 9g / Protein: 10g / Carbs: 14g / Fiber: 2g / Sodium: 119mg

Harissa Lamb and Veggie Wraps

Serves: 4 / Prep time: 10 minutes / Cook time: 10 minutes

- 1 clove garlic, minced
- 2 teaspoons ground cumin
- 2 teaspoons chopped fresh thyme
- ¼ cup olive oil, divided
- 1 lamb leg steak, about 12 ounces (340 g)
- 4 whole-wheat pita rounds or naan (8-inch)
- 1 medium eggplant, sliced ½-inch thick
- 1 medium zucchini, sliced lengthwise into 4 pieces

- 1 bell pepper (any color), roasted and skinned
- 6 to 8 Kalamata olives, sliced
- Juice of 1 lemon
- 2 to 4 tablespoons harissa
- 2 cups arugula

1. Combine garlic, cumin, thyme, and 1 tablespoon olive oil in a large bowl. Marinate the lamb in this mixture for at least 1 hour in the refrigerator.
2. Preheat the oven to 400°F (205°C).
3. Grill or use a grill pan over high heat to cook the lamb for about 4 minutes per side, until medium-rare. Let it rest for 10 minutes, then slice thinly against the grain.
4. Wrap the pita rounds in foil and heat them in the oven for about 10 minutes.
5. Brush the eggplant and zucchini slices with the remaining olive oil and grill until tender, about 3 minutes. Dice the vegetables and combine with the bell pepper, olives, and lemon juice in a bowl.
6. Spread harissa on each warm pita, then layer with the grilled vegetables, sliced lamb, and arugula. Roll up the wraps, cut them in half, and serve.

Per Serving: Calories: 553 / Fat: 24g / Protein: 33g / Carbs: 53g / Fiber: 11g / Sodium: 531mg

Basil and Cucumber Tea Sandwiches

Serves: 2 / Prep time: 10 minutes / Cook time: 0 minutes

- 4 slices whole-grain bread
- ¼ cup hummus
- 1 large cucumber, thinly sliced
- 4 whole basil leaves

1. Spread hummus on 2 slices of bread. Arrange the cucumber slices on top and add basil leaves. Place the remaining slices of bread on top to form sandwiches.
2. Gently press down and serve right away.

Per Serving: Calories: 209 / Fat: 5g / Protein: 9g / Carbs: 32g / Fiber: 6g / Sodium: 275mg

Roasted Veggie Pita Pockets

Serves: 4 / Prep time: 15 minutes / Cook time: 9 to 12 minutes

- 1 baby eggplant, peeled and diced
- 1 red bell pepper, sliced
- ½ cup diced red onion
- ½ cup shredded carrot
- 1 teaspoon olive oil
- ⅓ cup low-fat Greek yogurt
- ½ teaspoon dried tarragon
- 2 low-sodium whole-wheat pita breads, cut in half

1. Toss the eggplant, bell pepper, red onion, and carrot with olive oil in a baking pan. Roast in the air fryer at 390°F (199°C) for 7 to 9 minutes, stirring once, until vegetables are tender. Drain if needed.

2. Mix the Greek yogurt and tarragon in a small bowl.
3. Combine the yogurt mixture with the roasted vegetables. Fill each pita pocket with one-fourth of the vegetable mixture.
4. Toast the pitas in the air fryer for 2 to 3 minutes until the bread is crispy. Serve hot.

Per Serving: Calories: 115 / Fat: 2g / Protein: 4g / Carbs: 22g / Fiber: 6g / Sodium: 90mg

Mediterranean Flatbread Pizza

Serves: 4 / Prep time: 5 minutes / Cook time: 20 minutes

- 1½ pounds (680 g) cherry or grape tomatoes, halved
- 3 tablespoons olive oil, divided
- ½ teaspoon salt
- ½ teaspoon freshly ground black pepper
- 4 Middle Eastern–style flatbread rounds
- 1 can artichoke hearts, rinsed, drained, and cut into thin wedges
- 8 ounces (227 g) crumbled feta cheese
- ¼ cup chopped fresh Greek oregano

1. Preheat the oven to 500°F (260°C). Toss tomatoes with 1 tablespoon of olive oil, salt, and pepper. Spread on a baking sheet and roast for 10 to 12 minutes until the skins blister. Reduce oven temperature to 450°F (235°C).
2. Brush flatbreads with the remaining olive oil. Top with artichokes, roasted tomatoes, and feta, dividing evenly.
3. Bake for 8 to 10 minutes until edges are browned and cheese is melted. Sprinkle with oregano and serve immediately.

Per Serving: Calories: 436 / Fat: 27g / Protein: 16g / Carbs: 34g / Fiber: 6g / Sodium: 649mg

Grilled Eggplant and Greek Salad Wraps

Serves: 4 / Prep time: 10 minutes / Cook time: 20 minutes

- 15 small tomatoes (such as cherry or grape), halved
- 10 pitted Kalamata olives, chopped
- 1 medium red onion, thinly sliced
- ¾ cup crumbled feta cheese (about 4 ounces / 113 g)
- 2 tablespoons balsamic vinegar
- 1 tablespoon chopped fresh parsley
- 1 clove garlic, minced
- 2 tablespoons olive oil, plus 2 teaspoons, divided
- ¾ teaspoon salt, divided
- 1 medium cucumber, peeled, halved lengthwise, seeded, and diced
- 1 large eggplant, sliced ½-inch thick
- ½ teaspoon freshly ground black pepper
- 4 whole-wheat sandwich wraps or tortillas

1. Mix tomatoes, olives, red onion, feta, balsamic vinegar, parsley, garlic, 2 teaspoons olive oil, and ¼ teaspoon salt in a bowl. Let it sit for 20 minutes, then add cucumber and let sit for another 10 minutes.
2. Meanwhile, heat a grill or grill pan to high heat. Brush eggplant slices with the remaining 2 tablespoons olive oil. Grill for 8 to 10 minutes per side, until tender. Season with remaining salt and black pepper.
3. Warm the wraps in a dry skillet over medium heat for about 1 minute on each side. Place 2 or 3 eggplant slices in the center of each wrap. Top with salad mixture, using a slotted spoon to remove excess liquid. Fold the sides of the wrap and roll up. Serve immediately.

Per Serving: Calories: 233 / Fat: 10g / Protein: 8g / Carbs: 29g / Fiber: 7g / Sodium: 707mg

Chapter 12: Delicious Desserts

Banana Pudding Parfaits

Serves: 2 / Prep time: 10 minutes / Cook time: 0 minutes

- 1 cup nonfat vanilla pudding
- 2 low-sugar graham crackers, crushed
- 1 banana, peeled and sliced
- ¼ cup chopped walnuts
- Honey for drizzling

1. In small parfait glasses or dishes, layer the pudding, banana slices, and crushed graham crackers, finishing with walnuts.
2. Repeat layers if desired. Drizzle with honey and serve chilled.

Per Serving: Calories: 312 / Fat: 11g / Protein: 7g / Carbs: 50g / Fiber: 3g / Sodium: 273mg

Mascarpone-Stuffed Figs

Serves: 4 / Prep time: 5 minutes / Cook time: 5 minutes

- ⅓ cup chopped walnuts
- 8 fresh figs, halved
- ¼ cup mascarpone cheese
- 1 tablespoon honey
- ¼ teaspoon flaked sea salt

1. Toast walnuts in a skillet over medium heat, stirring frequently for 3 to 5 minutes.
2. Place figs cut-side up on a plate. Create a small indentation in each fig and fill with mascarpone cheese.
3. Top with toasted walnuts, drizzle with honey, and sprinkle with a pinch of sea salt.

Per Serving: Calories: 200 / Fat: 13g / Protein: 3g / Carbs: 24g / Fiber: 3g / Sodium: 105mg

Nutty Baklava

Serves: 6 to 8 / Prep time: 40 minutes / Cook time: 1 hour

- 2 cups finely chopped walnuts or pecans
- 1 teaspoon ground cinnamon
- 1 cup (2 sticks) melted unsalted butter
- 1 (16-ounce / 454-g) package thawed phyllo dough
- 1 (12-ounce / 340-g) jar honey

1. Preheat oven to 350°F (180°C).
2. Mix chopped nuts with cinnamon in a bowl.
3. Brush the bottom and sides of a 9-by-13-inch baking dish with melted butter.
4. Cut phyllo dough to fit the dish. Place one sheet in the dish, brush with butter, and repeat for 8 layers.
5. Sprinkle ⅓ cup nut mixture over the phyllo layers. Add a sheet of phyllo, brush with butter, and repeat for 4 layers.
6. Add another ⅓ cup nut mixture and repeat layering with buttered phyllo sheets until all nuts are used. Finish with 8 buttered phyllo layers.
7. Cut the baklava into desired shapes before baking.
8. Bake for 1 hour or until the top is golden brown.
9. Warm honey until pourable and drizzle over baked baklava. Let absorb for about 20 minutes before serving.

Per Serving: Calories: 1235 / Fat: 89g / Protein: 18g / Carbs: 109g / Fiber: 7g / Sodium: 588mg

Apple Pastry Bites

Serves: 6 / Prep time: 5 minutes / Cook time: 15 minutes

- 1 sheet organic puff pastry, thawed
- 1 Gala apple, peeled and sliced
- ¼ cup brown sugar
- ⅛ teaspoon ground cinnamon
- ⅛ teaspoon ground cardamom
- Nonstick cooking spray
- Honey for drizzling

1. Preheat oven to 350°F (180°C).
2. Cut puff pastry into 4 equal discs. Toss apple slices with brown sugar, cinnamon, and cardamom.
3. Spray muffin tin wells with nonstick spray. Place pastry discs in the muffin tin and add 1 or 2 apple slices to each. Fold over the pastry and drizzle with honey.
4. Bake for 15 minutes, or until golden and bubbly.

Per Serving: Calories: 250 / Fat: 15g / Protein: 3g / Carbs: 30g / Fiber: 1g / Sodium: 98mg

Greek Yogurt Chocolate "Mousse" with Berries

Serves: 4 / Prep time: 15 minutes / Cook time: 0 minutes

- 2 cups plain Greek yogurt
- ¼ cup heavy cream
- ¼ cup pure maple syrup
- 3 tablespoons unsweetened cocoa powder
- 2 teaspoons vanilla extract
- ¼ teaspoon kosher salt
- 1 cup fresh mixed berries
- ¼ cup chocolate chips

1. Combine yogurt, cream, maple syrup, cocoa powder, vanilla, and salt in a stand mixer or large bowl with an electric mixer. Beat on medium-high until fluffy, about 5 minutes.
2. Spoon into 4 bowls and refrigerate for at least 15 minutes.
3. Top each bowl with ¼ cup mixed berries and 1 tablespoon chocolate chips before serving.

Per Serving: Calories: 300 / Fat: 11g / Protein: 16g / Carbs: 35g / Fiber: 3g / Sodium: 60mg

Tahini Protein Bars

Serves: 16 / Prep time: 5 minutes / Cook time: 0 minutes

- ¾ cup tahini
- ⅓ cup coconut butter
- ¼ cup virgin coconut oil
- 1 cup collagen powder
- ½ teaspoon vanilla powder or 1½ teaspoons unsweetened vanilla extract
- ½ teaspoon cinnamon
- ⅛ teaspoon salt
- Optional: low-carb sweetener, to taste

1. In a small saucepan, gently heat tahini, coconut butter, and coconut oil until softened. Remove from heat and allow to cool slightly.
2. Mix in the remaining ingredients and optional sweetener if desired. Stir until well combined. Pour the mixture into an 8 × 8-inch (20 × 20 cm) pan lined with parchment paper. Refrigerate for at least 1 hour or until set.
3. Cut into 16 bars and serve. Store in the refrigerator for up to 2 weeks or freeze for up to 3 months.

Per Serving: Calories: 131 / Fat: 13g / Protein: 2g / Carbs: 3g / Fiber: 1g / Sodium: 33mg

Vanilla Almond Milk

Serves: 6 / Prep time: 5 minutes / Cook time: 1 minute

- 1 cup raw almonds
- 5 cups filtered water, divided
- 1 teaspoon vanilla bean paste
- ½ teaspoon pumpkin pie spice

1. Place almonds and 1 cup of water into the Instant Pot®. Seal the lid, set the steam release to Sealing, press the Manual button, and set the timer for 1 minute.
2. When the cooking time is complete, perform a quick release and open the lid. Drain and rinse the almonds with cool water. Transfer almonds to a high-powered blender with the remaining 4 cups of water. Blend on high for 2 minutes.
3. Strain the mixture through a nut milk bag into a large bowl, squeezing out all the liquid. Stir in vanilla bean paste and pumpkin pie spice. Store in a Mason jar or sealed container and refrigerate for up to 8 hours. Stir or shake before serving.

Per Serving: Calories: 86 / Fat: 8g / Protein: 3g / Carbs: 3g / Fiber: 2g / Sodium: 0mg

Fruit Compote

Serves: 6 / Prep time: 15 minutes / Cook time: 8 minutes

- 8 ounces (227 g) dried apricots, quartered
- 8 ounces (227 g) dried peaches, quartered
- 1 cup golden raisins
- 1½ cups orange juice
- 1 cinnamon stick
- 4 whole cloves

1. Combine all ingredients in the Instant Pot®. Stir to mix. Seal the lid, set the steam release to Sealing, press the Manual button, and set the timer for 3 minutes.
2. After cooking, let the pressure release naturally for about 20 minutes. Open the lid and discard the cinnamon stick and cloves.
3. Press the Sauté button and simmer the mixture for 5–6 minutes. Serve warm or cool before covering and refrigerating for up to a week.

Per Serving: Calories: 258 / Fat: 0g / Protein: 4g / Carbs: 63g / Fiber: 5g / Sodium: 7mg

Rose Water Peaches

Serves: 6 / Prep time: 15 minutes / Cook time: 1 minute

- 1 cup water
- 1 cup rose water
- ¼ cup wildflower honey
- 8 green cardamom pods, lightly crushed
- 1 teaspoon vanilla bean paste
- 6 large yellow peaches, pitted and quartered
- ½ cup chopped roasted unsalted pistachios

1. Combine water, rose water, honey, cardamom pods, and vanilla bean paste in the Instant Pot®. Stir well and add the peaches. Seal the lid, set the steam release to Sealing, press the Manual button, and cook for 1 minute.
2. Once cooking is complete, perform a quick release and open the lid. Let the peaches rest for 10 minutes, then remove them with a slotted spoon.
3. Peel the skins off the peaches. Arrange peach slices on a plate and sprinkle with chopped pistachios. Serve warm or at room temperature.

Per Serving: Calories: 145 / Fat: 3g / Protein: 2g / Carbs: 28g / Fiber: 2g / Sodium: 8mg

Pears with Blue Cheese and Walnuts

Serves: 1 / Prep time: 10 minutes / Cook time: 0 minute

- 1 to 2 pears, cored and cut into 12 slices
- ¼ cup blue cheese crumbles
- 12 walnut halves
- 1 tablespoon honey

1. Arrange pear slices on a plate. Top each slice with blue cheese crumbles and a walnut half. Drizzle with honey.
2. Serve and enjoy!

Per Serving: Calories: 420 / Fat: 29g / Protein: 12g / Carbs: 35g / Fiber: 6g / Sodium: 389mg

Ricotta and Strawberry Layers

Serves: 4 / Prep time: 10 minutes / Cook time: 0 minutes

- 2 cups ricotta cheese
- ¼ cup honey
- 2 cups sliced strawberries
- 1 teaspoon sugar
- Optional: sliced almonds, fresh mint, and lemon zest for garnish

1. In a medium bowl, blend ricotta cheese and honey until smooth. Chill in the refrigerator for a few minutes to firm up.
2. In another bowl, mix strawberries with sugar.
3. In each of four small glasses, layer 1 tablespoon of the ricotta mixture, followed by a layer of strawberries, and then another layer of ricotta.
4. Add any optional toppings if desired and serve.

Per Serving: Calories: 311 / Fat: 16g / Protein: 14g / Carbs: 29g / Fiber: 2g / Sodium: 106mg

Honey Glazed Almonds

Serves: 4 / Prep time: 15 minutes / Cook time: 5 minutes

- ½ cup raw almonds
- 3 tablespoons honey, plus extra if needed

1. Boil water in a medium saucepan. Add almonds and cook for 1 minute. Drain almonds and rinse under cold water to cool. Peel the skins off the almonds using a clean towel. Dry on a paper towel.
2. In the same saucepan, heat almonds and honey over medium heat until almonds are lightly golden, about 4 to 5 minutes. Allow to cool completely, about 15 minutes, before serving or storing.

Per Serving: Calories: 151 / Fat: 9g / Protein: 4g / Carbs: 17g / Fiber: 2g / Sodium: 1mg

Cocoa-Coconut Banana Bites

Serves: 1 / Prep time: 10 minutes / Cook time: 0 minutes

- 1 banana, peeled and sliced
- 2 tablespoons shredded coconut
- 1 tablespoon unsweetened cocoa powder

- 1 teaspoon honey

1. Arrange banana slices on a parchment-lined baking sheet. Freeze for about 10 minutes, until firm but not solid. Combine coconut and cocoa powder in a small bowl.
2. Dip banana slices in honey, then coat with the coconut-cocoa mixture. Eat immediately or freeze for a cold treat.

Per Serving: Calories: 187 / Fat: 4g / Protein: 3g / Carbs: 41g / Fiber: 6g / Sodium: 33mg

Citrus Baked Rice Pudding

Serves: 6 / Prep time: 10 minutes / Cook time: 20 minutes

- Nonstick cooking spray
- 2 medium oranges
- 2 teaspoons extra-virgin olive oil
- ⅛ teaspoon kosher or sea salt
- 2 large eggs, beaten
- 2 cups 2% milk
- 1 cup 100% orange juice
- 1 cup instant brown rice
- ¼ cup honey
- ½ teaspoon ground cinnamon
- 1 teaspoon vanilla extract

1. Preheat oven to 450°F (235°C). Spray a large rimmed baking sheet with nonstick cooking spray.
2. Slice oranges into ¼-inch rounds. Brush with olive oil and sprinkle with salt. Roast on the baking sheet for 4 minutes per side until browned. Set aside.
3. In a medium saucepan, combine milk, orange juice, rice, honey, and cinnamon. Bring to a boil over medium-high heat, stirring frequently. Lower heat and simmer for 10 minutes, stirring occasionally.
4. Scoop out ½ cup of the hot rice mixture and whisk into the beaten eggs. Slowly stir the egg mixture back into the saucepan, continuing to stir to prevent scrambling. Cook on low heat for 1 to 2 minutes until thickened. Remove from heat and stir in vanilla.
5. Allow pudding to stand for a few minutes to soften the rice. For softer rice, let it sit for an additional 30 minutes. Serve warm or at room temperature with roasted orange slices.

Per Serving: Calories: 289 / Fat: 6g / Protein: 8g / Carbs: 52g / Fiber: 4g / Sodium: 118mg

Red Wine-Poached Figs with Ricotta

Serves: 4 / Prep time: 5 minutes / Cook time: 1 minute

- 2 cups water
- 2 cups red wine
- ¼ cup honey
- 1 cinnamon stick
- 1 star anise

- 1 teaspoon vanilla bean paste
- 12 dried mission figs
- 1 cup ricotta cheese
- 1 tablespoon powdered sugar
- ¼ teaspoon almond extract
- 1 cup toasted sliced almonds

1. Combine water, red wine, honey, cinnamon stick, star anise, and vanilla bean paste in the Instant Pot®. Add figs, seal the lid, set steam release to Sealing, press the Manual button, and cook for 1 minute.
2. After cooking, perform a quick release and open the lid. Remove figs with a slotted spoon and let cool for 5 minutes.
3. Mix ricotta cheese, powdered sugar, and almond extract in a small bowl. Serve figs with a dollop of the sweetened ricotta and a sprinkle of toasted almonds.

Per Serving: Calories: 597 / Fat: 21g / Protein: 13g / Carbs: 56g / Fiber: 9g / Sodium: 255mg

Apricot and Mint Cheesecake Jars

Serves: 6 / Prep time: 10 minutes / Cook time: 0 minutes

- 1 pound (454 g) apricots, washed, pitted, and chopped
- 2 teaspoons vanilla extract
- 4 ounces (113 g) Neufchâtel cheese or other light cream cheese
- 2 tablespoons fresh lemon juice
- 1 (7-ounce / 198-g) container 2% Greek yogurt
- ½ cup plus 2 tablespoons sugar
- 2 tablespoons finely chopped fresh mint, plus whole mint leaves for garnish if desired

1. In a stand mixer fitted with a paddle attachment, beat together the Neufchâtel cheese and Greek yogurt on low speed for about 2 minutes until well mixed. Add ½ cup of sugar, vanilla, and lemon juice, and continue to mix until smooth and lump-free, about 2 to 3 minutes. Set aside.
2. In a medium bowl, combine apricots, mint, and the remaining 2 tablespoons of sugar. Let sit until the apricots release their juices and soften.
3. Prepare six 6- to 8-ounce (170- to 227-g) glasses. Spoon 3 to 4 tablespoons of the cheesecake mixture into each glass. Add a layer of apricots over the cheesecake mixture. Repeat the layers, finishing with apricots on top. Garnish with mint leaves if desired.

Per Serving: Calories: 132 / Fat: 2g / Protein: 5g / Carbs: 23g / Fiber: 2g / Sodium: 35mg

Cinnamon Apple Brown Rice Dessert

Serves: 6 / Prep time: 10 minutes / Cook time: 20 minutes

- 1 cup long-grain brown rice
- 2 cups almond milk
- ½ cup golden raisins

- 1 Granny Smith apple, peeled, cored, and chopped
- ¼ cup honey
- 1 teaspoon vanilla extract
- ½ teaspoon ground cinnamon

1. Combine all ingredients in the Instant Pot®. Stir well, then close the lid, set the steam release to Sealing, press the Manual button, and cook for 20 minutes.
2. When the cooking time is up, allow the pressure to release naturally for 15 minutes, then perform a quick release for any remaining pressure. Open the lid and serve warm or at room temperature.

Per Serving: Calories: 218 / Fat: 2g / Protein: 3g / Carbs: 51g / Fiber: 4g / Sodium: 54mg

Mediterranean Citrus Yogurt Cake

Serves: 4 to 6 / Prep time: 10 minutes / Cook time: 3 to 5 hours

- Nonstick cooking spray
- ¾ cup all-purpose flour
- ¾ cup whole-wheat flour
- 2 teaspoons baking powder
- ¼ teaspoon salt
- 1 cup coconut palm sugar
- ½ cup plain Greek yogurt
- ½ cup mild-flavored extra-virgin olive oil
- 3 large eggs
- 2 teaspoons vanilla extract
- Grated zest of 1 orange
- Juice of 1 orange

1. Coat the slow cooker with nonstick spray or line it with parchment paper or aluminum foil.
2. In a large bowl, mix together all-purpose flour, whole-wheat flour, baking powder, and salt.
3. In another large bowl, whisk together coconut palm sugar, Greek yogurt, olive oil, eggs, vanilla extract, orange zest, and orange juice until smooth.
4. Combine the dry ingredients with the wet ingredients and mix until just blended. Pour the batter into the prepared slow cooker.
5. Cover and cook on Low heat for 3 to 5 hours, or until a knife inserted in the center comes out clean.

Per Serving: Calories: 544 / Fat: 33g / Protein: 11g / Carbs: 53g / Fiber: 4g / Sodium: 482mg

Greek Yogurt Pears with Pistachio

Serves: 8 / Prep time: 10 minutes / Cook time: 3 minutes

- 2 cups water
- 1¾ cups apple cider
- ¼ cup lemon juice
- 1 cinnamon stick
- 1 teaspoon vanilla bean paste
- 4 large Bartlett pears, peeled

- 1 cup low-fat plain Greek yogurt
- ½ cup unsalted roasted pistachios

1. Combine water, apple cider, lemon juice, cinnamon stick, vanilla bean paste, and pears in the Instant Pot®. Seal the lid, set steam release to Sealing, press the Manual button, and cook for 3 minutes.
2. When cooking is complete, quick-release the pressure and open the lid. Transfer pears to a plate and let cool to room temperature.
3. To serve, cut pears in half and remove the core with a melon baller. Place halves on plates or shallow bowls. Top with Greek yogurt and sprinkle with pistachios. Serve immediately.

Per Serving: Calories: 181 / Fat: 7g / Protein: 7g / Carbs: 23g / Fiber: 4g / Sodium: 11mg

Dark Chocolate Hazelnut Truffles

Prep time: 5 minutes / Cook time: 50 minutes / Makes: 12 truffles

- 1¾ cups blanched hazelnuts, divided
- ¼ cup collagen powder
- ½ cup coconut butter
- 4 tablespoons butter or ¼ cup virgin coconut oil
- 1 teaspoon vanilla powder or cinnamon
- ¼ cup raw cacao powder
- Optional: low-carb sweetener, to taste
- For Chocolate Coating:
- 2½ ounces (71 g) 100% dark chocolate
- 1 ounce (28 g) cacao butter
- Pinch of salt

1. Preheat oven to 285°F (140°C) with fan or 320°F (160°C) conventional. Spread hazelnuts on a baking tray and roast for 40 to 50 minutes until lightly golden. Let cool.
2. Place 1 cup of roasted hazelnuts in a food processor and blend for 1 to 2 minutes until chunky. Add coconut butter, butter, collagen powder, cacao powder, vanilla, and sweetener if using. Blend until combined. Chill dough in the fridge for 1 hour.
3. Reserve 12 hazelnuts for the centers and crumble the remaining.
4. For the coating, line a baking tray with parchment. Melt dark chocolate and cacao butter together using a double boiler or in a heatproof bowl over simmering water. Let cool to room temperature before use.

5. Scoop about 1 ounce (28 g) of dough, press a whole hazelnut into the center, and roll into a ball. Freeze for about 15 minutes.
6. Skewer each truffle and coat with melted chocolate, turning until the coating sets. Place on the lined tray and drizzle with remaining chocolate. Roll in crumbled hazelnuts before the coating hardens. Refrigerate for at least 15 minutes to set.
7. Store in the refrigerator for up to 1 week or freeze for up to 3 months.

Per Serving: Calories: 231 / Fat: 22g / Protein: 4g / Carbs: 8g / Fiber: 4g / Sodium: 3mg

Spanish Flan

Serves: 6 / Prep time: 5 minutes / Cook time: 0 minutes

- 3 large eggs
- 1¼ cups unsweetened almond milk, divided
- 1 tablespoon gelatin powder
- 1¼ cups goat's cream, heavy cream, or coconut cream
- 1 teaspoon vanilla extract or 1 tablespoon vanilla powder
- 1 teaspoon cinnamon, plus extra for garnish
- ½ ounce (14 g) grated 100% chocolate, for topping
- Optional: low-carb sweetener, to taste

1. Separate the egg whites from the yolks. In a small bowl, mix ½ cup (120 ml) of almond milk with the gelatin and let it sit to bloom.
2. Combine the yolks, cream, and the remaining ¾ cup (180 ml) almond milk in a heatproof bowl set over a saucepan of simmering water. Ensure the bowl doesn't touch the water. Stir constantly until the mixture thickens and becomes smooth.
3. Mix in the vanilla, cinnamon, any sweetener if desired, and the bloomed gelatin. Cover the surface with plastic wrap and refrigerate for 30 minutes. The mixture will appear runny at this stage but will firm up.
4. Using a hand mixer or stand mixer, beat the egg whites until stiff peaks form, then gently fold them into the cooled mixture. Pour the mixture into six serving glasses and refrigerate for 3 to 4 hours until set. Top with grated chocolate and, if desired, additional sweetener and a sprinkle of cinnamon.
5. Keep covered in the refrigerator for up to 5 days.

Per Serving: Calories: 172 / Fat: 13g / Protein: 5g / Carbs: 7g / Fiber: 1g / Sodium: 83mg

Crunchy Greek Yogurt Dip

Serves: 2 to 3 / Prep time: 5 minutes / Cook time: 0 minutes

- 1 cup full-fat Greek yogurt, plain and unsweetened
- ½ cup diced cucumber, peeled and seeded
- 1 tablespoon fresh lemon juice
- 1 tablespoon chopped fresh mint
- 1 small garlic clove, minced
- Salt to taste
- Freshly ground black pepper to taste

1. In a food processor, blend the yogurt, cucumber, lemon juice, mint, and garlic until well combined, leaving some cucumber pieces visible.
2. Season with salt and pepper according to taste.

Per Serving: Calories: 128 / Fat: 6g / Protein: 11g / Carbs: 7g / Fiber: 0g / Sodium: 47mg

Herb-Infused Butter

Prep time: 10 minutes / Cook time: 0 minutes / Makes: ½ cup

- ½ cup (1 stick) room temperature butter
- 1 garlic clove, finely minced
- 2 teaspoons finely chopped fresh rosemary
- 1 teaspoon finely chopped fresh oregano
- ½ teaspoon salt

1. Combine the butter, garlic, rosemary, oregano, and salt in a food processor and blend until smooth and creamy, scraping down the sides as needed. Alternatively, use an electric mixer to combine the ingredients.
2. Transfer the butter mixture to a small bowl or container, cover, and store in the refrigerator for up to 1 month.

Per Serving: ⅛ cup: Calories: 206 / Fat: 23g / Protein: 0g / Carbs: 0g / Fiber: 0g / Sodium: 294mg

Balsamic Vinaigrette

Serves: 4 / Prep time: 5 minutes / Cook time: 0 minutes

- 2 tablespoons balsamic vinegar
- 2 large garlic cloves, minced
- 1 teaspoon dried crushed rosemary
- ¼ teaspoon freshly ground black pepper
- ¼ cup olive oil

1. Whisk together the balsamic vinegar, garlic, rosemary, and black pepper in a small bowl. Gradually whisk in the olive oil until the mixture is well combined and emulsified.
2. Store in an airtight container in the refrigerator for up to 3 days.

Per Serving: 1 cup: Calories: 129 / Fat: 1g / Protein: 3g / Carbs: 0g / Fiber: 0g / Sodium: 2mg

Pickled Turnips and Beet

Serves: 2 / Prep time: 5 minutes / Cook time: 0 minutes

- 1 pound (454 g) turnips, peeled and cut into 1-inch sticks
- 1 small beet, roasted, peeled, and cut into 1-inch sticks
- 2 garlic cloves, smashed
- 1 teaspoon dried oregano
- 3 cups warm water
- ½ cup red wine vinegar
- ½ cup white vinegar

1. Place the turnips, beet, garlic, and oregano in a jar. Pour the warm water and both types of vinegar over the vegetables. Seal the jar, shake well, and refrigerate. The pickled turnips will be ready in about 1 hour.

Per Serving: Calories: 3 / Fat: 0g / Protein: 1g / Carbs: 0g / Fiber: 0g / Sodium: 6mg

Green Salsa

Prep time: 5 minutes / Cook time: 0 minutes / Makes: about 1½ cups

- 4 cups fresh parsley leaves
- 8 garlic cloves, minced
- ¼ teaspoon salt
- ¼ cup sherry vinegar
- 1 cup extra-virgin olive oil

1. In a food processor, pulse the parsley, garlic, and salt until the parsley is coarsely chopped, about 10 pulses. Add the vinegar and pulse briefly to mix.
2. Transfer the mixture to a bowl and slowly whisk in the olive oil until fully combined. Let sit at room temperature for at least 30 minutes to let the flavors blend. (Refrigerate for up to 2 days and bring to room temperature before serving.)

Per Serving: ¼ cup: Calories: 341 / Fat: 36g / Protein: 1g / Carbs: 4g / Fiber: 1g / Sodium: 121mg

Minted Olive Vinaigrette

Prep time: 5 minutes / Cook time: 0 minutes / Makes: ½ cup

- ¼ cup extra-virgin olive oil
- ¼ cup pitted and finely chopped olives
- ¼ cup white wine vinegar
- 2 tablespoons minced fresh mint
- ¼ teaspoon kosher salt
- ¼ teaspoon freshly ground black pepper
- ¼ teaspoon honey

1. In a bowl, whisk together the white wine vinegar, honey, salt, and black pepper. Gradually whisk in the olive oil until well combined. Stir in the chopped olives and minced mint. Store leftovers in an airtight container in the refrigerator for up to 5 days.

Per Serving: 2 tablespoons: Calories: 135 / Fat: 15g / Protein: 0g / Carbs: 1g / Fiber: 0g / Sodium: 135mg

Traditional Basil Pesto

Prep time: 5 minutes / Cook time: 13 minutes / Makes: about 1½ cups

- 6 garlic cloves, unpeeled
- ½ cup pine nuts
- 4 cups fresh basil leaves
- ¼ cup fresh parsley leaves
- 1 cup extra-virgin olive oil
- 1 ounce (28 g) finely grated Parmesan cheese (½ cup)

1. Toast the garlic cloves in an 8-inch skillet over medium heat, shaking occasionally, until softened and lightly browned, about 8 minutes. Let the garlic cool, then peel and chop coarsely. In the same skillet, toast the pine nuts over medium heat until golden and fragrant, about 4 to 5 minutes.
2. Place basil and parsley in a 1-gallon zipper-lock bag. Use a rolling pin or meat pounder to bruise the leaves.
3. In a food processor, blend the garlic, pine nuts, and herbs until finely chopped, about 1 minute. With the processor running, slowly add the olive oil until well combined. Transfer the pesto to a bowl, mix in the Parmesan, and season with salt and pepper to taste. (Refrigerate for up to 3 days or freeze for up to 3 months. To prevent browning, cover with plastic wrap directly on the surface or top with a thin layer of olive oil. Bring to room temperature before use.)

Per Serving: ¼ cup: Calories: 423 / Fat: 45g / Protein: 4g / Carbs: 4g / Fiber: 1g / Sodium: 89mg

Sesame Tahini Dressing

Serves: 8 to 10 / Prep time: 5 minutes / Cook time: 0 minutes

- ½ cup tahini
- ¼ cup freshly squeezed lemon juice (about 2 to 3 lemons)
- ¼ cup extra-virgin olive oil
- 1 garlic clove, finely minced or ½ teaspoon garlic

powder
- 2 teaspoons salt

1. In a mason jar with a lid, combine the tahini, lemon juice, olive oil, garlic, and salt. Cover and shake vigorously until the mixture is smooth and creamy. Store in the refrigerator for up to 2 weeks.

Per Serving: Calories: 121 / Fat: 12g / Protein: 2g / Carbs: 3g / Fiber: 1g / Sodium: 479mg

Lemon Citrus Dressing

Serves: 4 / Prep time: 2 minutes / Cook time: 0 minutes

- Zest of 1 lemon
- 3 tablespoons fresh lemon juice
- Pinch of kosher salt
- Pinch of freshly ground black pepper
- 2 tablespoons olive oil

1. In a small bowl, mix together the lemon zest, lemon juice, 3 tablespoons of water, salt, and pepper. Gradually whisk in the olive oil until the dressing is fully emulsified. Store in an airtight container in the refrigerator for up to 3 days.

Per Serving: Calories: 65 / Fat: 7g / Protein: 0g / Carbs: 2g / Fiber: 0g / Sodium: 146mg

Spiralized Zucchini

Serves: 4 / Prep time: 5 minutes / Cook time: 0 minutes

- 2 medium to large zucchini

1. Trim the ends off each zucchini. Using a spiralizer set to the smallest blade, create zucchini noodles (zoodles).
2. To serve, place about ½ cup of the spiralized zucchini into each bowl. Top with a hot sauce to slightly soften the zoodles to an al dente texture. Pair with your favorite sauces or simply toss with warmed pesto for a quick and easy meal.

Per Serving: Calories: 27 / Fat: 1g / Protein: 2g / Carbs: 5g / Fiber: 2g / Sodium: 13mg

Whole-Wheat Pizza Crust

Prep time: 10 minutes / Cook time: 10 to 12 minutes / Makes: 1 pound (454 g)

- ¾ cup warm tap water
- ½ teaspoon sugar
- 1 packet rapid-rise yeast (2¼ teaspoons)
- 1 tablespoon olive oil, plus additional for greasing the bowl
- 1 cup whole-wheat flour
- 1 cup all-purpose flour
- 1 teaspoon salt

1. Preheat your oven to 500°F (260°C).

2. In a non-reactive bowl, mix the warm water and sugar. Sprinkle the yeast on top, stir, and let it sit for about 10 minutes until it becomes frothy. Stir in 1 tablespoon of olive oil.

3. In a food processor or stand mixer fitted with a dough hook, combine the whole-wheat flour, all-purpose flour, and salt. With the machine running, gradually add the yeast mixture until the dough forms a soft, tacky ball. If the dough is too dry, add warm water 1 tablespoon at a time until the desired consistency is reached. If too wet, add all-purpose flour, 1 tablespoon at a time. Continue processing for about 1 minute to knead the dough.

4. Lightly grease a large bowl with olive oil. Place the dough in the bowl and turn it to coat with oil. Cover with a clean dish towel and let it rise in a warm spot for about 1 hour, or until doubled in size.

5. Shape the dough as desired using your hands or a rolling pin. Add toppings and bake in the preheated oven for 10 to 12 minutes, or until crisp and lightly browned.

Per Serving: 2 ounces / 57 g: Calories: 135 / Fat: 2g / Protein: 5g / Carbs: 24g / Fiber: 3g / Sodium: 294mg

Herb Citrus Sauce

Serves: 6 / Prep time: 5 minutes / Cook time: 0 minutes

- 1 cup fresh mint leaves
- ½ cup fresh flat-leaf parsley
- 2 garlic cloves, minced
- 2 scallions, chopped
- 2 tablespoons pomegranate molasses
- ¼ cup olive oil
- 1 tablespoon lemon juice

1. Place all ingredients in a blender and blend until smooth. Transfer to an airtight container and refrigerate until needed. Can be kept in the refrigerator for up to 1 day.

Per Serving: Calories: 90 / Fat: 9g / Protein: 1g / Carbs: 2g / Fiber: 0g / Sodium: 5mg

Anchovy Garlic Dip

Serves: 8 to 10 / Prep time: 5 minutes / Cook time: 20 minutes

- ½ cup extra-virgin olive oil
- 4 tablespoons (½ stick) butter
- 8 finely chopped anchovy fillets
- 4 large garlic cloves, minced
- ½ teaspoon salt
- ½ teaspoon freshly ground black pepper

1. In a small saucepan, heat olive oil and butter over medium-low heat until the butter melts.

2. Add the anchovies and garlic, stirring to combine. Season with salt and pepper, then reduce the heat to low. Cook, stirring occasionally, until the anchovies are very tender and the mixture is aromatic, about 20 minutes.

3. Serve warm over steamed vegetables, as a dip for raw veggies or cooked artichokes, or as a salad dressing. Store leftovers in an airtight container in the refrigerator for up to 2 weeks.

Per Serving: Calories: 145 / Fat: 16g / Protein: 1g / Carbs: 0g / Fiber: 0g / Sodium: 235mg

Red Wine Sweet Vinaigrette

Serves: 2 / Prep time: 5 minutes / Cook time: 0 minutes

- ¼ cup plus 2 tablespoons extra-virgin olive oil
- 2 tablespoons red wine vinegar
- 1 tablespoon apple cider vinegar
- 2 teaspoons honey
- 2 teaspoons Dijon mustard
- ½ teaspoon minced garlic
- ⅛ teaspoon kosher salt
- ⅛ teaspoon freshly ground black pepper

1. In a jar, combine olive oil, red wine vinegar, apple cider vinegar, honey, Dijon mustard, garlic, salt, and pepper. Shake well to mix.

Per Serving: Calories: 386 / Fat: 41g / Protein: 0g / Carbs: 6g / Fiber: 0g / Sodium: 198mg

MEASUREMENT CONVERSION CHART

VOLUME EQUIVALENTS(DRY)

US STANDARD	METRIC (APPROXIMATE)
1/8 teaspoon	0.5 mL
1/4 teaspoon	1 mL
1/2 teaspoon	2 mL
3/4 teaspoon	4 mL
1 teaspoon	5 mL
1 tablespoon	15 mL
1/4 cup	59 mL
1/2 cup	118 mL
3/4 cup	177 mL
1 cup	235 mL
2 cups	475 mL
3 cups	700 mL
4 cups	1L

VOLUME EQUIVALENTS(LIQUID)

US STANDARD	US STANDARD (OUNCES)	METRIC (APPROXIMATE)
2 tablespoons	1 fl.oz.	30 mL
1/4 cup	2 fl.oz.	60 mL
1/2 cup	4 fl.oz.	120 mL
1 cup	8 fl.oz.	240 mL
1 1/2 cup	12 fl.oz.	355 mL
2 cups or 1 pint	16 fl.oz.	475 mL
4 cups or 1 quart	32 fl.oz.	1L
1 gallon	128 fl.oz.	4L

TEMPERATURES EQUIVALENTS

FAHRENHEIT(F)	CELSIUS(C) (APPROXIMATE)
225 °F	107 °C
250 °F	120 °C
275 °F	135 °C
300 °F	150 °C
325 °F	160 °C
350 °F	180 °C
375 °F	190 °C
400 °F	205 °C
425 °F	220 °C
450 °F	235 °C
475 °F	245 °C
500 °F	260 °C

WEIGHT EQUIVALENTS

US STANDARD	METRIC (APPROXIMATE)
1 ounce	28 g
2 ounces	57 g
5 ounces	142 g
10 ounces	284 g
15 ounces	425 g
16 ounces (1 pound)	455 g
1.5 pounds	680 g
2 pounds	907 g

The Dirty Dozen and Clean Fifteen

The Environmental Working Group (EWG) is a nonprofit, nonpartisan organization dedicated to protecting human health and the environment Its mission is to empower people to live healthier lives in a healthier environment. This organizaation publishes an annual list of the twelve kinds of prod≠uce, in sequence, that have the highest amount of pesticide residue-the Dirty Dozen-as well as a list of the fifteen kinds ofproduce that have the least amount of pesticide residue-the Clean Fifteen.

THE DIRTY DOZEN

The 2016 Dirty Dozen includes the following produce. These are consid-ered among the year's most important produce to buy organic:

Strawberries	Spinach
Apples	Tomatoes
Nectarines	Bell peppers
Peaches	Cherry tomatoes
Celery	Cucumbers
Grapes	Kale/collard greens
Cherries	Hot peppers

The Dirty Dozen list contains two additional itemskale/collard greens and hot peppers-because they tend to contain trace levels of highly hazardous pesticides.

THE CLEAN FIFTEEN

The least critical to buy organically are the Clean Fifteen list. The following are on the 2016 list:

Avocados	Papayas
Corn	Kiw
Pineapples	Eggplant
Cabbage	Honeydew
Sweet peas	Grapefruit
Onions	Cantaloupe
Asparagus	Cauliflower
Mangos	

Some of the sweet corn sold in the United States are made from genetically engineered (GE) seedstock. Buy organic varieties of these crops to avoid GE produce.

30-Day Meal Plan

	Breakfast	Lunch	Dinner	Snack/Dessert
Day 1	Greek Egg and Tomato Scramble	Paella with Shrimp and Chicken	Saffron Rice with Cod	North African-Spiced Grilled Sweet Potatoes
Day 2	Peach Sunrise Smoothie	Herb-Marinated Grilled Lamb Loin Chops	Greek-Inspired Turkey Burgers	Muhammara from Lebanon
Day 3	Mini Shrimp Frittata	Crispy Oregano Tilapia	Red Wine Mushroom Sauce Filet Mignon	Crispy Roasted Chickpeas
Day 4	Egg Salad with Red Pepper and Dill	Turkey Tenderloin with Paprika and Garlic	Quinoa-Stuffed Pork Tenderloin	Zesty Lemon Garlic Hummus
Day 5	Savory Breakfast Oats	Rosemary Salmon	Herb-Infused Lamb Meatballs	Ricotta and Orange-Raisin Flatbread
Day 6	Egg Baked in Avocado	Greek-Style Pork and Vegetables	Honey-Glazed Chicken Thighs	Crispy Baked Potato Sticks
Day 7	Ricotta and Fruit Bruschetta	Roasted Cornish Hen with Fresh Figs	Greek-Style Pork Kebabs	Greek-Inspired Mini Tacos
Day 8	Greek Yogurt Parfait	Steamed Clams	Spanish Garlic and Lemon Sautéed Chicken	Cinnamon-Dusted Apple Crisps
Day 9	Tomato and Feta Egg Skillet	Chilean Sea Bass with Olive Relish	Mussels with Potatoes	Herb-Infused Italian Chickpea Crepes
Day 10	Yogurt with Granola and Citrus Compote	Lamb and Herb Stew	White Wine–Sautéed Mussels	Citrus-Infused Melon Salad
Day 11	Amaranth Chocolate Almond Bowl	Smoky Herb Lamb Chops with Lemon-Rosemary Dressing	Your Favourite Sheet Pan Fish Dinner	Lemon-Feta Olive Medley
Day 12	Nutty Pear Oatmeal	Fast and Tasty Shrimp Risotto	Pork Skewers with Onion	Crispy Sweet Potato Sticks
Day 13	Blue Cheese and Apricot Toast	Chicken and Freekeh with Cilantro and Preserved Lemon	Grilled Chicken Gyros with Vegetables and Tzatziki Sauce	Spicy Air-Fried Bok Choy
Day 14	Hearty Veggie Breakfast	Pork Milanese	Simple Cod Gratin	Flaxseed Tortillas
Day 15	Powerhouse Peach Smoothie Bowl	Tuscan Braised Pork	Delicious Spicy Steamed Chili Crab	Maple-Baked Cherry Tomatoes

	Breakfast	Lunch	Dinner	Snack/Dessert
Day 16	Tuna and Pepper Spanish Tortilla	Quick Ouzo Mussels	Moroccan-Spiced Meatballs	Provençal Artichokes
Day 17	Egg and Veggie Pita	Shrimp Foil Packets	Spiced Citrus Chicken	Lentil Salad with Herbs and Citrus
Day 18	Red Pepper Feta Egg Cups	Roasted Greek Chicken and Potatoes	Mixed Seafood Soup	Cucumber and Avocado Stuffed
Day 19	Tahini and Apple Toast	Turkey Breasts with Lemon and Basil	Garlic Beef Meatballs in Creamy Sauce	Sicilian Roasted Cauliflower with Capers, Currants, and Crispy Crumbs
Day 20	uinoa Breakfast Bowl with Figs and Walnuts	Moroccan-Spiced Flank Steak with Harissa Couscous	Lemon Salmon with Dill	Dill-Infused Rice Pilaf
Day 21	Sweet Potato Toast with Spinach and Pesto	Spiced Beef Skewers	Chicken Cacciatore with Fennel and Wild Mushrooms	Cheese and Herb Flatbread
Day 22	Mediterranean Pita Breakfast Sandwiches	Cashew Chicken and Snap Peas	Italian Halibut with Grapes and Olive Oil	Goat Cheese and Mushroom Delight
Day 23	Smoked Trout and Avocado Toast	Linguine with Clams and White Wine	Chicken and Vegetable Fajitas	Sweet Potato Mash Bites
Day 24	Italian-Style Egg Cups	Braised Striped Bass with Zucchini and Tomatoes	Goat Cheese-Stuffed Flank Steak	Rosemary and Sage White Beans
Day 25	Tropical Peach Smoothie Bowl	Pesto Chicken with Slow-Cooked Potatoes	Italian Tuna Roast	Classic Greek Salad
Day 26	Avocado Toast with Flax Seed Bread	Balsamic-Glazed Pork Roast	Red Wine-Braised Short Ribs with Potatoes	Spicy Lemon Potatoes
Day 27	Smoked Trout Crostini	Baked Swordfish with Herbs	Pork Stew with Cannellini Beans	Cabbage Rolls with Barley, Pine Nuts, and Currants
Day 28	Almond Banana Cocoa Smoothie	Chicken and Olives with Couscous	Mediterranean Garlic and Herb-Roasted Cod	Caramelized Fennel Wedges
Day 29	Spiced Berry Smoothie	Lamb Shanks with Tomatoes and Potatoes	Butternut Squash and Lentil Chicken	Summer Peach and Tomato Salad
Day 30	Greek Tomato and Egg Cups	Cucumber and Salmon Salad	Dill-Coated Chicken Strips	Charred Zucchini with Kimchi Herb Sauce

INDEX

Printed in Great Britain
by Amazon

58080625R00051